GLOBAL MEETINGS AND EXHIBITIONS

THE WILEY EVENT MANAGEMENT SERIES

SERIES EDITOR: DR. JOE GOLDBLATT, CSEP

GLOBAL MEETINGS AND EXHIBITIONS

Carol Krugman, CMP, CMM
Rudy R. Wright, CMP

BICENTENNIAL
1807
WILEY
2007
BICENTENNIAL

JOHN WILEY & SONS, INC.

Published by John Wiley & Sons, Inc., Hoboken, New Jersey
Published simultaneously in Canada

Limit of Liability/Disclaimer of Warranty: While the publisher and author have used their best efforts in preparing this book, they make no representations or warranties with respect to the accuracy or completeness of the contents of this book and specifically disclaim any implied warranties of merchantability or fitness for a particular purpose. No warranty may be created or extended by sales representatives or written sales materials. The advice and strategies contained herein may not be suitable for your situation. You should consult with a professional where appropriate. Neither the publisher nor author shall be liable for any loss of profit or any other commercial damages, including but not limited to special, incidental, consequential, or other damages.

For general information on our other products and services or for technical support, please contact our Customer Care Department within the United States at (800) 762-2974, outside the United States at (317) 572-3993, or fax (317) 572-4002.

Wiley also publishes its books in a variety of electronic formats. Some content that appears in print may not be available in electronic books. For more information about Wiley products, visit our web site at www.wiley.com.

Library of Congress Cataloging-in-Publication Data:

Krugman, Carol, 1948–
   Global meetings and exhibitions / Carol Krugman and Rudy R. Wright.
      p. cm.
   Includes index.
   ISBN-13: 978-0-471-69940-8 (cloth)
   ISBN-10: 0-471-69940-3 (cloth)
   1. Congresses and conventions—Planning—Handbooks, manuals, etc. 2. Meetings—Planning—Handbooks, manuals, etc. 3. Exhibitions—Planning—Handbooks, manuals, etc. 4. International relations—Miscellanea.   I. Wright, Rudy R.   II. Title.
   AS6 K795 2007
   658—dc22

                                                            2006010268

DEDICATION

To my extraordinary parents, Saul and Sylvia Stern Krugman, in loving memory and with profound admiration for the sacrifices they made to provide me with the kind of education that resulted in my being the only kid on my block to know what a participle was—dangling or otherwise. Among the many gifts I received from them, two of the most precious were the undying love of learning and passion for the written word that made this book possible.

And to my beloved husband, Alex Maller, who entered my life as I was beginning this book, stayed in my life in spite of it and without whose love, support, abiding patience and killer fruit salad, I never could have finished it.

—Carol Krugman, CMP, CMM

To my friend, valued colleague and giant in the meetings industry, Mel Hosansky, who had a profound influence on my professional career. It was he who first suggested, "You should write a book, Rudy." Thanks, old friend—I did!

—Rudy R. Wright, CMP

CONTENTS

SERIES EDITOR FOREWORD

This is the first book to provide the essential knowledge needed for planning and managing global meetings, conventions and exhibitions.

The term *global* is derived from the term *sphere*. The latter term is derived from the Greek word *sphaera* (ball), which is akin to the term *spairein* and literally means "to quiver." A ball is of course a sphere, and therefore the Greek definition evolved from the process of playing with it, as in making it quiver such as a spinning globe. You are about to explore many global opportunities in international meetings, conventions, and exhibitions.

The coauthors, Carol Krugman, CMP, CMM and Rudy R. Wright, CMP, have traveled the world in search of the best practices in international meetings, conventions, and exhibitions. Their extensive careers, along with their rich cadre of global industry contacts, have produced the first truly international guide to the modern meetings and exhibitions industry. Together, they have produced the very first book in the history of this industry written from a global perspective.

Each chapter not only addresses the local, state, regional, provincial, national, and international perspectives, it also provides the reader with a "Passport" to the future of this expanding profession. The Passport provides dozens of helpful resources for future study and exploration.

Only a few weeks ago I was in Almaty, Kazakhstan, helping that government conduct a feasibility study to build the first convention center. While in that beautiful land I could sense a feeling of hopefulness about the global meeting industry discovering the great silk road once traveled by the explorer Marco Polo.

Thanks to the excellent research, experience, and wisdom provided by Carol Krugman, CMP, CMM and Rudy R. Wright, CMP you now can create your own road around the world as you become a global expert in the worldwide meetings, conventions, and exhibitions industry. As you circle the globe or sphere, may you also expand the frontiers of this industry. Through this advancement you will be fulfilling an even nobler purpose by connecting the world through the events you produce. And perhaps you will produce a few global "quivers" of your own making in the future.

Dr. Joe Goldblatt, CSEP
Series Editor
Professor and Executive Director for Professional
  Development and Strategic Partnerships
Temple University
Philadelphia, Pennsylvania

FOREWORD

As one who has dedicated his career to the growth and development of global events, I am privileged to introduce this, first ever comprehensive and much-needed reference work. Although there are many books on meeting management, only a few address the demanding task of planning and conducting events in other countries and involving multicultural delegates. As organizations recognize the need for a global perspective and seek to master multicultural interaction, they also recognize that international meetings are the most effective medium for communications.

This book is the synthesis of the combined experience of Carol Krugman, CMP, CMM, president and CEO of Krugman Group International, Inc., and Rudy R. Wright, CMP, charter member and past president of Meeting Professionals International and a veteran Professional Conference Organizer (PCO). The two have been planning, managing, and implementing multinational, multicultural events throughout the world for over two decades. Much of their knowledge has been shared over the years with their colleagues in seminars and workshops sponsored by meeting industry associations as well as academic institutions. It also has been documented in a variety of industry publications, including articles written by Carol for *Successful Meetings, Meeting News, Insurance Conference Planner, Association Planner,* and *The Meeting Professional,* the official journal of Meeting Professionals International (MPI), the world's largest association of professional planners and supplier partners, with over 20,000 members in 68 chapters throughout the world. Rudy's contributions to a variety of industry publications have been equally prodigious. A series of 55 columns written for *The Meeting Professional* were later syndicated in a number of international trade publications, including the following:

- *Asian Meetings & Incentives*—Southeast Asia
- *Delegates*—United Kingdom
- *Congress & Convention*—Japan
- *Convention & Incentive Marketing*—Australia
- *Meeting & Congressi*—Italy
- *Meetings & Incentive Travel*—Canada
- *Meeting News*—USA
- *Successful Meetings & Incentives International*—USA/Europe

That body of knowledge, along with Carol's ongoing experience as a practicing international meeting planner, has been distilled and updated for this book. I am especially pleased to recommend *Global Meetings and Exhibitions* to the generation of meeting professionals who are just now discovering the excitement and challenge of our industry. They are fortunate to have a comprehensive text to guide them through the labyrinth of multinational, multicultural event management, and it could not have been written at a more propitious time.

Multinational operations ability and cross-cultural awareness are critical requirements in today's business environment. At last, both students and practicing meeting professionals alike have the resource they need to enter the global arena with confidence.

> *Ray Bloom*
> *Chairman*
> *IMEX—The Worldwide Exhibition for*
> *Travel, Meetings & Events*

Currently chairman and founder of IMEX, Ray Bloom developed both EIBTM (European Incentive Business Travel and Meetings Exhibition) and Incentive World, before selling them to Reed Elsevier. He has devoted his time, energy, and resources to numerous industry associations, receiving their highest honors and recognition along the way, including induction into the Convention Industry Council's (CIC) Hall of Leaders and the International Congress and Conventions Association (ICCA) Presidents Award. In addition, he has served on the Board of Trustees for both the Meeting Professionals International (MPI) Foundation and the Society of Incentive & Travel Executives (SITE) Foundation, and he is currently a member of the MPI Global Strategy Task Force.

PREFACE

During the Industrial Age, the emphasis was on raw materials, labor, manufacturing, product, and distribution. With the transition to the information age came dramatic changes in that traditional relationship. Raw materials became data, labor went from predominantly blue-collar to administrative and technical, and the computer assumed the responsibility for manufacturing the product, which is information. Distribution options took on many new forms: telex, copiers, fax, e-mail, cellular, and personal data assistants. A principal medium for the distribution of that new product—information—proliferated: meetings!

Yes, meetings flourished throughout the latter part of the last century. The United States alone witnessed a dramatic growth in total meetings industry revenues from millions of dollars in the 1970s to over $2 billion by millennium's end. The compelling force behind that growth was the recognition that meetings, conventions, and exhibitions are highly effective media for communicating information.

As the meetings industry grew in volume and sophistication, the professionals responsible for planning and staging those events had to learn new skills and develop a different mind-set. Thus, meeting planners became meeting managers, and with certification, they became meeting *professionals*.

Concurrently, during that transitional period we witnessed another dramatic evolution: the change from a national to a global perspective. Meeting professionals found it necessary to think beyond their borders, to develop new skills and discover new places to stage their events for participants from diverse cultures.

International events have come into their own as our changing world has moved toward an increasingly global economy. As national and political barriers fall, countries that once were fiercely independent have come to realize that they are also interdependent. There are powerful forces at work today that affect all of us on a global scale. The bridges being built between continents, between nations, and between peoples and cultures challenge us all to learn not only from but about one another.

Like governments, corporations and associations must achieve a global perspective. This is no longer a question for debate; it is a matter of survival. An experiment in superconductivity in Kyoto affects a manufacturing process in Dresden. A computer glitch on the London stock exchange causes panic in the Hong Kong, New York, and Tokyo markets. A breakthrough in microsurgery at a Houston medical center saves a life in Adelaide, Johannesburg, or Kuala Lumpur.

On any given day, from Singapore to Salzburg, from Rio to Rome, a wide variety of meetings and events take place on a global scale. Whether it be trade fairs or world congresses involving thousands of delegates, scientific colloquiums on specific topics addressed by a select panel of experts, corporate management meetings, or government conferences discussing issues of mutual concern, all have certain characteristics in common. They must be planned carefully, targeted to a specific audience, infused with compelling and relevant content, convened at a thoroughly researched venue, organized meticulously, implemented impeccably, and evaluated carefully at their conclusion.

Although there are thousands of such events occurring each year in venues around the world, there is no single reference available to guide the organizers responsible for planning and managing them. There are several excellent books on the planning of meetings, conferences, exhibitions, and special events, but most are written under the assumption that a meeting is a meeting regardless of where it is convened or who attends.

Look in the business section of any bookstore and you will find several texts on meeting and event planning. However, most of them do not focus on meetings overseas or provide a truly global perspective by specifically addressing the critical differences that characterize international events. Meeting professionals confronting the challenge of working outside the comfort zone of their home country, culture, and language have not had the benefit of a definitive text on the subject. Until now!

Global Meetings and Exhibitions is the comprehensive reference for a planner responsible for organizing programs both inside and outside his or her home country. It provides readers with the tools they need to plan effective programs, while outlining the crucial distinctions between domestic and international events by explaining the dynamics of how people from differing cultural backgrounds communicate, learn, react, and interact.

The purpose of this book is twofold. Corporate, association, and independent meeting professionals experienced in domestic events but faced with the need to plan an international meeting, convention, or exhibition will find the book a valuable asset in achieving a higher degree of professionalism in those disciplines. Students of meeting and event planning will learn the fundamentals of their discipline within the global context that is critical to business in the twenty-first century. As with computer proficiency a decade ago, the ability to communicate effectively and work successfully across national, cultural, and linguistic boundaries is quickly becoming a requirement for all of us rather than the special interest of just a few.

The meetings sector has adapted to this demand for a global outlook. Look at the history of just one—albeit the largest—industry association: Meeting Professionals International (MPI). Founded in 1972 by 52 charter members, MPI began its global expansion in 1977 by adding chapters in Canada. It held its first transnational annual congress in 1981 in Toronto, followed by educational conferences in Monaco and Hong Kong. The first European chapter—in Italy—was chartered in 1990, and two years later the MPI-Europe office opened in Brussels. Today MPI boasts over 20,000 members in 68 chapters throughout the world. Its educational programs are offered worldwide in international conferences and via distance learning on the Web. One of the authors of this book is a past international president of MPI.

EMPHASIS ON EDUCATION

The unique skills and knowledge required for proficiency in the meetings field are being met industrywide not only in North America but throughout Europe and Asia. The Professional Convention Management Association (PCMA) conducts extensive educational events for its planner, supplier, and student members. The annual Conference Management Program sponsored by the International Congress and Convention Association (ICCA) and the Seminar on Professional Congress Organization presented annually by the International Association of Professional Conference Organizers (IAPCO) provide students and practitioners alike with valuable opportunities to learn and advance their professional development.

Other organizations offering similar educational programs in the United States and Canada are the Association for Convention Operations Management (ACOM), and the International Special Events Society (ISES). Overseas they are the European Society of Association Executives (ESAE), the Association of Conferences and Events (ACE) in the United Kingdom, and the Meetings Industry Association of Australia (MIAA) in the South Pacific. Many of these organizations have substantial student memberships.

Although much of the educational emphasis has been directed at meeting and exhibition planners, there is a commensurate effort at developing professional competence on the part of facilitators. Professional education in event management is becoming a major emphasis in the hospitality industry. In the past, event management was learned through hands-on experience; the expertise was shared by many areas, from sales to catering to convention services. At major hotel chains they are implementing a career in event management, with all the appropriate training, professional development, and growth opportunities.

Universities and colleges recognize this important career field, and although only a few offer a four-year curriculum in hotel, travel, and meeting management, some 300 schools offer some aspects of this specialized discipline in their curricula. All have expanded their curricula to encompass event management.

This learning is not confined to traditional venues such as meeting rooms and classrooms. Such tutorial methods are defined as synchronous instruction in which the instructor and the students share the same time frame as well as physical space. With the proliferation of computers worldwide there has come a form of asynchronous instruction. Distance learning—or online learning—allows a student to access courses by computer at a time and place of his or her choosing. Thus, a hotel banquet staff member in Alexandria, Egypt, wanting to learn the finer points of servicing meetings can sign up for an online course in event management offered by assorted universities and colleges throughout the world. The student learns the body of knowledge, completes assignments and tests, and interacts with the instructor much as in a traditional course except that this is done by computer at times that are convenient for the student. Online learning is now an essential part of several universities' and associations' professional curriculum.

This book is not a theoretical treatise but a practical guide for active meeting professionals and those who aspire to work in the profession. With over 50 years of combined experience in the field and an undying enthusiasm for cross-cultural, transnational challenges, the authors' goal is to enhance the wisdom of the seasoned meeting professional and to impart the necessary knowledge to the learner contemplating a career in meeting and event management.

Carol Krugman, CMP, CMM
Rudy R. Wright, CMP

ACKNOWLEDGMENTS

Reflecting on whom to thank and how to thank them, I realized that my life is composed of a series of concentric families. There is my immediate family, my office family, my professional family, and the extended family of colleagues in the global meetings industry, all of whom made significant contributions to this book whether they knew it or not. Now is the time to let them know how much I appreciate their support and thank them for enriching these pages.

The life of an international meeting planner who also happens to own and manage her own company is lived at a very fast pace and usually far from home. In fact, a good part of this book was written either in airport lounges or at 35,000 feet. I must first thank my husband, Alex Maller, for sharing our precious "home time" with this book. As a professor with a string of publications to his credit, he understood firsthand the demands of writing and left me alone to work when it was often the last thing either of us wanted.

The members of my office family in the United States and United Kingdom—Agnès Canonica, CMP, Jeanette Ferrara, and Louise D'Aguilar—were similarly patient, flexible, and supportive of my need for writing time. These three talented, dedicated, and loyal professionals carried on the work of the company without missing a beat while their boss disappeared (frequently whining) to write . . . and write . . . and write some more, further proving that the job of the CEO is to interfere as little as possible with great people who know what they are doing and love doing it.

Since 1995, Meeting Professionals International (MPI) has been the source of professional and personal relationships that have changed my life. The exhilaration and satisfaction of working with a group of one's peers to raise the level of professionalism in our industry is unsurpassed. Among my extended MPI family, Richard Aaron, George Aguel, Mark Andrew, Steve Armitage, Ray Bloom, Betsy Bondurant, Terri Breining, Katie Callahan-Giobbi, Coleman, David DuBois, Christine Duffy, Barbara Dunn, Joan Eisenstodt, Marsha Flanagan, John Foster, Ann Godi, Tyra Hilliard, Jonathan Howe, Dave Johnson, Paul Kennedy, David Kliman, Susan Krug, Evelyn Laxgang, Hugh Lee, Jaap Liethof, Larry Luteran, Carole McKellar, Michael Owen, the late Chris Pentz, Angie Pfeifer, Alan Pini, Mary Powers, Colin Rorrie, Eric Rozenberg, Didier Scaillet, Michael Shannon, Ed Simeone, Charlotte St. Martin, and Jerry Wayne are just a few of people who continue to enrich both my life and my career and whom I am especially proud to call my friends. And to the denizens of the Café La Krug who were there in the very beginning, especially the late Jim Whitehead and the ever-present, effervescent Mollie Newton and Louise Felsher, my love and thanks for taking over cheerleading duty from my mom and revitalizing the wordsmith in me.

To make the content of this book even more current and relevant, colleagues who are recognized experts in specific areas have graciously contributed additional information and insights to selected chapters. We who are dedicated to the progress of the meetings industry thank them for their generosity of spirit and expertise, as well as for their time and their commitment to the profession. The contributions of Rick Werth to this book were especially significant, and I remain in perpetual awe of his encyclopedic knowledge and incisive insights. Rick, you are not only the guy I want to have with me in the dark alley, on the desert island, and everywhere else spooky (because I know you will have checked everything out and I'll be safe) but also the guy I want to learn from and teach with until we can't anymore.

Our colleagues in the industry media were most generous in granting permission to use or reprint material originally written for their publications by me or Rudy or by others. These trade publications are a font of education and important information for all of us in the profession, and we are fortunate to have so many dedicated writers and editors keeping us up to date. Many thanks to Betsy Bair, Barbara Scofidio, Sue Pelletier, Tamara Hosansky, Regina Baraban, and Paula Hill from The Meetings Group publications; Robert Carey and Sara Welch at *Successful Meetings;* Sarah Braley from *Meetings & Conventions;* Dave McCann from *Meeting News;* and the talented staff at *The Meeting Professional.*

My extended global family is also numerous, and their knowledge and expertise resonate throughout this book. Profound thanks to Richard White, Myles McGourty, Andreas Nauheimer, Christophe Lorvo, Michel Morauw, Gordon Fuller, Xavier Destribats, Claudio Salgado, Jean Franken, Sean Mahoney, the late Jan Loeff, and Chris Stanley for setting unparalleled standards of professionalism, perfection, and partnership over the years. *Muito obrigada, muchissimas grácias,* and *grazie mille* to Vera Joppert, Liliana Couto, Anne Grauer, Maria Alcina Santos, Merina Begg, Ana Maria Montes, and Piera Doria, who taught me everything I know about working successfully with DMCs and PCOs abroad. They also taught me that trust and respect are the true currency of cross-cultural, transnational business, and I am privileged to be the beneficiary of their continuing advice, counsel, and support.

Last and absolutely not least, if it were not for Rudy R. Wright, Dr. Joe Goldblatt, and Melissa Oliver at John Wiley & Sons, I would not have the privilege of writing these acknowledgments. It was Rudy who honored me by asking me to coauthor this book with him. Thank you, "Tarzan," for allowing me the pleasure of reviewing 20 years worth of your excellent articles and giving me the opportunity to join you in this most important endeavor. It is not often that one gets asked to write a book, much less one that will be so useful to so many people.

Joe Goldblatt, you are part Yoda, part Simba, and all mensch. Your wise counsel, incisive editing, continuous cheerleading, and willingness to pitch in and help us out of the deadline trenches were invaluable. There is a reason why you are an icon in the industry, and I am honored to be associated with this series of texts you have helped create.

And to Melissa Oliver and the team at Wiley, special thanks for understanding the challenge of writing a book while you are boarding your house up against hurricanes (four times in six weeks), running a business, running to the airport, and trying to be available to both the man and the Chihuahua puppy (in that order, of course), while fulfilling your volunteer commitments all at the same time. Your patience and assistance have been invaluable and are greatly appreciated.

Carol Krugman, CMP, CMM

Any author would be privileged to have at his disposal the network of friends and colleagues who make up the meetings industry. I was more fortunate than most, having spent some 28 years meeting and working with true professionals around the world. My circle of support included hoteliers, airline people, destination representatives, producers, PCOs, and of course fellow meeting professionals.

I mentioned Mel Hosansky in the Dedication. As editor-in-chief of *Meetings & Conventions* and, later, *Successful Meetings,* Mel encouraged me to write. He also stimulated my interest in the global scope of this industry. Interviewing me after I had been elected president of Meeting Professionals International, Mel urged, "Focus on the 'international' in MPI, Rudy." That was the foundation for a series of some 50 articles and this book.

The book would not have been possible had not Joe Goldblatt taken an interest and convinced Wiley, our publishers, that it was needed in the Wiley Event Management Series and then sweated it out through endless rewrites. And Carol . . . dear Carol Krugman, who spent untold hours turning my articles into gems of wisdom while bopping around the world running her own business.

I would be remiss if I didn't point out others who were influential in the book's development. Contributing advice and lending encouragement were Terri Breining, Tony Carey, Christine Duffy, Peter Haigh, and Rodolfo Musco. Other colleagues provided the wisdom of their own experience, such as Lori Cioffi, Jim Daggett, Tyra Hilliard, Dave McCann, Diane Silberstein, Sara Torrence, and my son Andrew, our family's AV wizard and a professional in his own right.

And speaking of family, I owe much to my wife, Sarah, whose love, patience, and devotion are reflected in every page. Thank you, one and all.

Rudy R. Wright, CMP

Chapter 1

FUNDAMENTALS OF MEETINGS, CONVENTIONS, AND EXHIBITIONS

A community is like a ship; everyone ought to be prepared to take the helm.
—**Henrik Ibsen**

IN THIS CHAPTER

We will explore:

- The generally accepted definitions of meetings, conventions, and exhibitions.
- The vocabulary and key phrases commonly used in this industry.
- The differences and similarities between a domestic meeting and an international meeting.
- Identifying the purpose for an event.
- Determining event frequency and duration.
- Developing an organizational timetable.
- Developing and implementing effective communications.
- Managing program dynamics.
- The role of the organizer/planner.
- Networking effectively throughout the world.
- Guidelines for selecting the best site.
- Interfacing with destination marketers, hotels, and other venues.
- Selecting and working with destination management companies (DMCs) and Professional Congress Organizers (PCOs).
- Understanding the role of a DMC and a PCO.
- Assessing and planning entertainment.
- Guidelines for producing a safe and secure meeting, convention, or exhibition.
- New technology and its role in managing events.
- Understanding international currencies.
- Developing budget procedures to produce the greatest return on investment (ROI).

A global meeting, convention, or exhibition forms a temporal community. This temporary society has all the challenges and opportunities of more permanent societies. However, because it is temporary, it is different, and when a meeting, convention, or exhibition takes place in a foreign land, it can be very different indeed. This is the first book to provide the knowledge necessary to plan temporary global communities and/or societies that produce consistently successful, sustainable outcomes for the participants.

For the student or for the professional new to this type of event, it will be comforting to know that most of the planning parameters and operations methods that characterize domestic events also apply to those held in other countries. Meeting rooms and exhibit halls in most of the world are much like those at home. Menus and venues in Salzburg are not much different from those in Salt Lake City, and motorcoaches are pretty much the same the world over. After all, a meeting is a meeting whether it is held in Alexandria, Virginia, or Alexandria, Egypt, though some facets vary significantly according to venue. It is in the cultural variations, values, and customs that the main differences lie, and identifying those variants and learning how to manage them is the main purpose of this book.

This chapter is devoted to basics; it is written for meeting organizers who are planning a transnational or multinational meeting for the first time as well as for students enrolled in a hospitality/meetings curriculum. It is designed to serve as an overview of the basic elements that characterize international events.

There is no denying that a meeting convened in another country demands specialized knowledge on the part of the organizer. However, like any skill, this can be learned readily if one is given the necessary facts. A large proportion of the discipline in planning and staging the event applies, regardless of the site. It is the remaining specialized knowledge that pertains specifically to international events that needs to be learned. What follows is an overview of the fundamentals that characterize meetings, conventions, and exhibitions that are global in scope.

Before addressing those elements, it is important that there be consensus on the semantics. Terms such as *domestic, foreign, overseas, international, offshore,* and *multicultural* are used extensively and often erroneously. For the purpose of this book, they are defined as follows.

Overseas generally is used in North America to describe an event in which participants from, say, Canada or the United States travel offshore to another country. A more apt term would be *transnational.* Thus, a Canadian group meeting in Belize or Italian delegates convening a conference in Copenhagen would be deemed to be attending a transnational conference. In both instances, citizens of one country meet in another country.

International applies to events in which participants from two or more countries meet in a specific destination. Thus, a meeting of delegates from Canada, Mexico, and the United States held in Los Angeles would be an international event. However, because in common usage *international* applies to all these situations, this text will use the term *multinational* or *multicultural* to describe such meetings.

To distinguish the nature of the event further, the authors have limited the scope of this book to international events that meet the following criteria:

- Involves crossing national borders
- At least two days' duration in addition to travel days
- Fifty or more attendees
- A business agenda utilizing presenters

SHARPENING YOUR MEETING VOCABULARY

Understanding the meaning and proper use of terminology in one's own native tongue is difficult enough. Arriving at a consensus on the connotation of terms in a multinational context demands even greater accuracy on the part of organizers managing international events. For instance, a common misuse occurs even among experienced meeting professionals with respect to *podium.* That word has its roots in the Latin *pod,* referring to the foot. Hence the podium is what one stands on (also called a rostrum); one stands *behind* a lectern.

The term *congress* often is applied to international meetings in general, leading to confusion and misinterpretation. It is not a generic word like *meeting,* though it sometimes is substituted for it erroneously even by professionals who should know better. A congress is a scheduled, periodic meeting of delegates or representatives of interested groups to discuss a subject. Outside the United States, it is substituted for *convention.* The administrative staff of the organization sponsoring an international congress is the *secretariat.*

The *Manual of Congress Terminology,* published by the International Association of Professional Congress Organizers (IAPCO), tries to clear up some of the confusion, although this respected work uses *congress* in a generic sense. The manual's definitions encompass *assembly, colloquium, conference, congress, convention, exhibition, forum, seminar, symposium,* and other meeting formats in seven languages.

Other common terms evolve from usage. A *kick-off* or *launch,* for instance, generally describes a meeting organized to introduce a product and its marketing plan. Such an event is also motivational. In the United States, the term *convention* usually implies a meeting combined with an exhibition. Large conventions whose housing needs require several hotels in a location often are referred to as "citywides." Are those distinctions only a matter of terminology? Not really. Every type of meeting has its own purpose, format, requirements, timetables, and characteristics.

TYPES OF MEETINGS

Rodolfo Musco, CMP, CMM, founder of the Italian Association of Meeting Planners, analyzes several meeting types according to their objectives and parameters.

1. *Purpose.* A meeting may be held to inform, organize, debate, motivate, educate, communicate, or reach a decision. There is a similarity of purpose among a congress, a forum, and a symposium, which seeks to inform, communicate, and provide opportunities to debate issues. A conference is useful to inform and reach decisions, whereas a convention may be called to organize, inform, motivate, communicate, debate, and vote. The purpose of a seminar is to inform and educate. These distinctions are important because they influence timetables, room setups, speaker selection, and many other program decisions.

2. *Number of Participants.* Conferences, forums, and seminars usually are attended by a few dozen, whereas congresses and conventions have a large number of delegates. A symposium may have a large or relatively small attendance. Though these are subjective terms, one would not refer to a meeting of fewer than 100 persons as a congress.

3. *Frequency.* A convention usually is held annually, whereas a congress may be held annually, biannually, or on an ad hoc basis. A symposium also is held periodically, but conferences, forums, and seminars have no established frequency. They are called as needed or when deemed advisable.

4. *Duration.* Conferences normally last one day or more. Seminars can cover anywhere from one to six days. Symposia and conventions tend to last three to four days, and congresses may be three to five days, depending on the location and the topics to be covered.

5. *Organization Timetable.* There is no consensus on the time required to organize an event. A conference could be planned in as little as a few weeks. A forum or seminar requires two to six months. At least one year is needed for a symposium, and from one to four years for a congress or convention.

6. *Communications before the Event.* Premeeting communication for forums and conferences is minimal: Location, date and time, topics, speakers, and registration data are usually adequate. Conventions use a dedicated Web site and/or a series of mailings because program details are not included in the early information. Communications for symposia, seminars, and congresses must be very detailed because they influence the recipient's decision to attend.

7. *Program Dynamics.* There is an essential relationship between speakers and attendees that, if overlooked, could result in a failure. Delegates attend a seminar, symposium, or congress because they are interested in the subject and the speakers. Speakers are perceived as authorities. In most cases, a participant at such events has chosen to attend and has paid a registration fee. Interest in the issues, a need to form one's own opinion, and a desire to contribute to the ultimate decision move people to attend a conference or forum. Convention delegates, in contrast, have been called on to participate, with little or no opportunity to influence the dates, location, duration, or program content. Consequently, they tend to be more critical and analytical in their relationship to speakers.

It is important to understand the characteristics of various kinds of meetings and identify them correctly in communications, in promotional materials, and at industry educational events. For that matter, even journalists and authors of event-related texts should demonstrate a knowledge of the terminology in order to contribute to a better understanding of the profession.

▌GOING GLOBAL

A growing number of organizations convene meetings in other countries or organize in their own nations' events that are attended by people of diverse cultures. Corporations with global markets or affiliates, international associations, and professional societies and government entities involved in world affairs have an ongoing need to interact with a worldwide audience. The nature of those entities imposes on them an obligation to convene events in other countries or host multinational attendees in their own homelands. Thus, the meetings industry finds a British government agency exhibiting at a trade show in Japan; a Latin American pharmaceutical firm attending a medical congress in Zurich; a trade association based in Washington, DC, hosting its international membership at the Denver Convention Center; and a Taiwanese auto manufacturer convening its dealer network in Vancouver.

Aside from the usual matters applicable to choosing a destination, international events may be influenced by a variety of factors that may not apply to domestic meetings, such as the following:

- Visa and passport requirements
- Shipping and customs regulations
- Currency exchange fluctuations
- Host country political and threat issues
- Government-imposed travel restrictions
- Language considerations
- Cultural differences and taboos
- International protocol

NETWORKING

Nowhere is a network more valuable than in researching international meetings. Admittedly, one's most objective source of information is colleagues who have been there.

Meeting professionals begin with their personal database of acquaintances in industry organizations such as Meeting Professionals International (MPI), the Professional Convention Management Association (PCMA), and the American Society of Association Executives (ASAE) (see Appendix 1 for Web sites). They seek out fellow members who have planned events abroad or represent international hotels and destinations. They assess their experience and attendance at meetings industry educational events. Who were the presenters who spoke at international meetings? This is where the network begins.

Meetings industry publications periodically run updated destination features that offer helpful information, from cultural differences and travel tips to hotel and convention facility construction. Most of these magazines also publish annual directories as well as an annual index to articles. By the same token, attendance at industry expositions can be a valuable research tool if they happen to fall during the research phase. Annual tradeshows such as the Motivation Show (formerly IT&ME, the International Travel and Meetings Exposition) held in Chicago, IMEX in Frankfurt, EIBTM in Barcelona, LACIME in South America, and AIME in rotating cities in Asia are well attended by international exhibitors representing destinations, airlines, congress centers, hotels, and support services.

SITE SELECTION

Researching, studying, and evaluating a variety of destinations and venues within those destinations can seem an awesome task when the entire world is under consideration. However, there are a limited number of cities or regions that have the facilities and services needed to sustain the average international meeting.

The selection process begins with focusing on a particular region such as the Asia-Pacific region, Europe, or Latin America. Often the demographics or distribution of attendees will influence that choice. Time of year and climate also may influence the choice. Within the chosen region, several sites are selected for research.

Research starts with defining the event's parameters. The meeting's objectives and proposed dates, along with the number of attendees, their geographical distribution, and their profile, influence destination and venue choices. Other factors to be considered at this point are the following:

- *Requirements.* Estimated initial room block: the number of guest rooms, meeting rooms, exhibit space, food and beverage functions (F&B), support services, and special requirements.
- *Meeting history.* This is based on research and documentation of previous meetings of similar design, including date, site, room block and pickup (rooms actually occupied), room rates, and F&B expenditures. This information also allows prospective venues to estimate the meeting's value and provides negotiating leverage. Armed with these data, the meeting organizer narrows the scope of study by focusing on a specific region and country. Within each destination, research is concentrated on two or three sites or cities. It is those cities which will be the subject of further exploration.

The old burden of digging through voluminous files or thick directories has been lightened by the nearly universal accessibility of Web sites that feature comprehensive details, function space floor plans, pictures, and even virtual tours. Using the resources of the Internet, a meeting planner usually selects three or four hotels in each venue that have the required room capacity and meeting space and are within the budget parameters. This research customarily is followed by a Request for Proposal. The RFP usually is e-mailed (occasionally faxed) to select venues, to DMCs, or to convention and visitors bureaus (CVBs). If international chain hotels are in the select list, their regional sales representatives often are contacted for rates and available dates.

Venues that have the necessary dates, space, and rates specified in the RFP respond with a detailed proposal. Upon reviewing these documents, most meeting organizers narrow the choices to those they feel best fit their needs. At that point a physical inspection of the destination and candidate venues is arranged, usually through an intermediary such as a convention bureau, a DMC, or a particular hotel property.

SCHEDULING SITE INSPECTIONS

As choices are refined further on the basis of responses, a site visit is scheduled to the city and the properties that best meet the organization's needs. Hotel and CVB representatives are advised and are given meeting histories in advance. The meeting organizer contacts support services on site to ascertain reputation, fees, and capabilities.

DESTINATION MARKETERS

To aid event planners, most meeting destinations have an active tourist office and/or convention bureau staffed by competent, multilingual professionals. They also tend to staff offices in major cities, and most attend and exhibit at industry trade shows. These organizations assist planners with detailed information on their city or region and arrange for site inspection visits. Destination marketers also assist with promotional support: shells (four-color printed destination flyers or brochures with blank spaces for imprinting sponsor's logo or text), brochures, maps, CDs, and DVDs as well as mailing services.

Federations of convention bureaus such as the Asian Association of Convention and Visitors Bureaus (AACVB) and the European Federation of Conference Towns (EFCT) serve their members by focusing their marketing efforts. They sponsor comprehensive databases on their member cities' resources for events. Similarly, independent marketing entities that represent various destination resources, such as hotels and DMCs, are a valuable source of general information.

PROGRAM PLANNING

As a rule, the meeting program for an association is a joint effort of a program committee, which is designated for each event, and the meeting planner. Corporate meeting programs usually are developed by the sponsoring department or division in conjunction with a meeting planner who is an employee of the company or an independent professional who provides planning services on a contract basis. The program is the rationale for the meeting and its most important element. After all, people attend because they are interested in hearing what the meeting sponsor has to communicate.

In multicultural events, language is a key consideration. English has become the universal language of business and communications; however, the organizers must take into consideration the audience demographics and comprehension levels of the attendees. If the official language of the conference is not the native language of the majority of the attendees, it is advisable to arrange for professional translation of conference materials and provide simultaneous interpretation of select presentations, if not the entire program.

PROGRAM ELEMENTS

Following is a basic overview of program elements as they pertain specifically to international events:

Scheduling flexibility. Because attendees may have traveled long distances over several time zones, it is customary for the first day to be free of any demanding social or educational programming, although a welcome reception is in order. The same principle applies to presenters. Unless they are local, they should plan to arrive a full day before their presentations. The subsequent business agenda should be flexible, and its content should provide added value for delegates whose costs are substantially higher at transnational events. It is important to avoid overprogramming so that attendees can interact with one another and so that they and their companions can shop, sightsee, and enjoy the attractions of an international venue.

By the same token, it is customary at international association events to offer delegates the option of pre- and postconference travel opportunities. It would be counterproductive to assemble a large number of travelers in another country and deny them the opportunity to see some of its primary attractions. Unfortunately, this is often the case with corporate meetings.

Session formats. At international congresses the emphasis is on plenary sessions, although some small group conferences may be scheduled as well. Corporate meetings run the gamut from general session presentations to numerous small breakout group workshops and often combine the two.

Program materials. To avoid or minimize shipping costs, meeting professionals find it cost-effective to have program materials such as attendance rosters, programs, handouts, and evaluation forms printed on-site. They verify during the site inspection that competent printing services are available. Masters and camera-ready graphics or discs containing those elements are mailed or downloaded to the designated printer, who produces and returns proof sheets. On approval, the material is printed and delivered to the site.

A resource that is appreciated by delegates is a meeting syllabus. Presenters are asked in advance of the meeting to submit a written résumé of their topics. The résumés are reproduced, bound, and distributed on-site, provided on a CD or occasionally available on the organization's Web site for the attendees to download at leisure. As a rule, they are published in the conference language, but translations may be offered if there is sufficient demand to cover the cost. Audio and video recordings may be available to attendees for the same purpose.

LANGUAGE APPLICATIONS

In all multinational meetings the organizers designate the official conference language. However, depending on attendee demographics, the organizers may arrange for interpretation and translation into other languages when the demographics indicate that some delegates, although multilingual, are not fluent in the conference vernacular.

Translation. Written materials intended for multinational audiences may need to be translated as the numbers in each language group dictate. Those items may include marketing literature, the conference program, the attendee roster, handouts, proceedings, exhibit literature, and other printed matter germane to the conference. In addition to the cost of translation, proofreading and printing costs call for a higher budget.

Interpretation. For seminars and breakout sessions at which audiences are smaller and only two language groups are represented, consecutive interpretation may be employed. This requires the presenter to pause frequently to allow the interpreter to translate. However, in general assemblies, simultaneous interpretation (S/I) is the rule. For these sessions, the program will designate available languages with each one's channel number, and delegates are given multichannel headsets.

Professional interpreters in sound isolation booths interpret the speaker's message as it is presented. Because this is very demanding, each language requires two interpreters who work as a team, giving each other breaks when necessary. As a general rule, a skilled professional can interpret highly technical material for 20 to 30 minutes before requiring a break. To facilitate accurate interpretation, presenters are required to provide interpreters with a copy of their talks and any visuals in advance. Budgeting for S/I includes interpreter fees, travel, and lodging as well as equipment rental.

CULTURAL CONSIDERATIONS

Even experienced meeting planners need to be reminded to consider cultural differences as they pertain to program planning. For instance, the "working lunch" that is often a part of North American gatherings is anathema at multicultural assemblies. Program organizers and speakers alike need to be aware of differences in learning styles among various cultures.

Those differences also influence audience participation. For example, the members of some Asian cultures are reluctant to speak out among foreigners for fear of losing face. Meeting organizers find that interaction and discourse are best achieved in small, informal discussion groups at social events away from the meeting room.

PREPARING PRESENTERS

Speakers, panelists, and discussion leaders who are not accustomed to addressing multinational audiences need to be briefed. To ensure that their messages are received and understood, use the following checklist (Figure 1-1) to prepare the presenters.

SOCIAL AND RECREATIONAL PROGRAMS

A meeting in a distant venue is an added value for delegates and guests. It would be counterproductive to have people travel great distances to an exciting destination and then spend all their time in meeting rooms. Therefore, meeting planners give visitors an opportunity to interact. It is customary at such events to schedule an international reception on the arrival night. Delegates also should be afforded the opportunity to enjoy, historical, cultural, and recreational sites at or near the conference venue. An afternoon or evening at leisure enables visitors to enjoy the area's restaurants, entertainment, and cultural amenities. As a rule, planners contract with a local DMC to organize and supervise these activities.

ENTERTAINMENT

DMCs also can be helpful in contracting entertainment at distant venues. This may run the gamut from a dance band, a comedian, or a magician to a complete folkloric show. Meeting professionals are sensitive to cultural taboos and are careful to avoid acts that may offend the audience. They routinely audition performances before engaging entertainment. Because booking entertainment involves contracts, it is best to work through a local DMC who is familiar with contract laws.

- Make use of visual aids to illustrate and clarify key points
- Use distinct, idiom-free language. Avoid slang and colloquialisms
- Adopt a global perspective and forgo provincial references
- Provide handouts and an outline or abstract
- Repeat questions to ensure they were heard and understood
- Summarize key points
- Conform to protocol

Figure 1-1 Checklist for Preparing Presenters

SAFETY AND SECURITY

Safety and stability of the meeting venue are among the organizers' prime criteria in site selection. For international destinations, they routinely consult U.S. State Department advisories and country-desk officers. Some contract with professional security services for threat assessments of sites under consideration. On site, depending on the sensitivity of the event, they consult local law enforcement officials and may contract for appropriate security resources. Law enforcement personnel also can be helpful in identifying unsafe areas in metropolitan centers. During site inspection visits, the meeting professional also conducts a safety inspection of the meeting venue and meets with facility security officers to evaluate their emergency response plans.

Health problems and medical crises can be minimized if they are anticipated. Delegates routinely are given predeparture information on basic security and safety precautions. They are advised of travel necessities such as prescription copies, allergies, travelers medical insurance, and spare eyeglasses. Emergency notification information is solicited at registration.

Even the safest meeting venue can be subject to unanticipated weather conditions, natural disasters, labor disputes, terrorist acts, and similar calamities. Anticipating those contingencies, many organizations routinely include event cancellation insurance in their meeting budgets.

CUSTOMS, CURRENCY, AND CONTRACTS

Attendees who are new to foreign travel and even some who are not should be advised well in advance of departure of the host country's customs and immigration regulations, especially those covering passports, visas, and prohibited items. They need to know about currency exchange and be aware that many countries charge a flat tax on purchases that may range as high as 25 percent. Called VAT, IVA, or GST, these taxes sometimes can be reclaimed by the individual and/or the meeting planner when he or she leaves the country. However, VAT reclaim is not offered everywhere, the paperwork can be daunting, and the length of the reimbursement process can range from months to years, depending on the country and the complexity of the claim.

Those rules are also important for the meeting staff in terms of payment for goods and services, shipping and customs fees, and documentation for shipments and restricted items. With regard to shipping and customs fees, most planners find it expedient to work with a freight forwarder who will prepare the necessary documents and oversee shipments. The most useful and reliable freight forwarders have corresponding customs brokers in the destination country who will receive the shipment, process the required customs documents, and arrange delivery to the meeting venue. This is especially important when exhibits are a part of the meeting.

Currency fluctuations can have a dramatic impact on meeting budgets, especially those which involve months or even years to implement. Meeting professionals routinely budget a contingency of 15 to 25 percent and use a variety of financial tactics to protect the budget from cost overruns. Multinational accounting firms, currency brokers, and the international departments of commercial banks are reliable sources of information on banking abroad, paying suppliers, and general financial management.

MARKETING

Marketing the event entails attracting delegates, providing them with detailed information on the program and speakers, and supplying appropriate forms for responding. Although e-mail and Web site utilization are virtually universal, many organizations continue to augment them with print media. Use the checklist in Figure 1-2 to incorporate the best practices into your marketing marketing messages.

Marketing media and literature should reflect the same cultural sensitivity as program presentations. If the material is in English, the designer needs to recognize that the recipient may not have a good command of the language. Acronyms, words with a double meaning, colloquial speech, and the term *foreign* should be avoided.

REGISTRATION AND HOUSING

Design of the registration form should reflect cultural competence. Nicknames and terms such as *first* and *last names* are inappropriate for multicultural events. *Given name* and *family name* are the proper terms in this context. In designating an address, *state/province* and *postal code* are proper usage. If registration fees are charged, details should include the amount for each delegate, early registration discounts, guest fees, currency, and forms of payment and deadlines.

The same thing applies to housing reservations. In addition, registrants should be advised that one group rate for singles and doubles is rare. In some countries double occupancy entails a premium for the second person. This is the case because outside the United States, hotel room rates routinely include

---

- A theme graphic incorporating event name, location, and dates
- Motivational message describing benefits of attending
- Overview of the business agenda and social and recreational programs
- Program highlights including presenters and a précis of each topic
- Information about the destination, accommodations, and travel options
- Host country's historical, language, and cultural characteristics
- Passport and visa requirements and health information
- Currency exchange, banking hours, and holidays
- Telephone and Internet access, electrical voltage, required adapters
- Response forms for registration and lodging, including fees and room prices

Figure 1-2 Checklist for Marketing Messages

breakfast, and in older European hotels especially, a double room is usually larger than a single room, which often contains only one twin bed. Housing request forms should explain such differences and list all rate options.

As in domestic venues, planners frequently find that the total number of rooms listed for a hotel may not be a reliable gauge of its capacity for a meeting group. The number of guest rooms a hotel will commit to group business varies with season and other commitments such as tour groups.

FOOD AND BEVERAGE

Meal functions can give attendees an opportunity to experience some of the unique cuisine of the host country. Serving local specialties and beverages also can effect savings in food costs. Serving times also vary according to local custom. In Spain, for instance, no cosmopolitan person would consider having dinner before 10 P.M.

Dietary customs vary greatly in some cultures. It is the meeting planner's responsibility to ascertain attendees' dietary restrictions (such as shellfish allergies and gluten or lactose intolerance) and convey that information to the chefs. Although vegetarian regimens are readily accommodated in most venues, albeit subject to interpretation, low-carbohydrate menus most likely will not be prevalent.

To take full advantage of the benefits of another culture's cuisine, meeting professionals arrange with the DMC to offer off-site functions. This may take the form of a dinner at a historic site, a museum, a castle, or a riverboat cruise. Another popular activity is a conducted dine-around that allows participants to enjoy some of the area's restaurants. In briefing delegates on local customs, it should be pointed out that in many countries the total cost of the meal is *service compris,* meaning that tax and gratuities are included. However, a nominal tip for good service is customary.

TRAVEL RESOURCES: AIR AND GROUND

Airline Services

Qualifying and selecting an official carrier for international flights is just as useful as it is for domestic travel. The designated airlines make concessions on fares and other services in anticipation of volume passenger revenues. However, this is not as simple with global travel. For a meeting convened in, say, Helsinki, with delegates departing from points in the Americas, Europe, Africa, and the Middle East, there may not be a single airline that serves all gateways. Code sharing among noncompeting carriers reduces the problem, but some travelers may have to take flights that do not make fare concessions. Destinations served by multiple carriers offer more competitive fares or more flexible terms.

Time of year also has an impact on airfares, just as it does with hotel rates, although this varies with the destination. Buenos Aires in July (midwinter) will be far more competitive than Amsterdam, where July is the height of the tourist season.

There are concessions other than low fares available from airlines, including marketing assistance, discounted freight rates, upgrades for VIPs, and complimentary or reduced-fare staff travel. The airlines also may offer passenger amenities such as use of club lounges, assistance with customs clearance, and group baggage handling.

Meeting professionals prepare for negotiating with potential carriers before meeting dates are firmed up, knowing that time of travel can have an impact on pricing. Other data they need to have include the following:

- Range of acceptable dates
- Originating gateways and approximate numbers from each one
- Percentage of coach, business class, and first class passengers

WORKING WITH PCOS AND DMCS

A PCO or DMC can be an invaluable asset to a meeting planner, particularly in another country. Their knowledge of the language and customs and familiarity with the destination, its attractions, and its support services relieve the organizer of much of the stress an unfamiliar site can engender.

PCOs who specialize in international meetings are generally experienced independent entrepreneurs. They can serve as an adjunct to the meeting staff, offering management and financial services as well as liaison with suppliers.

A reliable DMC has the same professional traits and serves as an expert coordinator of transportation and recreational services. In addition, DMCs frequently provide an on-site hospitality desk staffed by multilingual professionals who are thoroughly familiar with the destination and its attractions.

MEETING TECHNOLOGY

Dependable communication technology, which is vital at domestic events, becomes critical when the meeting venue is in another country. The need to communicate, illustrate, and convey information in an effective way takes on a higher meaning when the organization is in an unfamiliar locale conveying information to a multicultural audience or accessing data from sources around the globe.

DATA TRANSMISSION

High-speed broadband Internet connection is a valuable asset when an organization operates at its home base. Halfway around the world, it is indispensable. There is considerable variance in access, quality, and cost of services in meeting venues around the world. This asset is so important to the success of a meeting that it often is foremost on a corporate meeting professional's checklist at the RFP phase. Corporate planners especially often disqualify an otherwise acceptable venue if broadband connectivity is not available to the attendees in both the meeting space and the sleeping rooms.

The Internet plays a vital role in the management, logistics, and administration of the event, enabling organizers to access vital data from the home database and industry Web sites. It also has become an essential resource in conveying information to attendees and presenters alike.

PRESENTATION TECHNOLOGY

Laptop computers and streaming video for the most part have replaced the formerly ubiquitous slide and overhead projectors. Speakers are able to prepare elaborate presentations using computers or access a vast network of visual images from a wide variety of data banks to enhance their presentations.

Most meeting venues around the world offer the customary audiovisual and technical products as well as the technicians needed to operate them. Professional-quality sound systems, video projection, wireless interpretation networks, and interactive response systems, which once were considered advanced technology, are now standard fare in many countries.

There is a caveat, however. Meeting organizers need to be aware of differences in electrical current and video standards (including DVD) and related technological variances. A video recorded in Canada or the United States, whether on tape or on a DVD, is not compatible with a system in Germany or Australia.

EXHIBITIONS

If any single feature sets exhibition centers in Asia and Europe apart from their counterparts in North America, it is their immense size. Amsterdam, Berlin, Hamburg, Hong Kong, Nice, Singapore, and Tokyo are among the cities that boast megacenters that dwarf even Chicago's McCormick Place, the largest in America.

These megacenters, most of which expanded or came on line in the past two decades, are distinguished not only by their size but by their technological advances. Designed to cater to international exhibitors and audiences, they are equipped with sophisticated systems that include state-of-the-art auditoriums with dedicated simultaneous interpretation capability, subfloor channels for exhibit utilities, and data transmission and security systems that permit remote monitoring of all areas. Some offer rental of PDAs, which can be programmed with full data on any exhibition, replacing the traditional printed exhibit manual.

There are differences as well in how exhibitions operate and how they are configured. In most of Europe, the customary "pipe and drape" so familiar in the U.S. exhibit booth (called a "stand") is replaced by a hard-wall structure built on site.

IN CONCLUSION

This chapter has pointed out some of the many characteristics of international meetings from both a philosophical and a logistical viewpoint. When Christine Duffy, CEO of Maritz Travel and a world-class conference organizer, was asked to characterize the consummate global meeting executive, she provided the following profile: "Successful international event planners anticipate the learning process. They study their industry colleagues' attitudes, their culture, their values. And they adapt accordingly in order to build a mutually rewarding relationship."

That distinction has to do with the meeting professional's attitude. Most planners exhibit an inquisitiveness about the regions and cultures in which they function. They genuinely care about the people. This concern is communicated to those with whom they interact and is reciprocated. Europeans and Latin Americans have an expression for this kind of person: "simpatico." The most successful international planners are those who recognize that *different* does not mean better or worse; it just means different. By embracing the diversity of the countries in which they work rather than expecting everything to be "just like home," these professionals enrich not only their own professional careers but also the programs they plan and manage.

KEY POINTS

Global events may take many different forms, depending on locale, objective, format, program dynamics, and attendee demographics.

Factors that distinguish such events from their domestic counterpart include immigration and customs regulations, currency, political climate, and language and cultural differences.

Organizers research and make use of a variety of networks and resources during the planning stage to select a site for the event.

The program is the main focus of any meeting or convention. When the audience composition includes people of various nationalities, factors such as interpretation and speaker orientation must be taken into consideration.

The presence of participants with different cultural backgrounds affects all aspects of the event, including registration, program content, audience dynamics, protocol, meal planning, and entertainment.

To the customary risks characteristic of domestic events must be added a thorough assessment of potential threats and emergencies that are specific to a foreign destination, including safety, health, weather, crime, and political stability.

Comprehending currency instruments and differences in contract law and practices is essential to avoid budget overruns and misunderstandings.

Marketing to multicultural audiences requires a distinct perspective and methods that account for language and cultural differences.

Attention to detail at the preevent planning stage pays dividends during operations.

When planning exhibitions, organizers need to be aware of differences in facilities, exhibit configurations, nomenclature, and operations.

In planning and arranging air travel, consideration is given to widely dispersed origination points. Long-haul flights and multiple-time-zone travel have an impact on the program.

Variances in electric current, bandwidth access, and video standards affect data transmission and audiovisual technology. Advance knowledge of those variations is essential.

CHAPTER GLOSSARY

APEX Fare. Reduced advanced purchase excursion fare offered by international air carriers.

Bank draft. A bank document authorizing the holder to draw on funds through another financial institution.

Banquet event order (BEO; now called event order). A form prepared for each event by the facility confirming room setup, meals, beverages, staging, equipment, price, and related details. Also called a function sheet or résumé.

Carnet. A customs document that permits the holder to import merchandise or equipment duty-free for a defined period. A bond is posted to guarantee reexport. This is essentially a visa for goods and equipment.

Committed capacity. The number of guest rooms a hotel will commit to a meeting group at any given time.

Delegate. Voting representative at a meeting. A generic reference to person attending an international meeting.

Demipension. A room rate that includes breakfast and dinner. In North America it is called the Modified American Plan (MAP).

Destination. Country, region or city under consideration for an event.

Destination Management Company (DMC). Usually a locally based firm staffed by experienced, multilingual guides and operations personnel familiar with the area's attractions. DMCs organize theme events, leisure activities, and off-site tours and also provide airport transfers and ground transportation to and from off-site events.

Family name. The preferred term for "last name" on registration documents.

Force majeure. A contract clause limiting liability for event cancellation due to circumstances beyond both parties' control: war, strike, natural disaster, acts of terrorism, and so on.

Ground operator. Similar to a DMC. A company or individual providing ground transportation.

Head count. The total number of people attending a meal or event.

Head tax. A fee charged in some countries for arriving and departing passengers.

Interpretation. Oral translation to another langauge or several languages.

Long haul. Flights involving more than five time-zone distances.

Pickup. The number of guest rooms actually occupied in a room block.

Plenary session. General assembly of all participants. Also called a general session.

Proceedings. An official published transcription of all full conference sessions.

Satellite meeting. A seminar or symposium on a related topic occurring before, during, or after the main meeting.

Service compris. A menu designation indicating that a gratuity is included in the price.

Threat assessment. An analysis of an area or venue that is conducted by a professional security firm to identify risks and potential dangers.

Translation. Conversion of written material to another language.

Turnaround (turnover). Time required to break down and reset a room for an event.

VAT. Value-Added Tax charged on products and services. Also known as IVA in Spain, Portugal, Italy, and Latin America and GST in Canada.

Venue. Physical meeting site: a hotel, conference center, and/or facility such as a congress center.

PASSPORT

Books

Goldblatt, Dr. Joe, and Nelson, Kathleen S., *The International Dictionary of Event Management*, John Wiley & Sons, New York.

International Association of Professional Congress Organizers (IAPCO), *Manual of Congress Terminology*, IAPCO, Brussels.

Internet

IAPCO: www,congresses.com/iapco.

Meeting Professionals International: www.mpiweb.org.

Professional Convention Management Association: www.pcma.org.

APEX Glossary of Terms: www.conventionindustry.org.

Chapter 2

DECISION FACTORS

The great decisions of human life have as a rule far more to do with the instincts and other mysterious unconscious factors than with the conscious will and well-meaning reasonableness.

—Carl Jung

IN THIS CHAPTER

We will explore:

- How to define meeting, convention, and exhibition objectives carefully and precisely.
- Methods for determining a meeting's return on investment (ROI).
- Anticipating potential problems and determining how to avoid them.
- Formulating the meeting profile.
- Researching the demographics of the participants and matching them to the program.
- Determining the financial philosophy for an event and developing a budget that corresponds to it.
- How to develop the Meeting Prospectus.

All events, domestic or international, begin with an analysis of the rationale or purpose and the type of event that will serve that purpose best. Once those parameters are defined, thought is given to questions such as who is to attend, what organizational goals are to be achieved, and what tasks must be completed to attain those goals. Only after those questions are answered do the organizers consider where the event should take place. If those goals can be served by convening at a domestic venue, is there a valid rationale for going abroad?

Whether to hold a meeting overseas is often not a matter of choice. In the corporate arena, especially in multinational companies with subsidiaries, distributors, and customers around the world, a planner may be asked to organize a meeting in Athens, Georgia, one week and in Athens, Greece, the next. As companies grow, merge, and globalize, "business as usual" is becoming more multinational and multicultural than ever before. The need to connect on a global scale has stimulated dynamic growth in international events. Corporate and independent planners with corporate clients must be prepared to work in any country at any time.

Association planners also are becoming increasingly conscious of the need to be globally aware as more and more associations and nonprofit groups look toward global alliances to increase their membership, enrich their educational programs, and diversify networking opportunities for their members. However, before venturing overseas, associations and nonprofit groups should have valid reasons for doing so and should analyze the costs and benefits carefully.

Whatever the type of organization, the individual responsible for planning such events must be a consummate planner with the skills of a manager, strategist, educator, creative director, financial analyst, and diplomat. During the planning and subsequent phases, that person will call on all those skills.

▌MEETING OBJECTIVES

If you are considering taking a meeting overseas, carefully weigh the pros and cons and formulate a meeting profile as you would for a domestic event. Consider the meeting objectives, participant profile, time and distance allowances, tax impact, social and business agendas, time of year, and organizational policy. Isolate some of the factors that support those objectives, such as the following:

- Meeting with affiliates or counterpart organizations
- Studying innovative techniques, products, and facilities
- Tying in with other events, such as an exposition
- Sharing knowledge, perspectives, and technology with others
- Increasing the potential for new or expanded markets
- Forming new alliances

Having defined and articulated the objectives (there can be more than one), the meeting professional and management must ask the pointed question: "Can this be achieved by means other than a meeting?

It takes a great deal of fortitude and integrity for a meeting planner to talk management out of having a meeting. However, if one accepts the premise that meeting professionals are also financial managers, that decision must be made at times. Assuming that the indications are positive, the next step is to prepare a comprehensive document that outlines the variables on which the decision will be made, whether for domestic or for international. Some call this a Meeting Prospectus, others a Meeting Analysis, but whatever the name, the document presents management with key decision factors, including the following:

- Defined objectives and benefits to the organization
- Analysis of comparable recent events
- Estimate of attendance volume
- Attendee demographics and geographic distribution
- Benefits of attendance to stakeholders

- Estimated budget differential (domestic versus transnational)
- Best practices to support organizational objectives

WEIGHING THE BENEFITS AND ANTICIPATING PROBLEMS

Will the objectives of the meeting be better achieved in an international venue? Will the attraction of visiting another country increase attendance and, as a result, revenue? Will the meeting program attract new members, provide positive press, and/or improve the group's influence in the region? Will the added costs of managing and implementing the meeting in another country offset any of the potential advantages or projected revenue? These are all questions that should be asked and answered before a decision is made to go offshore.

The benefits then must be weighed against certain complexities and challenges of going abroad. Consider the increased travel time and cost as well as the effects of jet lag, which will affect both attendees and speakers. Language and cultural differences, different business practices, protocol, and etiquette can cause problems if they are not dealt with appropriately. What about the tax impact? Many international organizations are governed by tax codes that require proof that a meeting is directly related to the taxpayer's trade or profession to qualify as a legitimate business expense.

Will your attendees welcome the opportunity to experience another culture, or will they want everything to be just the way it is at home no matter where they are in the world? If this is the case, you might as well just stay home or at the very least be prepared to devote additional time, resources, and creativity to educating, motivating, and managing the expectations of your attendees before their departure.

▌RETURN ON INVESTMENT

ROI as it relates to meetings could also be termed ROE (return on event) and can encompass a return on marketing (ROM) expressed by attendance as well as a return on objectives (ROO) established by the sponsor and participants. It is an expression of the relationship between the cost of a program and the benefit to all those involved. The ROI process measures the success of a meeting by comparing desired outcomes to stated objectives, using a quantitative measurement. In the past, meeting evaluations often focused on impressions and subjective opinions about the venue, speakers, program, entertainment, and so on. Even today, many organizations continue to evaluate the success of their meetings in qualitative terms. Although this information is interesting and useful for logistics planning, it does not provide the substantive data required to make strategic cost-benefit decisions about future meetings.

Faced with increasingly tight budgets and competition for attendees' time and attention, meeting professionals today understand the importance of providing data rather than impressions to the various stakeholder groups. What constitutes an acceptable ROI for the meeting sponsor? For the attendee? For an exhibitor? Whether it is an increase in revenue, the acquisition of new skills, change in behavior, growth of market share, or greater influence in a particular area, the planner must ensure that the objectives are clear so that the outcomes can be measured accurately.

To know what to measure, one must have a clear understanding of members' expectations before the event. Establish measurement parameters: satisfaction, learning, performance, income potential, and the like. Then conduct surveys and/or focus groups ahead of the meeting to ascertain attendees' needs. This may be best done at the end of the preceding event, when you have an active audience. This will allow you to construct an experience that meets attendees' expectations, addresses their needs, and provides management with qualitative metrics. The data thus generated can become a valuable marketing tool for subsequent events.

Some event organizers schedule a follow-up survey to verify the results well in advance of the upcoming event. This survey is addressed to the entire stakeholder group, not just to previous attendees. Various incentives, such as drawings for gifts, free registration, air fare, and postevent trips, assure a good response.

THE MEETING PROFILE

The character and nature of the event and its various elements are determined by the objective and are formulated in the Meeting Profile: what an architect might describe as the meeting manager's blueprint. In its simplest form, it covers the Five W's as articulated by journalists but applied to meetings, conventions, and exhibitions:

What? Type of event: annual convention, incentive meeting, exhibition, seminar, Web conference, symposium, etc.

Why? Objective: rationale for holding the meeting and expected results.

Who? Participants: a brief description of who will attend, such as corporate and sales staff, association membership, delegates, presenters, dealers, field managers, spouses and guests, nonmembers, and user groups (includes an estimate of the accommodations required).

When? Proposed dates: targeted month or range of dates, including arrival-departure pattern and specific dates if known.

Where? Destination: domestic or international, city hotel or resort, conference center or specific venue if established.

Ideally, the *when* and *where* at this stage should be as broad as possible to provide the organization with maximum discretion and negotiating leverage.

It is possible to begin some of the initial planning by using the Meeting Profile as a guide. The PCO can start researching sites and facilities, since the time of year and rooming needs are known. However, at this point one may have to speculate on the program and, consequently, the required meeting space. Meeting history can be a valuable guide in estimating space requirements.

At the initial planning phase, the following tasks are performed by the meeting staff or in concert with the organization's executives:

- Review the objective
- Establish a time frame and agenda
- Develop an overall theme
- Prepare a task analysis and master timetable
- Determine the anticipated number and profile of attendees
- Set up appropriate internal and external communication procedures
- Prepare the initial budget and get approval as needed
- Formulate a tentative program in concert with participating departments
- Prepare a Meeting Profile and Prospectus

During this phase, research potential destinations by utilizing Web sites and/or directories, industry shows, professional colleagues, and, if appropriate, past histories. Identify and evaluate venues, hotels, and other facilities to fit the type of meeting, paying particular attention to conference facilities, services, and room capacity. Consider likely candidates' reputation for political stability and safety as well as climate and other conditions during the proposed dates. Research and evaluate support services and verify this information by networking. Finally, narrow the choices to three or four destinations that best fit your parameters and prepare and convey a Request for Proposal (RFP) to likely venues.

The late comedian Fred Allen defined a meeting as "a group of men who individually can do nothing but as a group decide nothing can be done." When beholding this immensity of detail, it is difficult for a meeting professional to realize that not everyone holds meetings in the same reverence.

| FINANCIAL CONSIDERATIONS

A common concern for organizations planning an international meeting is whether they can afford the cost, with the assumption being that it invariably will be more costly than a domestic event. An organizer faced with the decision to go offshore may ask, "Where do I have to beef up my budget?" An association executive may want to know, "What will it cost my members, and how do I justify the added cost to them?" Another planner may want to know, "Are there any cost-effective destinations left in the world?" It is true that meetings held abroad tend to be more expensive. However, they pay unique dividends that justify the higher cost. The opportunities to visit a foreign country, interact with people of other cultures, and broaden one's horizons to encompass a global perspective are tangible, value-added benefits that justify the additional cost to participant and sponsor alike.

HEDGING ONE'S BETS

In all international events, it is wise to add a contingency factor of 10 to 20 percent over the basic cost estimates to cover currency fluctuations if services are contracted for in the local currency. Even if services are quoted in dollars, some expenditures will have to be in foreign currency. Contact the international department of your bank or a dedicated foreign currency exchange and management company for information on currency hedges. Ask about which ones allow you to lock in prices at today's exchange rates. A premium is charged for the privilege, but it simplifies budgeting. (See Chapter 5 for an indepth discussion of these and other currency issues.)

Excluding airfare, the expense of attending a meeting abroad may not be any higher than that of a domestic event at a comparable venue. Five-star hotel rooms and meals are no more expensive in Geneva or Singapore than they are in New York or San Francisco. Indeed, in popular meeting destinations such as Athens, Buenos Aires, and Hong Kong, rooms, meals, shopping, and entertainment may be more affordable than they are in comparable U.S. cities. Hotels in Asia, Europe, and other parts of the world routinely levy a charge for meeting space. In hotels all over the world, rates are based on guest room occupancy and may be negotiable depending on the season.

Meeting managers can help keep participants' costs in line by alerting travelers to conditions in advance of their trip. Provide advice on tipping, ground transportation, shopping, and value-added tax (VAT) refunds, as well as currency exchange rates, bank locations, and banking hours. Negotiate favorable group rates for hotel rooms, car rentals, and other amenities that benefit the traveler.

Whatever the spot price or the strength of the dollar, some destinations are perennial favorites because they continue to offer value in the price of services, accommodations, dining, and consumer goods. If you as the meeting manager are concerned about cost—and who isn't?—assess several destinations that otherwise meet your meeting parameters in terms of cost savings. The romance of Paris can be had for considerably less in Vienna or Budapest. The rich historical tapestry of culture that is Rome's can be found at substantial savings in Athens or Istanbul. South American cities such as Buenos Aires, Rio de Janeiro, and Santiago de Chile combine both romance and culture at even more cost-effective prices.

Apart from budget considerations, a conscientious meeting manager should consider several factors in selecting an overseas venue. Does a foreign destination support the meeting's objective? Are the proposed sites attractive to participants, thus assuring a favorable response? Are these places safe, politically stable, and friendly toward foreigners?

Are there adequate first-class hotels and meeting facilities as well as cultural and leisure attractions? Is there a trained multilingual infrastructure and competent support services? Only if those criteria are met can budget requirements be addressed. As with any domestic meeting, cost is a relative factor. It is not the main criterion by which destinations are judged.

PARTICIPANT DEMOGRAPHICS

For a meeting to be a medium for communication, the audience must be receptive to the message. Therefore, it is contingent on the meeting organizers to know the composition of the audience, the needs of the attendees, and their motivation. When a meeting involves a multicultural audience, added considerations are engendered by the characteristics of delegates coming from several different countries. An analysis of participant demographics based on several factors is essential before planning can commence. Those factors and the way they affect operations are as follows:

- *Organizational.* If prospective delegates are all members of the sponsoring organization, it simplifies marketing and registration. If they are not, additional time and a larger budget are needed for market research.
- *Socioeconomic factors* influence delegates' ability to afford transportation, registration fees, and housing.
- *Ethnic or cultural background* will have an impact on the conference program's format and food and beverage functions. Religion can be a factor if a large percentage of the attendees are affected by dates that conflict with their religious observances.
- Delegates' degree of *language proficiency* may influence several planning areas, including program planning and marketing. In terms of marketing, it is customary to produce Web site data, brochures, and announcements in multiple languages, depending on the regions that are involved. For European audiences, English, French, and German are traditional. Latin American events customarily require Spanish and Portuguese. For Asian delegates, Japanese and Chinese are advisable.
- Delegate personal values, attitudes, and lifestyle preferences.

THE PROSPECTUS

After you have determined that there is a valid rationale for the event, it is time to draw up a document that contains the particulars. Carrying the architectural analogy further, the meeting profile is no more than a rough floor plan. As decisions are made and information is gathered, it is refined to resemble an architect's rendering with elevations and detailed diagrams and becomes the Meeting Prospectus (some call it the Meeting Specifications.)

The Five W's are expanded as the planning continues and the following elements are added:

- *Theme:* Usually reflects the objective, the locale, or both.
- *Subject matter:* A list of topics in support of meeting objectives.
- *Format:* Method of presentation for each topic to achieve optimum results and efficiency, such as plenary sessions, breakouts or discussion groups, seminars, workshops, and case method.

- *Business agenda:* The program's continuity from the opening address to the closing session, delineating types of sessions and presentation formats; includes meeting enhancers, bridges, continuity links, and presenter names (if known) or profiles (e.g., "financial analyst").
- *Social agenda:* Receptions, meal functions, recreational events, and both organized and optional leisure activities.
- *Guest agenda:* Special programs for invited guests, spouses, and children.
- *Budget:* A tentative overall budget showing projected fixed and variable expenses. Project registration fees and income should be included if applicable.
- *Registration and reception:* Registration forms, policies and fees, and deadlines; online registration; on-site reception and registration of attendees, exhibitors, speakers, and guests.
- *Transportation:* Plans for transporting staff and participants to and from the site, official airline Web site, transfers and surface transportation; shipment of freight, exhibits, products, and meeting materials.
- *Support services:* Resources required on-site, such as clerical staff, telecommunications and computer systems, audiovisual equipment and technicians, exhibit contractor, decoration, security, convention aides, photographer, ground operator, and volunteers.

MEETING THE GLOBAL CHALLENGE

Globalization is the result of dynamics that are driving corporations to target sources of revenue in foreign markets, outsource services, and form affiliations with their counterparts in other countries. There is a trickle-down influence on associations to keep pace by forming international alliances.

The decision to meet abroad imposes new and significant challenges on meeting organizers who are accustomed to managing events at home-based venues. Even those meetings are increasingly affected by the presence of attendees from around the world. Not only must meeting professionals learn new skills, they need to develop a different mind-set when interacting with and among other cultures. This imposes an obligation on individuals, organizations, and institutions of higher learning to develop a multicultural perspective and acquire the skills needed to conduct activities on a global scale.

KEY POINTS

As companies expand and merge globally, overseas meetings are becoming essential in linking subsidiaries, shareholders, and owners.

Carefully weigh the pros and cons of having a meeting overseas before considering taking on the added cost and time needed to plan an overseas meeting. Determine whether the cost and complexity of holding an overseas meeting will outweigh the benefits of increasing attendance or attracting new members.

Have a clear understanding of the sponsors', attendees', and exhibitors' objectives for the meeting so that you can meet them and create a clear return on investment and a value-added experience.

Identify the meeting's objectives by using the Five W's: *what, why, who, when,* and *where.* Using your proposed objectives, begin to do research by utilizing your network of other planners and then submit a Request for Proposal to your top destinations and/or properties.

Plan on costs 10 to 20 percent higher than your estimates to account for currency fluctuations.

Meetings may not cost more overseas than at home, depending on the strength of the dollar in your destination. Cost is not the main criterion in choosing an overseas destination. The added value of experiencing another culture is a valuable draw.

When holding a meeting with a multicultural audience, consider the organizational, socioeconomic, ethnic, and language proficiency of the delegates.

PASSPORT

Books

Carey, Tony, CMM, ed., *Professional Meeting Management—A European Handbook,* Meeting Professionals International, 1999.

Wright, Rudy R., CMP, *The Meeting Spectrum: An Advanced Guide for Meeting Professionals,* San Diego, CA: Rockwood Enterprises 2005.

Internet

Destination Marketing Association International: www.dmai.org.

Chapter 3

DESTINATION ASSESSMENT

A destination management company (DMC) is like an architect, utilizing its unique knowledge and experience [of the destination] to design a blueprint that fulfills the meeting, convention, or incentive travel planner's needs and desires, optimizes the available resources, and adheres to the limitations and requirements of the area.

—Christopher H. Lee, DMCP

IN THIS CHAPTER

We will explore:

- How to assess and evaluate the destination for a meeting, convention, or exhibition.
- Identifying and using the resources needed to conduct the assessment and site inspection.
- Networking in professional meetings and events organizations to find and assess the best destination for an event.
- Working with destination marketing organizations such as convention and visitors bureaus and national tourism bureaus.
- Avoiding problems when working with various destination stakeholders.
- How to identify, select, and manage a destination management company.
- Interfacing effectively with sales professionals at international chain hotel companies and representatives of hotel marketing consortia.
- Selecting the best destination.
- Determining the best facility (hotel or conference, congress, or convention center) for the event.

Ask any experienced meeting planner what location has been the most difficult or challenging to work in and the answer often will be a location that was not chosen or even recommended by the planner. More often than not, the worst meeting destinations are those chosen by the boss, CEO, program chairperson, executive director, or board of directors and/or the decision maker's spouse or spouse equivalent, teenage children, or in-laws who have *always* wanted to go to there on vacation. Accessibility, infrastructure, communications, support systems, service levels, and emergency response facilities, not to mention adequate sleeping rooms and meeting space, rarely are taken into account by decision makers or family members whose primary responsibility within the organization is something other than meeting planning. For this reason, a professional planner's assessment of proposed destinations is critical to the decision process no matter where the meeting is to be held.

If you are told one day that your next meeting will be outside your home country or have been asked to submit a proposal for such a meeting, your first step should be a careful assessment of potential destinations. As with any domestic program, the venue's resources and image must fit the meeting objectives and parameters as well as the attendees' expectations. However, the choices available for an international meeting are considerably greater and more varied, since you now have the whole world from which to choose. Is it to be a dynamic cosmopolitan city such as Paris, Tokyo, Santiago, or Sydney? The exotic ambience of Bangkok or Rio de Janeiro? The multiple cultures and world-class facilities of Hong Kong or Singapore? The cultural riches of Florence, Beijing, Athens, Cairo, or Buenos Aires? Or does the nature of the event dictate a more tropical venue such as Ixtapa, Bali, Recife, or the Great Barrier Reef?

One of the main attractions of international meetings is that they provide both the sponsors and the attendees with an opportunity to travel to places they might not visit on their own. The more well known, popular, exclusive, or exotic the meeting location, the greater the chance that people will want to attend. Unfortunately, as a general rule, the more exotic and/or isolated the venue, the greater the chance that it will not be an optimal location for a meeting. The planner's task is to identify a venue that is exciting enough to attract sponsors and attendees but at the same time can provide the logistic infrastructure to support the technical aspects of the meeting. This is not always easy.

In evaluating international destinations, it is important to apply objective criteria to the site selection process. Since potential venues may not be well known to all the decision makers, it is important to present the critical logistic requirements without which the meeting cannot take place. This makes it easier to reinforce a logical choice in the face of someone's fantasy vacation spot. Nonetheless, the final decision may be made by the CEO's spouse, but at least you will be on record as having done everything possible to provide a professional evaluation and recommendation.

At this point, you probably are thinking, "Wait a minute. I've never been out of the country. I don't know the first thing about meeting venues overseas. How could I possibly evaluate potential destinations, much less recommend one? I don't even know where to start looking for help—HELP!" The good news is that a variety of resources are available to you, beginning with this book. Other resources are discussed below so that you can organize your contacts into a functioning network on which to call whenever you need information.

ESTABLISHING A RESOURCE NETWORK

Experienced meeting professionals will tell you that assiduous research, incessant focused networking, and a lifelong commitment to continuing professional education are the most important components of a successful career. For an international meeting planner, the availability of dependable resources and accurate, up-to-date information is essential. Fortunately, there are abundant resources available, and with the advent of both the Internet and increasingly sophisticated communications technologies, the task of locating, retrieving, and processing information has been accelerated and simplified considerably.

When you are establishing your resource network, think about what happens when one drops a pebble into a puddle of water. From the point of impact, waves of concentric rings form and move outward from the center. This is how you should approach the development of your resource network. Start with the people closest to you and move progressively outward, gathering information and making contacts at every opportunity, wherever you go.

FAMILY AND FRIENDS

Begin with your family and friends, people in your neighborhood who may be from other countries, and anyone in your personal circle who travels abroad frequently. Although these people may not be able to provide specific technical information about a venue, they often can provide a wealth of information about the local culture and attractions from a point of view similar to that of your attendees. If you are fortunate enough to have friends and neighbors from a variety of national and ethnic backgrounds, talk to them, ask them about their homelands, and learn as much as you can about their cultures and the business practices of their native countries.

PROFESSIONAL COLLEAGUES

Your innermost professional circle will consist of your co-workers and other meeting professionals with whom you meet and work in volunteer positions in industry associations. If you are a corporate planner in a multinational company or an independent planner for multinational corporate clients, you may have access to branch offices or subsidiaries in potential meeting destinations. Local company personnel can be very helpful, especially if you have never visited the country, do not speak the language, and are not familiar with the local customs.

You may or may not be required to work with the local office staff, and though it is tempting to rely on this resource, you must take care to define each of your roles and responsibilities clearly from the outset. Understand that the perspective, priorities, and preferred method of operations in the subsidiaries may be very different from those of headquarters, which you represent. You must move carefully and correctly through the equivalent of a cultural and political minefield to achieve the objectives of headquarters without offending your local colleagues. If you are an association planner working with a non-U.S. program chairperson or a local host committee, the same cautions apply, but the situation may be even more delicate because you are working with volunteers who are not being paid to cooperate with you.

Unfortunately, there is no set paradigm for how much or how little assistance should be requested, provided, or accepted, since every meeting is different and every situation is unique. Some local offices may not have the time, inclination, or available personnel to provide more than perfunctory assistance. Others may be offended that headquarters sent you to organize a meeting in their bailiwick rather than entrusting it to them. Still others may be so pleased to be the local hosts of the meeting and so eager to showcase their cooperation to headquarters that you find yourself inundated with suggestions and offers of assistance.

Similar situations occur when association planners work with their counterparts from an allied society or local host committee. Whatever the meeting and whatever your role, learning how to work effectively with local contacts is a fundamental requirement for successful offshore meeting management.

MEETINGS INDUSTRY ORGANIZATIONS

Colleagues you meet at industry association educational conferences, tradeshows, and social events are among your most valuable resources for both the short term and the long term. If you are not a member of one of the major meetings industry associations, you should join one, participate actively, and try to attend as many of the local chapter meetings, regional conferences, and international congresses as possible. In addition to these major organizations, a variety of smaller associations provide professional education and networking opportunities for planners in specific industries such as insurance, financial services, and medical/pharmaceutical; planners who specialize in government, military, university, or religious meetings; independent planners who work in a variety of industries; and planners who belong to special interest groups. See Appendix 1 for a list of such organizations.

If you are a student pursuing a career in event planning, you have a professional network, beginning with your instructors. Their knowledge and contacts within the industry are invaluable, and many of them are members of major professional associations that provide continuing education programs and networking opportunities at the local, regional, national, and international levels. These associations have student memberships and encourage close interaction among members at all levels of experience.

Whatever your interests and whatever type of planner you are or want to be, the more active you are in the industry, the more people you will meet and the more your chances of finding colleagues who have worked overseas, have contacts overseas, or can be of direct assistance to you overseas will increase. It may be a speaker at one of the sessions you attend. It may be the person standing next to you at the opening reception. It may be the people you meet at the tradeshow who just finished a meeting in the destination you are considering. These people are among the most valuable resources because your planner colleagues have no financial interest in your choice of a destination. They will give you their objective opinions; tell you what's good and what's bad, who works well and who doesn't; and generally share their expertise and experiences freely. Word of mouth among planners is very powerful. A positive opinion from a respected colleague is worth more than all the information in paid advertisements or slick marketing materials.

DESTINATION MARKETERS

There are also a number of international organizations within the meetings and events industry whose members are predominantly suppliers and thus can provide additional contacts to your resource network. These sources can be found in Appendix 1.

Most of these associations, such as the Society of Incentive Travel Executives (SITE) and the International Congress and Convention Association (ICCA), organize one or more tradeshows each year, usually in conjunction with one of their major conferences. There are also freestanding industry trade shows around the world that are organized by commercial exposition companies and focus on international destinations and suppliers. Some occur in the same location annually and others move from country to country, but attending one of these expositions can be very useful to a busy planner who needs as much information as possible in a short period. If you think of a tradeshow as a supermarket for destinations and destination support services, you can fill your basket with contacts from national tourist organizations, convention and visitors bureaus, hotels, resorts, cruise lines, destination management companies, airlines, transportation companies, audiovisual supply companies, and marketing and production companies—people and companies related to almost anything and everything associated with the meetings business.

This unique opportunity to make personal contact with scores of suppliers from all over the world in just two or three days is an extremely useful information-gathering tool with which to develop your resource network. In addition, attending one or more destination tradeshows annually is an excellent way to keep current on what is available in countries that are of interest to you. As a networking tool, these expositions, like the major industry educational conferences, provide an opportunity to make new contacts while maintaining existing relationships. A list of the major industry tradeshows in North America, Latin America, Europe, and the Asia-Pacific region can be found in Appendix 1.

NATIONAL TOURIST OFFICES AND CONVENTION AND VISITORS BUREAUS

If you have minimal or no knowledge of a country, the national tourist office (NTO) should be your first contact. If you are interested in particular city, you also may make inquiries to its convention and visitors bureau (CVB). Most countries interested in attracting tourists and increasing their meetings and convention business maintain offices in the major world capitals. The NTOs and CVBs of some countries have offices in the United States, usually in cities such as New York, Washington, Chicago, Dallas, Houston, Los Angeles, and San Francisco. These offices are staffed with knowledgeable English-speaking professionals who understand the needs of meeting planners and whose job is to promote their destinations and make it as easy as possible for you to organize a meeting there.

The services of NTOs and CVBs are free and include assistance with marketing efforts; promotional support in the form of brochures, maps, CDs/DVDs, and mailing services; specifications of hotels and meeting facilities; and lists of local suppliers to support your logistic needs. Some NTOs and CVBs are funded exclusively by their governments, and others by supplier members who pay an annual fee to be included in a destination's promotional activities; still others are supported by a combination of public and private funds. Ask your contact in the beginning how the organization is funded so that you will know how the list of suggested suppliers is generated. NTOs and CVBs are supposed to be unbiased sources of information and will not recommend one company over another. However, some supplier directories may list only paying members, and it is important to know this.

One of the most useful and helpful services offered by an NTO/CVB is to arrange a site inspection of multiple venues, facilities, and properties with a knowledgeable bilingual staff member or local guide, ground transportation, and an efficiently scheduled itinerary. There is a misconception among many planners that these services are available only to people who are planning major citywide conventions or large corporate events with hundreds of attendees. Although the traditional focus of these organizations has been and remains the association market, the services of an NTO/CVB are available to every planner, no matter how large or small the group.

HOTEL CHAIN REPRESENTATIVES AND HOTEL MARKETING CONSORTIA

If you work domestically with large international hotel chains such as Hilton, Starwood, Hyatt, InterContinental, Marriott, Four Seasons, Fairmont, and Sol Melia, you may already have a relationship with a regional or national sales representative. If this person does not also handle international sales, ask to be referred to the appropriate contact within the company or to specific properties overseas, as needed. Hotel sales personnel can be very helpful during the initial planning stages of a meeting and will work closely with CVBs, airlines, and local support service providers to arrange site visits and facilitate communications between you and the internal departments of their properties.

There are also multinational marketing organizations that represent groups of hotels that are independently owned and managed outside the major chains. Leading Hotels of the World, Preferred Hotels, Summit Hotels, Small Luxury

Hotels, Great Resorts and Hotels, and Relais & Chateaux all specialize in a portfolio of properties that have similar facilities, quality standards, and service levels. Sales representatives for these hotel consortia function exactly the way their counterparts in the international chains do.

Unlike CVBs, which are mandated to remain impartial, hotel sales representatives, especially those who work directly in the local property, routinely recommend suppliers for the services not offered in-house. Although this is a good start for your support list, it is important to remember that many hotels negotiate preferred vendor agreements with local suppliers who provide commission payments (known less elegantly as kickbacks) in return for a group's business. Ask the hotel sales representative what preferred supplier agreements, if any, exist so that you will have a better idea of the objectivity of his or her recommendations.

DESTINATION MANAGEMENT COMPANIES

These professionals have come a long way from the "ground operators" of old whose primary function at meetings and incentives was to coordinate ground transportation and social events. By all measures, today's DMC is a multifaceted company offering professional services that cover a broad spectrum and may include, in addition to transportation and theme events, audiovisual support, temporary help, entertainment, interpreters, and related assets. In some cases, international DMCs serve as prime contractors for organizations that have meetings abroad. They may act on behalf of the organizer to negotiate hotel and meeting facilities, as a travel agency, or as a subcontractor for whatever services are needed.

DMCs can provide a wealth of information and a variety of services that will save you time, money, and anxiety as you plan your meeting long-distance. The value of a good DMC cannot be overstated, and even the most experienced international planners rely on these professionals to ensure a successful meeting. Unfortunately, many meeting planners who are comfortable working in their home country where everything is familiar tend to shun DMCs, preferring to do everything themselves and thinking they are saving money in the process. Other planners are unaware of what DMCs can do for them and fail to see the need for additional help. When it comes to international meetings, however, even the most experienced domestic planner becomes a novice when faced with the complexities and challenges of working overseas, especially for the first time. The question is not "To DMC or not to DMC?" but "Which DMC and how soon can we get started?"

Think of your meeting as a new house that you must build within the next few months. You know exactly what it should look like, you know what you want and need to be comfortable in it, but you have never built a house from the ground up in this location. You need an architect, a building engineer, an interior designer, a construction engineer, a plumber, an electrician, a bricklayer, a roofer, a painter, a landscaper . . . did you forget someone? Each one must be licensed and insured, and you want the best, of course, and so you will need to get references and check out each one carefully. You will have to get estimates from each of them, negotiate costs and contract terms, supervise their work, coordinate the payments to all of them, and make sure the schedule and quality control requirements are adhered to rigorously and all the necessary permits are obtained. You can do all this yourself or expedite the process by hiring just one person—a general contractor—whose experience, contacts, and knowledge of the system will save you time, money, and aggravation in the long run. You still will be in control of the finished house, but your decision to let an expert coordinate all the details will make the process more efficient and more secure.

A DMC is a combination architect and general contractor for your meeting, a "one-stop shop" for almost all the logistic arrangements you will need in a specific destination. To determine whether you need the assistance of a DMC at a meeting overseas, ask yourself the following questions:

- Do I have the time, ability, and expertise to identify the best transportation company, audiovisual equipment provider, simultaneous interpreters, entertainment, tour guides, production company, security personnel, off-site venues, restaurants, art galleries, hot new boutiques, and leisure activities in this unknown destination?
- Will I be able to negotiate prices that are as favorable as those given to a long-term local customer that provides volume business all year rather than just during the three days of my meeting?
- If something goes wrong, will I get a better response than will a local preferred client who works with these suppliers all the time and can leverage his or her relationship to ensure performance, demand action, and/or provide crucial emergency assistance if necessary?

The answer to all these questions is most certainly no. For this reason, you need the help of an established DMC who speaks the language, understands the culture, maneuvers within the local business practices every day, and has significant clout with the people who can make or break your meeting.

During the planning and coordination phase, the DMC also can assist a planner with matters such as program enhancements, arranging for proclamations, contact with local dignitaries, and advice on protocol. He or she can act as a liaison with local government agencies and arrange special government services such as security and tax assistance. Destination management companies that have travel departments can recommend and administer pre- or post-conference tours and assist with reservations, ticketing, itinerary changes, and VIP coordination. Many have media experts who can coordinate publicity and media relations before and during an event.

In terms of specific on-site support services, a full-service DMC can offer the following during an event:

- Meet and greet attendees on arrival; assist with customs clearance, baggage, and freight expediting; and provide hotel transfers.
- Conduct a group orientation on local culture and attractions, currency exchange, banking hours, postage, shopping, protocol, and program overview.

- Maintain an information desk staffed by multilingual personnel.
- Arrange car rental, restaurant, and theater reservations if requested.
- Coordinate and supervise recreational and leisure events and off-site theme parties and functions, including motorcoach supervision for group movement.
- Supply uniformed, licensed, articulate guides for group excursions.
- Arrange with local restaurants for group meal functions and dinner at leisure or dine-around programs.
- Recommend, contract with, and supervise entertainers, technical staff, conference aides, temporary help, and administrative staff.

PROFESSIONAL CONFERENCE ORGANIZERS

PCOs abroad tend to be associated with large meetings and congresses, and their services often overlap with those offered by DMCs. Like DMCs, they are extremely knowledgeable and well-connected local professionals who have extensive business relationships and the ability to support your meeting with a variety of services. Unlike DMCs, they are noted for their particular expertise in the area of congress organization and management, where they are involved in everything from program development, to speaker management, to registration, to budgeting, to final evaluation and postconference analysis. More information on the role and services of the PCO can be found in Chapter 4—*Organizing and Hosting International Events.*

How do you find a good DMC or PCO, and how do you know that this person or company is right for you and your meeting? Figure 3-1 provides suggested selection criteria. Begin with planner colleagues whom you know personally. If they do not work overseas, do they know anyone who does who could recommend a DMC or PCO experienced with your type of meeting? Ask suppliers you know and trust, especially local hotel contacts who are familiar with all the companies in town. If you are a member of Meeting Professionals International (MPI) or another professional association, your membership directory will list suppliers geographically. NTOs and CVBs often can provide

---

- In business at least three years
- Verifiable bank references
- Verifiable client references, especially from groups, meetings, and events similar to yours
- Professional association memberships (ADME, IAPCO, ICCA, ISES, MPI, PCMA)
- Government licensing, where applicable or required
- Appropriate insurance coverage, where applicable or required
- Sufficient number of trained, multilingual staff to meet project needs

Figure 3-1 Selection Criteria for an International DMC/PCO

lists of DMCs without recommending one over another, as they must remain neutral. There are also consortia of DMCs that attend the major international trade shows regularly.

Once you have identified a company or companies that fulfill your selection criteria, you will want to schedule time during your first site visit to meet with the candidate or candidates to confirm your choice. Insist on visiting the DMC or PCO's office so that you can see the scope of the operation firsthand. Does the company have the communications equipment, infrastructure, and personnel to support your event? What is the level of English proficiency of the office staff and the operations staff with whom you and your team will be communicating regularly? If only the salesperson is proficient in English and neither you nor your coworkers speak the local language, you may need to look elsewhere. From the standpoint of operations and risk management, you cannot afford to have any lack of comprehension or misunderstanding with your support team, especially in the event of an emergency.

Specific questions you may want to ask are as follows:

- Does the DMC have a large enough staff? Are they professional, personable, and fluent in the applicable languages?
- What is the proposed staff allocation? The usual formula is 1 staff member for every 40 or 50 attendees.
- Do they have good rapport with hotel personnel and ongoing contacts with the applicable establishments, organizations, and services to support the event?
- Are they able and willing to customize their programs to your group's needs?
- Are they flexible and responsive to last-minute changes?
- Are their liability coverage and staff training in emergency response situations adequate?

There is a consensus among planners of international events that the services of a competent, experienced DMC cannot be measured in cost alone. The value that these professionals bring to the meeting in terms of their knowledge of the venue, its business customs, and its resources is of particular importance when one is conducting an event in another country. Having people on hand who understand the influence of time, distance, language, and culture can help you avoid potential pitfalls and assure the successful operation of an event.

DESTINATION SELECTION CRITERIA

With the help of your resource network, you should be able to answer the following questions for each proposed destination to complete the first phase of the destination assessment:

- Does the venue support the objectives of the meeting?
- Is there broad appeal to the attendees?
- Is the area politically and economically stable?
- Are there any significant safety and security concerns?
- Are attendees from any specific country, ethnic group, or religion at a higher security risk than others?
- Is there a choice of airlines, direct flights, and adequate seating capacities from major international gateways?
- Is the location easily accessible from an international airport?
- Are hotels and meeting facilities adequate in number, quality, and rates?
- Are adequate, competent local support services, equipment, and personnel available?
- Are climate and seasonal factors favorable?
- Does the area offer a variety of cultural attractions and recreational activities?
- Are there organizations in related fields, if appropriate?
- Do customs and immigration procedures facilitate group travel?

When you have identified the destinations that meet these criteria, narrow the choice to one or two prospective locations. A site inspection trip is essential, and this is best arranged through the national tourist office or convention bureau or a DMC with a good reputation; if an official airline is to be designated, you can contact its convention representatives. You also may want to consult the national sales staff of hotel chains that have properties at the destination. Have the appropriate liaison make arrangements and accompany you. If possible, schedule the trip for the same time of year as the meeting so that you can observe conditions that may affect participants adversely, such as climate and tourism volume.

HOTELS AND MEETING FACILITIES

Hotel selection criteria are much the same abroad as at home, though the hotels may not be the same. Traditional hotels do not have the extensive meeting facilities one is accustomed to finding in newer ones. It was once customary in the capitals of Asia and Europe to have a room block at a hotel and hold meetings at a nearby conference center, a practice that persists to this day. As meetings and incentive travel have gained prominence, hotels built in foreign cities have increased their meeting space substantially. Recent hotel construction in Latin America and Asia has followed the North American model of standardized sleeping room sizes for both single and double occupancy as well as more abundant and flexible function space for both meetings and social events. In contrast, the older, more traditional hotels throughout Europe provide as much challenge as they do charm to an unsuspecting North American planner.

In negotiating with foreign hotels, as with domestic ones, it is best to negotiate for services rather than merely price. If the proposed hotel is part of a chain with international offices in major cities, it can be helpful to involve the national sales staff from the beginning if you have an existing relationship. As always, be sure that *all* the agreed-upon details, including specifics on meeting rooms, are in writing. Include in your contract specific meeting rooms, dates, and hours and provide a diagram of each room setup to avoid misunderstandings. Remember that throughout Asia, Europe, Latin America, and Australia, the metric system is used to designate distances and dimensions. If you want to work internationally and have difficulty thinking in terms of meters, grams, and kilometers, make it a point to get comfortable with those standards. Although you may ask for everything to be converted for you, do not expect that the rest of the world will automatically assume that you are "metrically challenged" and accommodate you accordingly.

Selection criteria applied to hotel and/or conference venues are similar to those for domestic meetings and should include the questions shown in Figure 3-2 and those listed here:

- Does the hotel have adequate sleeping room capacity on the required dates?
- Is there sufficient function space for meetings?
- Are the rooms suitable in size, quantity, and appointments to meet program specifications?
- Is the hotel of a quality consistent with participants' expectations?
- Are the room rates within the organization's budget range?
- Are management and staff trained and experienced in international events (e.g., key staff multilingual and trained in conference service operations)?
- Is the hotel readily accessible from the international airport? Is it close to the convention center if that facility is used?
- Can the facility meet technical program requirements for audiovisual support, simultaneous interpretation, and related meeting support services?
- Are food and beverage policies, staff, and facilities suited to groups?
- Are other potentially conflicting events scheduled for proposed dates?
- Does the venue have comprehensive emergency plans, and have they been disseminated?
- If this is a congress center, is the facility convenient to the hotels housing attendees?
- Are key staff members permanent, experienced, and multilingual?
- Are the facilities sufficient in capacity, size, number, and appointments?
- Are there adequate provisions for lighting, sound, utilities, and technical requirements?
- Will outside contractors be required for specialized services? Which ones?
- Do union rules and labor laws favor convention operations?

Destination Criteria
- Does the city (region) have a good range of conference hotels and facilities?
- Are there adequate direct flights from major gateways and a choice of airlines?
- Is the area politically stable and compatible?
- Are climate and seasonal factors favorable?
- Are there adequate ground transportation and support services?
- Does the destination enhance the objectives of the conference?
- Will attendees be attracted by the destination's assets?
- Is there a compatible host organization in a related field?
- Do customs and immigration facilitate foreign travelers?
- Are overseas liaison offices established in major cities?
- Does the destination offer a variety of cultural and recreational attractions?
- Are restrictions imposed by attendees' governments because of the destination?

Facility Criteria (Hotel Sites)
- Does the hotel have adequate room capacity on the dates required?
- Are there sufficient meeting rooms for the program on the dates scheduled? Are they adequate in size, number, and appointments?
- Is the hotel of a quality consistent with attendees' expectations?
- Are room rates within the organization's budget range?
- Are management and staff trained to handle international conferences (e.g., key staff members multilingual and trained for convention service?)
- Is the hotel readily accessible from the airport?
- Can the hotel meet technical requirements in terms of computers, simultaneous interpretation, audiovisual equipment, tables, platforms, and related meeting room needs?
- Are food and beverage policies and facilities suited to meeting groups?
- Will there be other meetings that may conflict?
- Does the hotel have a suitable emergency life safety plan and qualified security staff?

Facility Criteria (Halls and Auditoriums)
- Is the facility convenient to headquarters hotels?
- Is key staff well trained and permanent? Multilingual?
- Are facilities adequate in capacity, size, number, and appointments?
- Are there adequate provisions for lighting, sound, and technical support?
- Will outside contractors be required for specialized services?
- Does the secretariat office have suitable communications, computer, and office equipment?
- Are translation booths and systems provided?
- Does staging fit the needs of the program? Is the stage fully lighted and draped?
- Are catering facilities available at the site?
- Are medical, security, and other emergency facilities and trained staff available?

Figure 3-2 Selection Criteria

- Do the organizer's offices provide for communication; security, and equipment?
- Are interpretation systems provided? Are professional interpreters available?
- Do staging and stage equipment fit program needs (if applicable)?
- Are catering facilities available? Are the service standards suitable?
- Are medical and other emergency facilities and staff readily accessible?

As you can see, the essentials of meeting management and site selection are the same for any event. However, there are several planning considerations that are specific to international meetings. Among these are cultural differences, currency management, language, and government regulations. These criteria will be covered in greater detail in subsequent chapters.

KEY POINTS

Establish a network of well-traveled family, friends, colleagues, and meeting industry associations to gather information on specific destinations.

Attend trade shows hosted by international meetings and event organizations to access a wealth of information and meet contacts from all over the world.

Contact the national tourist office or convention and visitors bureau of the destination country to get a wealth of free services.

Speak with the national sales representatives of large international hotel chains who can arrange local services and support with logistics such as airline and ground travel coordination.

Contracting with a destination management company for logistical services will save you time and money because of its intimate knowledge of local businesses and inside contacts.

When selecting a DMC, consider its proficiency in the local language, reputation and rapport with your contacts, liability coverage, and flexibility.

In choosing an overseas hotel, make sure all your selection criteria are met and negotiate for essential services, not only price.

PASSPORT

Books

The Convention Industry Council Manual, 7th ed., Convention Industry Council, Fairfax, VA, 2004.

Professional Meeting Management, Professional Convention Management Association, Chicago, 2003.

Schaumann, Pat, CMP, CSEP, DMCP, *The Guide to Successful Destination Management,* John Wiley & Sons, New York, 2005.

Internet

Association of Destination Management Executives (ADME): www.adme.org.

Destination Marketing International (DMAI): www.destinationmarketing.org.

International Association of Professional Conference Organizers (IAPCO): www.iapco.org.

Chapter 4

ORGANIZING AND HOSTING INTERNATIONAL EVENTS

The world is a country which nobody ever yet knew by description; one must travel through it one's self to be acquainted with it.

—**Lord Chesterfield**

IN THIS CHAPTER

We will explore:

- How an international congress is organized.
- Planning parameters such as timing, funding, and venues.
- Functions of the program committee.
- The benefits of engaging a professional congress organizer.
- The timetable for a congress organization.
- Tips for hosting international visitors.

There are as many kinds of international meetings as there are of domestic ones, and they are similarly defined in great part by their sponsors or organizing bodies. Thus, we speak about a corporate or governmental meeting, an academic symposium or forum, a religious conclave, and, in the realm of global associations, an international congress.

To most North American planners, the word *congress* is synonymous with *convention,* connoting a large citywide event that often requires multiple hotels to house hundreds or even thousands of delegates, a convention center to provide thousands of square feet of meeting and exhibit space, shuttle service to and from the meeting venue, and a variety of ancillary events. This kind of meeting is indeed a congress, however, outside North America the word *congress* is used by many planners for smaller meetings as well.

As a rule, association meetings that involve multinational audiences are called congresses. The purpose of an international congress is to provide a forum for the exchange of information among counterparts worldwide, learn about recent advances in specific fields of knowledge or practice, address problems common to many nations and seek solutions, and establish dialogue with colleagues on a global scope. The sponsoring organization hopes that the attendees will depart feeling enriched by newly gained knowledge that will benefit them and others in their industry or field of endeavor.

INTERNATIONAL CONGRESS ORGANIZATION

Most congresses fall into one of two categories. The first is a congress sponsored by an international society that has a permanent secretariat responsible for administration. International society congresses generally are held at regular intervals, that is, annually, biannually, or in some cases every three or four years. The permanent secretariat may be responsible for planning and managing the society's congress in conjunction with the governing body and its appointed committees or in concert with an organizing committee in the host country. Alternatively, the function of planning and hosting the event is rotated among member countries, in which case the local organizing committee establishes its own secretariat devoted exclusively to the organization and management of a particular congress.

The second category includes congresses convened by members of an industry or discipline on a one-time or first-time basis. The sponsor may be a government, a university, a corporation, an interdisciplinary group, or an adhoc group organized for that particular meeting.

The organization and function of international congress committees tend to be somewhat different from those for domestic meetings, where committees often have an honorary role and most of the tasks are performed by paid staff. For international congresses, where the secretariat may be halfway around the globe, committees manage much of the planning and operations. They are structured along functional lines under an overall Organizing Committee.

The Organizing Committee has overall responsibility for planning the congress and setting tasks for the operating committees. It usually is composed of officers of the association, permanent staff members, and host country members representing the industry or discipline. The general chairman or chairwoman of an international congress may be an honorary designation. However, when that individual has the actual responsibility for the congress, he or she usually chairs the organizing committee. Because committee members are often geographically dispersed, this body meets infrequently, and so in most cases a smaller executive committee actually manages and makes the decisions. It meets regularly, usually is chaired by the general chairperson and oversees the actions of all operating task groups. In addition, it executes contracts in the name of the congress, approves disbursements, and directs the congress staff.

In domestic meetings, the host committee function may be incidental, with most of the work done by staff. In contrast, the local host organization of an international congress represents not only the host country but also the meeting sponsors to the foreign guests. This expanded role calls for a global perspective and imposes certain demands that are not characteristic of national meetings. Committee members will be involved in program content and will serve on other committees as valuable, knowledgeable resources.

SECRETARIAT

The secretariat of an international congress should not be confused with an association's headquarters. Headquarters frequently has management responsibilities granted by the bylaws and is overseen by the governing body. Its staff members plan and manage the organization's conventions. A secretariat is more of an administrative body that may or may not be heavily involved in the planning and management of the congress, though it performs critical administrative and fiduciary duties. It also provides staff support to the executive and operating committees and serves as the administrative center for correspondence, purchasing, accounting, and disbursements related to the congress.

When an international association maintains a permanent secretariat at its headquarters, the secretariat is managed by an administrative officer, a salaried professional who usually carries the title executive secretary. Under some congress arrangements, this position may be filled by a professional congress organizer retained for the course of the event. The secretariat fulfills all administrative duties during the planning phase and moves to the congress site before the event begins.

PLANNING THE CONGRESS

As occurs with all meetings, the planning process for an international congress begins with a statement of objectives. If the meeting is one of a series of congresses held regularly and alternating its venues among member countries, the objectives probably have been defined in the organization's charter. Nevertheless, each meeting in the series should have specific objectives. In the case of an ad hoc event, the objectives are established by the organizers and clearly communicated to all participants.

Once consensus is reached on objectives, the decision to proceed is made, and the committees are organized, the planning group addresses specific areas. Since languages and cultures at international meetings vary, the planners and staff need to be particularly sensitive to the ways in which cultural differences affect both communications and management functions. Clear and effective communication between the secretariat and attendees, the program committee and speakers, presenters, and delegates is an essential component of any international congress.

Planning decisions often are influenced by a variety of factors and determined by an analysis of participant profiles. For example:

- Additional time and budget allocations will be needed for market research and registration if all prospective delegates are not already members of the sponsoring organization with existing profiles in its database.
- Socioeconomic factors often influence delegates' ability to afford transportation, registration fees, and housing.
- Cultural background affect both the program format and the food and beverage functions. Religion can be a factor if the meeting dates conflict with religious observances important to many attendees.
- Language comprehension will influence the official conference language and the decision to provide simultaneous interpretation into one or more languages.
- Attendance criteria will determine whether the meeting is open to the public or restricted to a specific group. Who will be invited to the congress? Are there specific eligibility requirements?

TIMETABLE

The planning group selects the meeting dates by taking into consideration potential conflicting events or, conversely, possible congruent events that may benefit attendance. Registration deadlines are established, and a planning schedule evolves. Lead times for international congresses are generally longer than those for their domestic counterparts, with an average lead time of around two years. However, it can be substantially longer as the number of attendees increases. It is not unusual for an international association whose average attendance numbers in the thousands to block meeting and hotel space five or more years out. In light of the limited number of venues that can provide all the space and services required for these major congresses and the requirement of many associations that their congresses rotate among continents, cities that can support these types of meetings are limited and in great demand. Outside North America, it is rare to find large "convention hotels" with 500 to 1000 or more rooms attached to or within walking distance of a convention center that has flexible meeting and exhibition space. Thus, a meeting for 800 people that could be housed entirely in one hotel in Las Vegas might require multiple hotels in Milan, plus convention center space and shuttle transportation between venues.

Advances in communications technology have streamlined many planning components that were particularly labor-intensive and time-consuming in the past. Abstract collection and processing now are managed quickly and efficiently by a variety of software programs. Similarly, promotional and informational Web sites, online registration, and e-mail have revolutionized marketing and attendee communications. Translation, printing, and distribution of materials have been expedited similarly so that mail strikes and even political unrest no longer keep vital information from reaching potential or already registered attendees. Nevertheless, no matter how streamlined a process, an experienced international planner knows to build significant contingency time into the schedule. Differences in time zones, cultures, languages, business practices, and resources are bound to cause delays at one point or another in the planning process.

For a typical congress timetable, see Figure 4-1.

FUNDING

Although it is possible for a congress to be funded entirely from registration fees, this is rarely the case, and so a careful and comprehensive financial analysis is required. Funding sources must be identified, and additional revenue from sponsorships, grants, subsidies, and/or exhibits needs to be explored at the outset. Bridge funding—operating capital required for promotional and other expenses incurred before the receipt of registration revenues—may come from several sources. The international association, if one exists, may underwrite organizational expenses, or funding may be provided by a sponsor, a corporation, a federation of associations, or a government agency of the host country as an incentive for holding the congress there.

VENUES

Selection of the destination, hotels, and congress center for an international meeting is based on the criteria presented in Chapter 3. The attendee profile, along with the facilities and support requirements, influences the selection. Cities with large multicultural populations and a high percentage of multilingual staff in hotels and service industries have a distinct advantage. A key consideration may be the desirability of a gateway city (one that has an international airport) because of the international carriers serving the delegates' originating cities. However, the availability of connecting flights to most major international gateways allows consideration of secondary venues.

PROGRAM CONTENT AND POLICIES

Initially, the program committee prepares a tentative agenda identifying session formats for each day so that appropriate meeting facilities can be found. Subsequently, the committee attends to the following:

- Topics to be included and the session format for each topic.
- Selection and invitation of speakers, the keynoter, and dignitaries.
- Appointment of session chairmen or moderators and policy for their fees and/or expenses (e.g., complimentary registration for presenters).
- Call for papers. Technical and scientific congresses follow a set protocol and policy in inviting speakers. The invitation includes a request for a copy of presentations and abstracts of the topics to be presented. They

KEY:

Org—Organizing	Ex—Executive Committee
Pro—Program Committee	Reg—Registration Committee
Fin—Finance Committee	Arr—Arrangements Committee
T&T—Transport & Tours Committee	PR—Publicity Committee
Exb—Exhibition Committee	All—All Committees

Lead Time and Activity	Committee Responsibility	Secretariat Function
C (congress) minus (−)2 years: Form Organizing Committee, appoint chairman, document decisions, establish feasibility, dates, objective and theme. Begin destination assessment. Designate Executive Committee. Project expenses and arrange funding. Identify audience and determine attendance qualification.	Org	
C-20 months Form operating committees, appoint chairmen. Finalize destination and contact venues. Set-up secretariat. Refine timetable. Establish preliminary budget.	Org	Organize, establish headquarters and staff.
Develop congress timetable, committee budgets. Solicit sponsorships, prepare grant proposals. Open bank accounts.	Ex, Fin	Advise.
Analyze promotion media (website, mail, publications, etc.)	PR	Advise.
Research, inspect, select, negotiate and book hotel(s), meeting venue and exhibit facilities. Formulate tentative program, evaluate speakers.	Ex, Arr, Exb Ex, Pro	Assist, confirm contracts, initiate liaison. Advise and support.
Interview PCOs; select and contract.	Ex	Brief PCO.
Design, activate and publicize website. Send news releases to trade and society journals. Track publicity.	PR	Advise and assist.
C-18 months Design preliminary announcements for delegates, attendees, sponsors, exhibitors.	PR, Reg	Monitor website.
Write brochure text. Submit for translation. Update web design.	PR, Exb	Contract graphics and translation.
Verify translations, approve layouts, print, mail and post announcements.	PR, Exb, Ex	Contract printing and mailing services.
Screen and select Exhibition Contractor.	Exb	Advise and contract.
Develop business agenda. Issue call for papers. Begin exhibitor recruitment. Monitor and update website.	Ex, Pro, Exb	Advise and support.

Figure 4-1 Typical Congress/Convention/Exhibition Timetable

Lead Time and Activity	Committee Responsibility	Secretariat Function
C-15 Months		
Budget and planning review. Analyze attendee demographics/distribution. Report to Executive Committee.	All	Support and document.
Select and book congress interpreters. Refine business, social agendas.	Pro, Arr	Screen and contract.
Appoint official airline, travel agent, DMC.	T&T	Confirm, establish contact.
Second mailing to delegates and exhibitors. Second press release.	PR, Reg Exb	Print and mail.
C-12 Months		
Review delegate/exhibitor response. Review budget and meeting plan. Select DMC. Report to Executive Committee.	All	Support and document.
Finalize speakers and invite. Call for abstracts. Contract translations, printing.	Pro	Support; contract.
Appoint Customs broker.	T&T	Advise and assist.
C-9 Months		
Review delegate/exhibitor response. Review budget and meeting plan. Report to Executive Committee.	All	Support and document.
C-6 Months		
Deadline for abstracts. Translate, edit and print.	Pro	Support and document.
Review delegate/exhibitor responses. Review budget and meeting plan. Conduct site coordination visits.	All	Support and document.
C-3 Months		
Review delegate/exhibitor response. Review budget and meeting plan. Monitor room pickup. Provide F&B guarantees.	All	Support and document.
Finalize social agenda, reception plan. Report to Executive Committee.	Pro, T&T	Contract DMC services.
Abstracts and outlines to interpreters. Determine and order AV support, interpretation equipment. Print badges, registration lists and signage.	Pro Arr, Reg	Support and document. Contract and supervise.
One Month Out		
(Final pre-event activities much the same as domestic meetings.)		

Figure 4-1 *(Continued)*

must be submitted far enough in advance to allow time for translation, if needed, and reproduction for dissemination to delegates. The papers form the nucleus of the congress proceedings.

- Program support requirements, including audiovisual equipment and staff, special staging or environment, and special staff for security, room captains, and aides.

In any international meeting, program design should reflect the organizers' concern for attendees who may have traveled long distances. Adequate breaks should be scheduled between sessions, at lunchtime, and at the end of the day so that attendees can meet and network with colleagues from other countries. A half day at leisure on the second or third day and one or two open evenings are also advised. Although cultural perceptions of time vary from country to country, formal sessions should follow the printed schedule precisely as a courtesy to both the speakers and those in the audience who are able and willing to show up on time.

The program committee needs to recognize that participating groups want to see their countrymen represented on the program. Accordingly, speaker selection should reflect the international character of the event, although not all nationalities need be represented by speakers. The program committee can create the appearance of multinational program participation in the designation of session chairmen, panelists, moderators, and event hosts. If there is one overriding consideration in planning international congresses, it is precisely this sensitivity to the multinational, multicultural nature of the event and its participants. See Figure 4-2 for additional guidelines.

ROLE OF THE PCO

The PCO, introduced previously as a Professional Conference Organizer, is referred to abroad as a Professional Congress Organizer, especially when working with associations, and this role is understood and well established. Customarily independent businesspeople, PCOs are intimately familiar with the destination, including its language, customs, resources, and amenities, and at the same time thoroughly professional and skilled in the area of congress planning and management.

Once retained, the PCO becomes the liaison between the organization and the local convention bureau, the hotel, and other suppliers, which may include a DMC. However, unlike DMCs, which generally charge on a per person or percentage markup basis, PCOs generally receive a fee for their services. In return, they relieve the organizing committee and/or meeting manager of many of the logistic and administrative details involved in a meeting of international scope, leaving them free to concentrate on the program and participate fully. Services that a PCO provide include but are not limited to:

- Advice on accommodations or facilities and assistance in negotiations.
- Assistance with customs, taxation, and related government compliance.
- Consultation on the program relative to local influences, customs, and cultural considerations.
- Budgeting advice invoking the PCO's experience with similar meetings.
- Arranging foreign bank accounts and letters of credit, collecting fees and disbursing funds to vendors, and administering and auditing accounts.
- Establishing a secretariat or conference office with staff and administrative services.
- Liaison with local counterparts, offices, or host and organizing committees.
- Supervision, receipt, and processing of registrations.
- Contracting, organizing and supervising exhibit services and collecting of exhibitor fees and other exposition management functions.
- Providing interpreters and multilingual staff and arranging for translation, reproduction, and dissemination of proceedings and meeting materials.
- Advice on protocol, cultural differences, VIP treatment, and security.
- Assistance with risk assessment, analysis, and contingency planning, as well as preparation of emergency response and crisis management protocols.
- Supervision and coordination of support services and logistical and/or operational details.
- Coordination of postconference tasks, close-out of accounts, and preparation and supervision of return shipments.
- Postconference critique and reconciliation of budget and expenditures.

You would not attempt to run a domestic meeting without the help of professional audiovisual technicians or exhibition contractors. By the same token, if you need the specialized skills international events demand, look to a PCO. If you have wisely chosen to use a PCO, you may wish to get proposals from several firms and contract with the one that can best fulfill your meeting's needs. For recommendations on experienced PCOs, consult the convention bureau or hotel or network with colleagues who have held meetings in that venue. During the site inspection, you may want to interview more than one firm. At that time, provide prospective PCOs with a full résumé of the event and ask whether they have worked with similar clients. As with any supplier interview, ask for references from a colleague whose event and group profile are similar to yours.

During the premeeting coordination phase, look to the PCO as your principal liaison with other suppliers. Keep him or her apprised of all communications and arrangements as well as changes. At the meeting, utilize the PCO much as you would any independent meeting planner. This is your chief of staff, and he or she should be given full authority to speak for your organization and carry out all the responsibilities you have assigned.

Stereotypes are useful when dealing with people in general, but they are at folly when dealing with individuals.

—Wu-Kuang Chu

1. Be aware of cultural differences in business etiquette, forms of address, relationships, learning styles, values, eating habits, and protocol.
2. Address visitors by title and family name until invited to use a less formal form. Learn or ask the proper pronunciation and avoid abbreviating given names or using nicknames.
3. Avoid slang, colloquial terms, and expressions. Shun sports references like "can't get to first base" or "you play ball with me." Don't use acronyms that may not be understood.
4. Certain English words may mean something else in another culture. Stick to basics.
5. Cultivate a basic understanding of metrics. Most of the world uses metric measurements and Celsius temperature references.
6. Be cautious in using gestures. Some that are prevalent in our culture, may be offensive in others. For instance, joining thumb and forefinger in the "OK" sign means money to Japanese, zero to the French, and an obscenity to Brazilians and Greeks.
7. Avoid national stereotypes. Just as United States regional characteristics and values differ greatly, other countries have widely divergent cultures and subcultures.
8. If you know some social phrases in the visitor's language ("hello, please, thank you," etc.), by all means use them. It will make visitors feel welcome and gratified that you are making the effort. But first, be sure to ascertain nationality, especially among Asians.
9. Seek out visitors who speak a language in which you have a degree of fluency and make use of your language skills. They will be appreciative and tolerant of occasional mistakes.
10. If drawn into conversations, avoid political topics and organized sports. Discuss business matters only after you have established a relationship. Family, individual sports, hobbies, and travel are good conversational openers.
11. Personal space varies with cultures. Latin Americans and Mid-Eastern visitors like close proximity during conversation. Most Asians and Northern Europeans prefer some distance.
12. Time sensitivity fluctuates with culture. As a rule, people in the Northern countries value punctuality and are time-conscious. Those in the Southern regions are more casual about time and view promptness with greater latitude.
13. If you anticipate spending some time with a particular visitor, brush up on his or her country's history, geography, culture, and current events. The Web is a great resource for that kind of information.
14. Humor is universal, but understanding of humor is not. Funny anecdotes and jokes that are *readily understood* can be great conversational gambits and enhance relationships.
15. Friendship precedes business. Take time to get to know your international visitor before getting down to business.

Rudy Wright, CMP, *Introduction to International Events*

Figure 4-2 Guidelines for Hosting International Visitors

It is not unusual in international congresses to contract for both a PCO and a DMC. Occasionally the same company provides both functions, but it is more common for a PCO to perform in concert with an independent DMC, coordinating its services as would be done with any other support element. In some instances, you will contract for both a PCO and a DMC and delineate their responsibilities so that there is no overlap other than in the coordination of activities. In other cases, the PCO will already work with an already established DMC partner.

Although the foregoing information is specific to congresses, other aspects of program development apply to international meetings in general and are covered in later chapters. Likewise, the topics involving planning, operations, and logistical activities covered in later chapters are generally applicable to congresses as well as other international events.

▌KEY POINTS

An international congress has a permanent secretariat to provide planning at regularly scheduled meetings. Meetings held on a one-time basis are organized by an organizing committee that is responsible for planning the congress.

Lead time for planning should be one to five or more years for international congresses.

When preparing a tentative agenda for speakers, panelists, and staff, include a wide range of nationalities to create the appearance of a multinational event.

A local PCO should be hired as a liaison between the organization and its suppliers to give consultations on budget, emergency response, interpreters, and local protocol and culture.

▌PASSPORT

Books

Convention Industry Manual, 7th ed., Convention Industry Council, Fairfax, VA, 2004.

Torrence, Sara R., CMP, *How to Run Scientific and Technical Meetings,* Van Nostrand Reinhold, New York, 1996.

Wright, Rudy R., The Meeting Spectrum, HRD Press, Boulder, CO, 2005.

Internet

Confederation of Latin American Congress Organizers: www.bicca.com.br/cocal.

International Association of Professional Congress Organizers (IAPCO): www.congresses.com/iapco.

International Congress and Convention Association (ICCA): www.iccaworld.org.

Union of International Associations: www.uia.org.

Chapter 5

MANAGING CURRENCY AND FINANCES

A penny saved is a penny earned.
—Benjamin Franklin, International Statesman

IN THIS CHAPTER

We will explore:

- Effective management of currencies and the overall finances related to meetings, conventions, and exhibitions.
- How to develop a budget for an event.
- Where to obtain advice from professionals to reduce financial risk.
- How to coordinate different currencies to achieve maximum financial yield.
- Identifying and managing various tax obligations, including value-added tax.
- Navigating the international currency marketplace to produce a greater return on event.

Experienced meeting, convention, and exhibition organizers who venture boldly into air and ground travel, food and beverage planning, program development, and multicultural communications sometimes exhibit extreme reluctance to face the intricacies of currency fluctuations, taxes, and fiscal transactions.

This need not be the case. As long as one understands a few basic principles and seeks expert assistance with some of the more complex aspects of international finance, it is possible to create and manage meeting budgets anywhere in the world. As with other areas of meeting planning that may be somewhat specialized and/or technical in nature, it is neither required nor possible to know everything but important to know enough to ask the right questions and ask for help when necessary.

❙ BUDGETING

The cost of an offshore meeting usually is greater than that of an equivalent meeting implemented domestically. Figure 5-1 lists the items that require special consideration in budgeting for an international program.

For a meeting organizer and patron, the first budget item to be increased is transportation. In general, promotional fares notwithstanding, international travel tends to be more expensive than domestic. This is due in part to bilateral agreements between governments that restrict fare concessions, though promotion-minded carriers have found ways around them. Request proposals from international carriers and apply them in computing staff travel, shipping, attendee fares (if borne by the company or meeting sponsor), and speaker expenses.

If exhibits are part of the event, increase lead times and shipping costs. Budget for the services of a freight forwarder and customs broker, as well as for the cost of documentation such as carnets, commercial invoices, and bonds (see Chapter 11). Exhibit services may be higher in some countries because of value-added taxes, which are discussed in detail below.

Meeting materials may or may not increase costs. Many countries offer high-quality printing at prices substantially lower than those in North America. Sending camera-ready materials for digital reproduction abroad can effect savings in shipping and customs duties.

Translation and interpretation are budget factors customarily associated with international events that have multinational attendance. Translation, which applies to the written word, may affect promotional and marketing budgets as well as meeting materials such as programs, handouts, and proceedings. Interpretation pertains to the spoken word. If professional simultaneous interpreters are required, determine the number of languages and budget ac-

- Anticipate higher air travel costs.
- Anticipate higher communications costs.
- Anticipate a longer and increased number of site visits.
- Anticipate higher shipping costs.
- Investigate potential customs and duty payments.
- Investigate simultaneous interpretation/translation costs.
- Investigate potential taxes (VAT, IVA, GST, or equivalent).
- Allow for appropriate contingency/emergency funds.
- Anticipate changes in the local political situation where the meeting, convention, or exhibition will be held.
- Monitor changes in the local economy where the meeting, convention, or exhibition will be held.
- Monitor currency fluctuations (exchange rates, volatility).

Figure 5-1 Budget Considerations for Global Meetings, Conventions, and Exhibitions

cordingly. Interpreters' fees are high, and because the task is demanding, interpreters work in shifts, necessitating two interpreters per language. Contact a language service at the site to ascertain availability and fees. Budget for interpreters' meals and, possibly, travel and accommodations if qualified interpreters are not available locally.

Responsible fiscal management requires no more than common sense and expert advice. The first means simply understanding monetary exchange principles and having a passing familiarity with the terms. The second entails knowing where to seek expert advice.

▌GETTING ADVICE

Major international banks and currency brokers that buy and sell currency in the interbank market are in a unique position to assess future exchange rates and recommend strategies to protect against adverse fluctuation. In fact, any bank with an international department can advise its clients on currency strategies, fund transfers, and monetary instruments. International accounting firms and stockbrokers are also aware of currency market trends and knowledgeable about things such as hedging and forward contracts; these strategies are described in detail later in this chapter. Planners in the corporate sector who work in these types of companies and planners who work in multinational companies often begin their search for assistance in-house.

Many experienced global planners prefer to work with international currency management and foreign exchange specialists such as Travelex Financial Services, Eide Inc., Thomas Cook Foreign Exchange, and Ruesch International. Unlike banks, which offer a variety of services and charge for each one, these companies specialize in moving currency around the world. They either do not charge a transfer fee or charge fees considerably lower than those of banks, since they move large sums around the world all the time and profit from what is called "the float," that is, the interest earned during the period of time during which transferred funds are held in one bank before being sent to another. The greater the number of transactions and sums of money that are managed and moved for you, the lower the fees.

These companies also have dedicated account managers who can provide up-to-date exchange information and advice and can facilitate the transfer of funds. In many respects, it is similar to having a specialized private banker, but at a fraction of the cost.

At the destination, PCOs and DMCs familiar with their markets and the country's fiscal regulations can be valuable assets during both planning and operations. For noncorporate groups that may not have a local office, PCOs often act as fiduciary agents in the collection, disbursement, and accounting of funds for the sponsoring organization. Another benefit of these local connections is that they are current on tax requirements and can facilitate tax refunds where applicable.

CURRENCY STRATEGIES

Astute managers usually seek expert advice on subjects outside their area of expertise. However, a basic familiarity with currency terms is valuable, if only to understand what questions to ask. Following are some of the common methods for international currency management with which you should be familiar. Since even experts cannot predict currency fluctuations accurately, no strategy is foolproof, but it is important to take steps to ensure that today's budget will be adequate for tomorrow's expenses; this is what money managers call capital preservation.

Some planners, gambling that exchange rates will be less favorable in the future, actually purchase the currency required for expenditures. They may offset the cost of tying up funds over a long period by investing them in the destination country or depositing them in an interest-bearing account established for that purpose. The drawbacks are that this requires the availability of funds well in advance and that if the exchange rate improves, they will have lost the additional buying power. But at least they have protected their capital and ensured the budget.

A viable alternative to buying currency is to buy options on the futures market or lock in an exchange rate in advance by buying what is known as a forward contract. These strategies require less capital outlay and may be appropriate when the meeting date is uncertain. Following are the methods most commonly used by international planners:

> *Options contract.* The most flexible method of locking in an exchange rate in advance, this contract gives you the option to purchase foreign currency at a predetermined price during a specified period as a hedge against currency fluctuations. You may choose not to exercise the option at the due date; however, the fee charged for this flexibility can be significant.
>
> *Forward contract.* This is a more binding transaction that is an agreement to purchase a stipulated amount of currency on a specified future date. It is based on a $10,000 minimum, and the exchange rate is locked in and secured by a deposit, usually 15 percent of the total amount requested. Forward contracts customarily are purchased a year before the program date, although shorter-term contracts can be negotiated. This is probably the most common strategy for capital preservation, as it offers a high degree of protection without tying up a large amount of capital as currency purchase would.
>
> The main drawback is that if the rate of exchange at the value date—the effective date when the funds are purchased—is more favorable, the organizer derives no financial benefit. If you purchase a contract for more money than you eventually need or if the meeting is canceled, what is left can be sold at any time. The selling price, however, will be at the rate of exchange in effect at that time.
>
> Forward contracts should be viewed as insurance policies, not as currency speculation. They offer the sponsor the security of knowing

that the budget established today will be adequate to cover anticipated expenses in spite of an adverse exchange rate.

Layering. This strategy that involves purchasing currency (or forward contracts) at intervals when exchange rates are favorable, thus averaging the rate of exchange. This can be useful when it is anticipated that your currency will strengthen over time, making the rate of exchange more favorable. It is also a useful strategy for association planners who may not be certain how many attendees will register, since forward contracts can be purchased if the numbers grow.

Spot price. This term refers to the current price at which a currency trades. The spot price fluctuates hourly and is expressed in U.S. dollars, pounds sterling, or euros.

PLANNING GUIDELINES

It is important for planners to recognize that these strategies are not available for all currencies, only those which are traded routinely on the world money markets or are pegged to Special Drawing Rights established by the International Monetary Fund. Some currencies are not convertible, and so it is important to decide in advance in which currency contracts will be written. Depending on the country or region, euros, swiss francs, pounds sterling, U.S. dollars, or yen will be the most widely acceptable currency for exchange. (For a list of major world currencies, see Figure 5-2.)

If the event, such as a congress or exhibition, entails the collection of registration fees, it is essential to establish acceptable currencies at the outset, especially in Asia. Consideration should be given to currencies that are available for purchase in the delegates' countries. Most organizations set registration fees in the destination country's currency if they are to be used to cover local expenses. However, it is not uncommon to have registration fees set in euros or U.S. dollars if receiving deposits in local currency will require paying local taxes. It is best in all cases to verify the tax consequences.

When funds are to be collected in the host country and a surplus is anticipated, a thorough understanding of the national currency regulations is essential. Some countries restrict the amount of funds that can be repatriated; others levy excessive taxes on funds leaving their borders.

FINANCIAL PLANNING AND FISCAL MANAGEMENT

In almost every international event, organizers are cast in the role of financial managers. Not all of the program's expenses can be disbursed by advance deposits or later billing. Indeed, very few foreign venues or services will accept

COUNTRY	CURRENCY	SYMBOL
Australia	Australian Dollar	AUD
Austria	Euro	EUR
Belgium	Euro	EUR
Canada	Canadian Dollar	CAD
Chile	Chilean Peso	CLP
Cyprus	Cyprus Pound	CYP
Denmark	Danish Krone	DKK
Fiji	Fiji Dollar	FJD
Finland	Euro	EUR
France	Euro	EUR
Germany	Euro	EUR
Greece	Euro	EUR
Hong Kong	Hong Kong Dollar	HKD
India	Indian Rupee	INR
Indonesia	Indonesian Rupia	IDR
Ireland	Euro	EUR
Italy	Euro	EUR
Luxembourg	Euro	EUR
Malaysia	Ringgit	MYR
Mexico	Mexican Peso	MXP
Morocco	Dirham	MAD
Netherlands	Euro	EUR
New Zealand	New Zealand Dollar	NXD
Norway	Norwegian Krone	NOK
Oman	Omani Real	OIMR
Pakistan	Pakistan Rupee	PKR
Philippines	Phippine Peso	PHP
Portugal	Euro	EUR
Saudi Arabia	Saudi Riyal	SAR
Singapore	Singapore Dollar	SGD
South Africa	Rand	ZAR
Spain	Euro	EUR
Sweden	Swedish Krona	SEK
Switzerland	Swiss Franc	CHF
Tahiti	CFP Franc	XPF
Thailand	Thai Baht	THB
Turkey	Turkish Lira	TRL
United Arab Emirates	UAE Dirham	AED
United Kingdom	Pound Sterling	GBP

Figure 5-2 Major World Currencies

contracts that stipulate billing after the event. International collections can be extremely complex, expensive, and time-consuming.

There are numerous options available for disbursing funds. Assuming that large expenses are covered by advance deposits, as is the case in most international events, day-to-day expenses may be anticipated and disbursed by one of the following methods:

- Purchase of adequate currency to provide a cash fund.
- Financial instruments such as letters of credit, bank drafts, or traveler's checks.
- High-limit credit cards such as the American Express Corporate Card or the corporate credit cards issued by American Express exclusively for meeting expenses.
- A bank checking account established on-site and funded by advance deposits.
- For minor expenses such as gratuities, cash payouts from the hotel charged to the master account.
- Use of a fiduciary such as a PCO, a DMC, or, where available, a branch or affiliate office with local banking connections.

For those not familiar with monetary instruments, some that are in common use by international banks are:

Wire transfer (also known as electronic funds transfer, or EFT). Funds deposited into a foreign bank account by means of online financial data transmission and debited to the client's domestic bank account.

Bank draft. A check drawn on a domestic bank with a face value expressed in foreign currency. This is usually the most economical means of paying foreign vendors.

Letter of credit. A monetary instrument issued by a bank that permits the holder to draw on that account, up to a specific amount, at correspondent banks abroad it may be drawn in the currency in which it is issued or the equivalent foreign currency at the spot price in effect at the time the letter is dated.

These instruments are associated with transaction fees, which can be charged to both the sender and the receiver of the funds. Thus, it is important to factor these fees into the budget and look for the most cost-effective service provider. As was noted previously, banks tend to charge higher fees than do currency brokers. For this reason, many experienced international planners prefer to establish accounts with currency brokers that offer a variety of valuable services in addition to those already mentioned.

TAX ISSUES

Under U.S. and Canadian tax codes, a meeting held in a country outside North America must meet at least two primary criteria. First, it must be as reasonable to meet there as it would be to hold the meeting in North America. The "as reasonable" test is dependent on the purpose and activities of the meeting and its sponsor, the residence of the active participants or members, the organization's past meeting venues, and other relevant information. Such information might include a unique resource or site in the host country that enhances the meeting's objectives.

The second criterion is that the venue be related to the organization's mission or the participant's business or profession. *Note:* For U.S. tax purposes, Puerto Rico and all U.S. territories are included in this definition. See Chapter 9 for specific locations and additional details.

WHAT ABOUT VAT?

In Europe and Asia they call it VAT (value-added tax), in Canada it is the GST, and in Latin America it is known as the IVA. In most countries outside the United States, you will see these initials on your invoices, indicating a flat tax of anywhere from 5 percent to 25 percent on goods and services that you purchase. Although what is taxed can vary from country to country, meeting costs that are affected usually include transportation, hotel sleeping room and function room fees, venue rentals, catering, equipment rental, shipping, labor, professional fees, and restaurant bills. These charges can have a significant impact on the meeting budget and must be taken into account from the outset. Suppliers should be asked to include VAT charges on their quotes, and these charges should appear as a line item in the meeting budget worksheet. In this way, if a decision is made to apply for VAT reclaim, it will be clear what items are affected and how much may be refunded.

A few basic questions asked at the outset of the planning will save you considerable time and money along the way. Do not hesitate to ask your local suppliers and/or a VAT reclaim agency for help. At the very least, you will want to know the following:

- What is the level of VAT in the destination country?
- Is VAT levied on everything pertaining to the event, or are some items exempt?
- Can VAT be reclaimed by my company or organization? What are the requirements?
- Can VAT be reclaimed by the meeting attendees? If so, how?

Although it is possible to reclaim some or all of the VAT payment from certain countries, there is no uniform procedure, the process is complicated and time-consuming, and it is best outsourced to specialists. Even within the European Union, which has a common currency, taxes vary from country to country and are subject to change. Applications must be filled out in the official language of the country; only original invoices, vouchers, and receipts are accepted; and the required documentation is daunting. Fortunately, there are several VAT reclaim companies that have the patience, tenacity, and expertise to prepare and submit the necessary paperwork. In view of the high tax rates, the tax refund on major purchases may well be worth the effort in countries where reclaim is possible. VAT reclaim services charge commissions of 20 to 30 percent of the amount refunded; however, considering the complexity of tax laws and the potential savings, this is well worth it. If the claim is unsuccessful, there is no fee.

Meeting participants are also eligible for VAT refunds on personal purchases they make abroad. Depending on the country, refunds may be processed before departure, usually at refund centers at airports and border crossings.

KEY POINTS

Transportation is the biggest budget increase compared to domestic events, followed by shipping. Translation and interpretation are often a hidden cost but are needed.

To anticipate budget fluctuations due to exchange rates and fiscal regulations, seek the knowledge of international banks or currency management specialists.

Exchange rates can be controlled by buying the currency and paying ahead of time or using an options or forward contract to lock in rates.

Many countries will not accept billing after an event. To expedite cash flow, use wire transfers, bank drafts credit cards, or letters of credit.

Taxes vary from country to country, ranging from 5 to 25 percent on goods and services. It is wise to include tax charges on contracts and quotes.

PASSPORT

Books

Howe, Jonathan T., *U.S. Meetings and Taxes, 2005 Edition* (available on the MPI website at www.mpiweb.org).

Internet

Currency conversion information: www.xe.com/ucc.

Trancentrix (foreign currency exchange and management): www.trancentrix.com.

Meridian VAT Reclaim: www.meridianvat.com.

See the appendixes for additional currency and VAT reclaim resources.

Chapter 6

PROGRAM PLANNING AND DEVELOPMENT

Nature has given to men one tongue, but two ears, that we may hear from others twice as much as we speak.

—Epictetus

IN THIS CHAPTER

We will explore:

- The significance of the program in terms of the meeting's objective.
- The various steps in designing a meaningful program that addresses the meeting's objectives.
- How long-distance travel influences the timing of program elements.
- Various session formats and how they influence program dynamics.
- Techniques for influencing audience participation and maintaining interest.
- How visual aids and technology reinforce communication between speaker and audience.
- How to communicate with multicultural participants through translation and interpretation.
- Selection and briefing of speakers to ensure rapport with the audience.
- Factors that enable speakers to be effective and stimulating to the audience.
- The importance of the meeting room as a communication environment.
- Cultural considerations in the choice of entertainment for multinational audiences.
- Legal matters regarding professional speakers.
- How satellite events expand the scope of the meeting; their added value to organizers and attendees.
- Various sources and types of sponsorship of events and their advantages to the organization.

The program is the raison d'etre of a meeting and the vehicle by which its objectives are fulfilled. Designing a program is like building a house. The blueprint summarizes the program and reflects the principles of design. The program elements—presenters, audiovisuals, handouts—are the lumber, bricks and mortar, and structural components that result in a sound building that fulfills its stated purpose. Like a builder, a meeting professional needs to gain experience in specifying those elements, ordering them, and managing them after they arrive at the site.

Just as the logistics of international events differ from those involved in domestic meetings, the organizer and program committee need to be aware of the differences in planning the social and educational programs. Time changes, travel distance, the cultural background of delegates, and language affect program design.

Program planning responsibilities differ among various groups. Corporate meeting programs can be developed by one or two people, a team of people from one department or division, or a multidivisional team. International meeting agendas, especially for association meetings, very often are planned by a program committee. The role of the meeting professional in each case is to assist with the establishment of the meeting's objectives when necessary and to ensure that they are achieved through flawless execution of an appropriately designed program.

Whether or not you are involved in program design and content, it is important to understand the dynamics to manage the administrative and logistic needs of speakers, session chairmen, interpreters, and other program support components. For this reason, it may be valuable to review some of the design principles and see how they differ at international events before addressing specific program elements.

PROGRAM DESIGN

Because of the distances and time zones involved in global communications, the normal planning schedule needs to be extended. Some international planners add 50 percent to the timetable; others double it to accommodate communications on program logistics, calls for papers, receipt of abstracts, and the like. The same thing applies to the timing of the meeting agenda at distant venues. As you will see in Chapter 7, people from some countries and cultures move, act, work, and communicate at a slower or faster rate than what is considered normal in North America. When one is working in one of the more leisurely cultures, additional time must be scheduled for every component of the planning and on-site management process.

To carry the house analogy through to program development, the builder begins with an analysis of the objective. Is the house to be a single-family home or a duplex, rental property or owner-occupied? The meeting professional asks the sponsor, "Why meet? What's the purpose of the meeting?"

Once the meeting objectives are ascertained, meeting professionals need to know who will attend, where participants are coming from, and other demographics such as each person's nationality, language fluency, and relationship to the sponsoring organization (member, supplier, exhibitor, guest, or other categories).

Figure 6-1 Steps in Program Development

To ensure that the program meets participants' needs and expectations, meeting professionals survey their prospective audience. They may do so at the conclusion of the current meeting, prior to the one being planned, or both.

With these key factors known, planning can proceed to formulating a program that will meet its objectives and appeal to prospective participants.

Program content will also suggest a theme for the event. A theme is to a meeting what the cover design is to a book. The meeting theme should have an eye-catching graphic and a title that describes the event. It will be a key marketing element and a highly visible graphic on site.

Demographics and program elements play a pivotal role in evaluating media for disseminating program content. Speakers, interactive sessions, audiovisuals and exhibits are all communication media; each must be carefully assessed as to its relevance to the audience.

Finally, the meeting planner and the relevant committees determine the most dynamic ways to communicate the program so as to achieve maximum response (see Figure 6-1).

TRAVEL PLANNING

There are two major considerations with regard to international travel. The first is the length of the trip, that is, the actual amount of time—on the ground and in the air—attendees will be traveling from origin to destination. The second is the number of time zone changes between the points of departure and arrival. One attendee who flies overnight from Miami to Rio de Janeiro, for example, may be tired upon arrival from the eight-hour flight. However, depending on the time of year, the time difference will be only one or two hours, and so her biological clock will be more or less in sync with the local time zone.

Her colleague flying from Miami to Milan, however, not only will be tired from his eight-hour flight but also will have to adjust to a time zone difference of six or seven hours. His body will tell him that it is nine in the morning and he did not sleep much last night, while the clock on the wall will tell him that it is three in the afternoon. If he lies down for a nap to catch up on his sleep, he not only will wake up around dinnertime but also will be up most of the night, crashing just a few hours before the meeting is supposed to start.

No matter how people route themselves or break up the trip to make it less stressful, long-haul international travel (over five hours of travel time and/or five time zones) is exhausting for even the most seasoned road warrior. For this reason, experienced international event planners follow a few basic guidelines to ameliorate the inevitable fatigue:

- Avoid business sessions and/or formal, sit-down social functions on arrival day to give participants an opportunity to rest. A light reception and/or buffet dinner that allows people to eat, mingle a bit, and leave at their leisure is the most practical first evening event.
- Avoid "overprogramming," especially on the first full day. Allow adequate time for breaks and keep the program length reasonable so that attendees have an opportunity to network with their peers, sightsee, shop, and enjoy the venue.
- Consider postconference tour options to extend the experience.

SESSION FORMATS AND DYNAMICS

International corporate meetings tend to follow the same pattern as those held in the company's home country, especially when the program is being planned by a U.S. headquarters group. It may be anathema to a European, Asian, or Latin American to begin a meeting at 8:00 A.M. over breakfast and continue discussions through a "working lunch" (where no wine is served, no less). However, that happens all the time, especially when there is no culturally oriented meeting professional at headquarters to advise the meeting sponsor that this is both unproductive and distasteful for the attendees.

International association conferences tend to favor more formal plenary assemblies and a mix of concurrent meetings and smaller breakout sessions or workshops that expand on the general session themes.

In association meetings especially, where people are paying their own way to attend, it is important to incorporate program elements that reflect added value for delegates who are traveling long distances and spending substantially more to attend a transnational event. Provide ample opportunities for participants to network either in a buyer-seller mode at industry events or in knowledge exchange at educational or scientific conferences. Free periods and social events play a vital role in enabling participants of different backgrounds and cultures to interact, exchange ideas and perspectives, and share experiences. They provide an added dimension to the conference, underscoring some of the value-added benefits that characterize international events.

AUDIENCE INTERACTION

Soliciting audience participation at large general sessions poses several problems, particularly when simultaneous interpretation is employed. In such conditions, it is best to position microphones at various places in the aisles or have aides equipped with mobile microphones. Participants should be directed to make use of the microphones, which should be tied into the sound system in such a way that interpreters can hear the questions. One recent development can facilitate audience participation: the interactive response system. This technology makes use of remote devices that enable the audience to respond to multiple choice questions projected on a video screen. Because the system logic uses computer technology, translation into multiple languages is achieved by integrating translation software.

In breakout sessions the usual techniques apply, though session leaders should be aware of cultural differences in learning styles. However, greater two-way communication between speaker and audience ensures understanding, especially when language fluency is marginal. People from some cultures are uncomfortable with informal, extemporaneous speakers who employ case studies and small group dynamics that require audience participation. They prefer more structured lectures that portray the speaker as an authority figure. Asians in particular may be hesitant to take the initiative in responding to or asking questions, since avoiding loss of face is an essential part of their cultural makeup. Chapter 7 addresses these cross-cultural communications issues in greater detail.

TECHNICAL SUPPORT

It is well substantiated that visual aids ensure comprehension and enhance retention. When one is dealing with multinational audiences and varying language fluency, they are essential. Encourage presenters to use visual aids and to have their presentations follow the visuals. Diagrams and illustrations are favored over copy and should be substituted whenever possible. Handouts should summarize the presentation, and verbatim abstracts are especially valuable for attendees and interpreters. Translated into the various conference languages, they constitute the proceedings and are a helpful reference.

At meetings held in foreign venues, you will encounter differences in electrical current, equipment and accessories, sizes, dimensions, and weights. Develop a working knowledge of the metric system since most of the world uses that form of measurement. Be particularly aware of the video format employed at the destination. Videotapes recorded in the North American NTSC format will not play on equipment that employs PAL (used throughout Europe and South America) or SECAM (used primarily in France and former French colonies). This was a major challenge before multiformat VCRs were developed. However, the widespread use of digital media (CDs, DVDs, and streaming video) and the now standard multimedia data projector have made videotapes all but obsolete.

Similar technological advances have streamlined the production and dissemination of program materials. Electronic file transfer, Web-based applications, and desktop printing have saved hundreds of hours of what used to be the tedious manual task of collecting, organizing, printing, and collating large, heavy program and abstract books. Shipping costs, customs duty, and delays in receiving cleared materials are not a concern now that everything can be quickly and cost-effectively transferred digitally and produced on-site.

Some international associations and many corporate groups have replaced the ubiquitous paper handouts with CDs of presentations and/or password-protected Web sites from which participants can download meeting materials. Chapter 15 expands on the topic of event technology.

LANGUAGE CONSIDERATIONS

In an era of increased globalization, English has become the lingua franca of international business in general and of conferences in particular. This may be comforting to meeting professionals from English-speaking countries, but they must guard against a sense of complacency in assessing the language needs of international meetings attended by other nationals. Although the world has been compressed into a single global marketplace, we must not lose sight of the fact that nine-tenths of our neighbors communicate in languages other than English. Consequently, at any international event in which several nationalities are in attendance, it may be necessary to provide interpreters and interpretation systems. Understanding the function of interpreters and the logistic requirements that accompany their use is your responsibility as a meeting professional. During the planning phase, the major language groups represented by the target audience should be determined. This will affect the promotion and marketing as well as the event itself.

Attendees' demographics and presumed language proficiency may influence several planning elements. In terms of marketing, it is customary to produce brochures and announcements in multiple languages determined by the marketing regions. For European audiences, English, French, German, and either Spanish or Italian are most often employed. For Latin America, English,

Spanish, and Portuguese are required. For Asia, Japanese and Mandarin Chinese may be advisable. French-Canadians, even though most are fluent in English, insist—sometimes obstreperously—on bilingual materials, and by law, any printed material or signage in Canada must be in both English and French.

Although the word *translation* is used generically to refer to all language services, this usage is not technically correct. Translation refers solely to the written word. In conference use, it applies to the translation of promotional and registration materials, instructions to delegates, handouts, papers, and program proceedings. *Interpretation,* in contrast, is the verbal communication of a speaker's presentation or comments into one or more other languages. It can take one of several formats:

Simultaneous interpretation (S/I) is the technique used for most general or plenary sessions that require more than one language. It is conducted, as the presenter speaks, by skilled interpreters housed in soundproof booths and distributed in multiple languages to the attendees' headphones by means of a receiver that allows them to select the appropriate language.

Consecutive interpretation, which is suitable for smaller sessions, is a format in which the speaker pauses to allow interpretation. It generally is limited to one language and is time-consuming due to the need to repeat the speaker's message.

Whisper interpretation is used in social and small group situations in which just one or two participants require interpretation. The interpreter sits beside or right behind the participant and literally whispers into his or her ear. This has limited value for conference usage but is the most cost-effective and time-saving way to provide interpretation for one person.

Emphasis has been given to the importance of recognizing one's professional limitations and knowing when to ask for help. Few meeting planners have the time or expertise to assess, recruit, schedule, and contract for teams of interpreters. Fortunately, there are professional translation services in various countries that offer comprehensive coordination of language requirements for meetings. They have access to interpreters, including those who specialize in specific industries and disciplines, and can, for a fee, handle many of the details of this complex but vital function.

In contacting such services, provide them with the full range of conference activities and let them assist you in determining where their expertise may be needed. For instance, premeeting promotion and the business agenda are obvious areas of need, but don't overlook social events that may require interpreters for distinguished guests or media relations and the need for press releases in multiple languages.

When simultaneous interpretation is required, you will need to employ teams of two professionals for each language. Because of the demanding nature of this activity, interpreters work in shifts of 15 to 30 minutes, depending on the complexity of the material and the clarity of the speaker. Strict professional codes govern their fees and working conditions for good reason: Like thoroughbred racehorses, they are highly trained, high-strung, and exquisitely conditioned intellectual athletes who require optimal conditions to perform at their best.

To understand just how difficult and nerve-racking this work can be, try to repeat everything someone says immediately after he or she says it and do this for five minutes. Can you do it? Many people cannot, as it requires intensely focused concentration to repeat accurately in one's own language, much less interpret into a completely different one. For this reason, the AIIC (Association Intérnationale de Interprètes des Conference) established the guidelines under which professional interpreters operate, and experienced international meeting planners honor their conditions faithfully. After all is said and done—literally—the attendees must understand the presentations, and nothing ensures this better than highly qualified, thoroughly briefed, and well-prepared professional interpreters.

Since interpretation and translation services are expensive, you and the program committee must determine how many languages are to be designated for translating printed materials and for interpretation at each session that requires that feature. Some international organizations routinely provide simultaneous interpretation for major language groups in attendance and offer this service as an option to others that require it. In the latter case a premium is added to the registration fee. Sometimes a prominent speaker whose presentation is essential may not be fluent in the official language. Interpretation thus is required to assure understanding and program enhancement. It may be that all the required interpreters are not available in a given city. Thus, provisions must be made in the budget for travel expenses as well as fees.

INTERPRETATION TECHNOLOGY

S/I systems consist of the interpreters' headphones, which are fed from the PA system; their microphones; an audio distribution amplifier; and multichannel receivers equipped with earphones. In some facilities, the receivers are installed in armrests, much as they are on aircraft. In others, they are portable and provisions must be made for distribution to attendees. Fixed systems make use of hardwired transmission in which headsets are plugged into a receptacle built into auditorium seats. Others utilize wireless receivers that operate within an inductive loop antenna that transmits up to eight channels of sound to the headsets. A more recent development utilizes infrared radiators placed around the room. They transmit the signals from the amplifier to the delegate's headset and are readily portable.

In most of Asia and Europe, conference centers incorporate dedicated simultaneous interpretation facilities in their design. When that is not the case, portable sound booths are available, as is a wide range of systems, most of which are now wireless. Language services and some audiovisual rental firms offer both systems and trained technicians to install and operate them.

It is essential to brief presenters thoroughly and in advance when they are to be interpreted. Advise them that they are addressing a multinational audience and should adapt their content and presentation techniques accordingly. Whenever possible, speakers should be asked to provide transcripts of their presentations and/or copies of their visuals. They should incorporate any changes and indicate where they may depart from the text for extemporaneous comments. Such transcripts are a great help for the interpreters and assure accuracy.

Language experts seek to acquire a working understanding of their audience's expertise and its vocabulary. Thus, there are interpreters who specialize in science, engineering, management, finance, government, and so on. In sessions involving topics of a technical nature, meticulous advance preparation is called for on their part. Because they must be able to absorb the speaker's comments, interpret them simultaneously, and feed them back in another language, interpreters are under considerable stress. Having an advance copy of the speaker's text, with the technical terms highlighted, relieves some of the pressure and ensures seamless, accurate translation.

SPEAKER SELECTION

Meeting professionals recognize the fact that a meeting is a medium for communications. Good speakers are as essential to the success of a meeting as good performers are to entertainment. Extending that premise to meetings held abroad, it follows that greater care must be exercised in the selection of speakers, and to a lesser extent entertainers, when language is a consideration.

The responsibility for speaker selection is usually a joint function of the meeting planner and the program committee. For meetings held abroad, it is suggested that a local resource such as a counterpart organization, a PCO, or a speakers bureau be consulted as well. In contracting professional speakers from the host country, the bureau can be particularly helpful since it knows which speakers are available and understands the fine points of compensation and contract law as they pertain to that country.

Unless simultaneous interpretation is planned, it is essential that the speaker be fluent in English, which is generally the conference language even in multinational gatherings. It is always best to audition speakers in person. But if that is not feasible, be sure that your representative abroad—the speakers bureau or the host committee—thoroughly understands the meeting objectives and the organization's expectations. Don't hesitate to ask for references, a transcript, or an audiodisk. Check it for content and delivery and check handout materials, if any, for content and relevance.

If participants from several countries are in attendance, ensure that presenters represent a cross section of the audience. People like to see their fellow citizens on the program. They need not all be principal speakers; they can be given high visibility as session chairmen, moderators, introducers, panelists, or cohosts at social functions.

Many meeting programs abroad are enriched by the use of local dignitaries and/or celebrity speakers. The National Tourist Office, your DMC/PCO, or a local speakers bureau representative can assist you with speaker selection and advise you on customs and protocol. If you choose to invite dignitaries, it will be important to apply the following guidelines:

- Ascertain their availability through the principal aide and arrange for a backup. Such people are subject to the expediencies of their high offices, and unforeseen obligations may arise.
- Be sure that the speaker is articulate and that the topic is germane to the conference theme.
- Inquire into proper protocol such as honors, form of address, and seating and instruct all program participants and organization officers accordingly.

SPEAKER PREPARATION

If the meeting is multinational rather than merely involving a transnational destination or if a substantial number of foreign guests have been invited, speakers need to be alerted that it is a multicultural audience. If they are addressing an audience whose native tongue is not their own, they need to follow certain guidelines to ensure rapport and effective communication of their message. Even though listeners may be fluent in the speaker's language, certain nuances may elude them, resulting in misunderstanding or noncomprehension.

It is a good idea to include in your communications to the program committee and speakers information on the host country's geography, history, culture, and business practices. Research and incorporate current events in politics, sports, and cultural affairs and encourage program participants to use such references in their presentations. Nothing pleases people from other countries more than to discover that a visiting speaker has taken the trouble to learn about things that matter to them. Such rapport can go far in ensuring that the meeting program is perceived as a success by sponsor and participants alike.

Conversely, take added measures to prepare speakers, both domestic and the ones from abroad. Make sure they are familiar with your organization, the audience composition and expectations, the conference objectives, and their role in the program.

Once the selection of speakers is finalized, detailed information and frequent communication are essential. As a minimum, advise speakers on the following:

- The sponsoring organization, its goals, and its position in the field.
- Other speakers on the program, particularly those sharing the speaker's session, as in panels and joint presentations.
- Logistics and specifics such as location, meeting room, session chairman, audiovisual support, speaker briefing, and rehearsal, as well as confirmation on compensation, lodging, and travel.
- Guidelines for addressing multinational audiences. This is particularly essential for Americans, who tend to use idiomatic expressions and homespun humor that may not be understood by people of other cultures. Finally, encourage speakers, other than ceremonial ones, to make

use of visual aids. Visuals are universal and aid understanding and retention even when language fluency is a factor.

MEETING ENVIRONMENT AND STAGING

The dynamics of the program carry over to and are influenced by the environment in which they occur. A setting that facilitates group communications among participants is essential for a forum, seminar, or symposium. Staging is a major consideration for a conference, especially if extensive audiovisuals are used. If it is an international event, the stage setting is influenced by protocol as well.

Staging also plays an important role at conventions and congresses. The height of the platform imparts a sense of importance to speakers addressing a congress, stressing their authority and role. At a convention, a lower platform—one just high enough for the speaker's gestures to be seen—may be in order. This implies a commonality between speaker and listener. Lighting, seating of speakers and dignitaries, decorations and use of flags, and theme decor also vary according to the type of event. These topics are covered in Chapter 7.

ENTERTAINMENT

Selection of appropriate entertainment is influenced by meeting objectives, audience demographics, organizational profile, and the nature of the specific function.

Music always adds a valuable dimension whether as part of program continuity, for ambience at a social function, or for dancing. But because people's musical tastes vary, even in one's own culture, some care should be taken in music selection. A principle often neglected by meeting planners is that the purpose of music at a reception is to serve as background for conversation. Hyperamplified, audacious music and vocalists who tend to distract from social interaction are inappropriate even at domestic meetings. At international gatherings where people are mixing and conversing with various degrees of fluency, such music is obtrusive and is regarded as being in poor taste. In contrast, light classics, show tunes, and universally known popular music are appropriate at any event.

Don't overlook the music of the region, particularly for social events. Dance troupes, choral groups, folkloric shows, and musical acts reflecting the local culture underscore the international nature of the event and provide attendees with an enjoyable cultural insight. However, it is important that planners consider the tastes of the audience. What may be a country's outstanding artist may not appeal to your attendees. On the other hand, entertainment that local people consider trite and commonplace may be just the ticket for your group.

When working with multilingual groups, concentrate on visual entertainment such as jugglers, acrobats, magicians, and dancers, though choral groups are appropriate even when language may be a barrier. Unless you're confident about the group's language fluency, avoid comedians since humor tends to depend on nuances that may be elusive, even among English-speaking audiences.

A valuable asset worth considering is a practice called "patronage" in which municipal and national government agencies will provide a variety of valuable services and assets as an incentive for holding a meeting or exhibition at their site. Often this takes the form of entertainment featuring the country's or region's artists giving vocal, orchestral, and folkloric performances.

Contracting for speakers and entertainers in other countries can be tricky. However, bringing paid speakers abroad may cause problems. Labor laws and union regulations vary greatly from one country to another. Visa restrictions may apply to paid speakers, requiring them to have a business visa. Unless you are an expert in international law, it is best to work with a professional producer, a DMC, or a reliable talent agency.

▌SATELLITE EVENTS

International meetings provide delegates with an excellent opportunity to participate in a variety of associated events, including exhibitions, tradeshows, and, in the area of medical meetings, "satellite symposia." These are usually sponsored by pharmaceutical and/or medical device companies whose products are related to the overall program content. Frequently a key element of international congresses and exhibitions, sponsorships afford organizers a source of revenue and sponsors an opportunity to provide full or partial funding for special events and program elements.

The importance of satellite events to association meetings cannot be overstated. They are a significant source of additional income to the organizers and provide an opportunity for the association to maintain and enhance relationships with companies whose sponsorship support is critical to the success of the meeting. The financial contribution—a valuable source of income—can help ensure the viability of the event from the outset. The congress organizing and program committees ensure suitability for integration within the overall congress agenda.

SPONSORSHIP BENEFITS

Typical of the meetings industry are medical congresses, which sponsorship is an essential element and a time-honored tradition. These events are perceived as an opportunity—as well as an obligation—for pharmaceutical companies to communicate the results of their clinical research to delegates. Although sponsorship is by no means exclusive to medical meetings, those events serve as an ideal illustration for the often controversial relationship between sponsors and congress organizers.

The venue for a sponsored meeting within an international congress is, of course, predetermined. The meeting planner is also likely to be presented with a fait accompli regarding the room allocated for the satellite meeting. Dimensions, staging, and other key aspects that are crucial to a meeting's success may be less than satisfactory, and the opportunity to negotiate the ideal meeting room may be denied. Here lies the first of many challenges that test a meeting professional's flexibility and adaptability.

By the same token, the services hired for the main congress and usually part of the "package" offered to sponsoring companies could, in some parts of the world, not quite meet the standards envisaged for the proposed satellite. As a result, one might have to look to outside services, and this can be a sensitive area, especially in the case of unions.

Another service provided at major international medical congresses is simultaneous interpretation. Here again, the satellite meeting may take advantage of this or utilize external sources. The highly technical nature of the papers presented and their medical terminology usually necessitate specialist translators, calling for careful coordination by the meeting planner.

Although it is generally mandatory to open satellite meetings to congress delegates, a sponsoring company also may choose to extend invitations through its international subsidiaries. In this case the meeting planner could be involved in a computerized mailing operation on a wide scale. Accommodations may be required for invitees nominated by the subsidiary, but the congress is likely to have secured all suitable hotel rooms in the immediate area for its own delegates. Early decisions and advice regarding sponsored delegate numbers therefore must be sought from the sponsoring company to ensure that all accommodation needs are met.

When scheduling sponsored meetings, be sure that they do not impinge in any way on congress sessions. Although specific times are set aside for the satellites (several often running concurrently), turnaround time between the close of a congress session and the commencement of a sponsored meeting, in the same room, may be very tight indeed, a matter of minutes rather than hours.

Satellite meeting registration and document distribution must be effected efficiently, within the framework of the congress's own arrangements. Likewise, signs must be not only clear but obvious without conflicting with the main event's information and directional signs.

It is self-evident that attendance, and the registration fees associated with it, is of paramount importance to an organization staging such events. Equally important as a source of nondues revenues are the exhibitions that often are associated with scientific congresses. This too is sponsorship in a sense, one that carries a quid pro quo. Not only do the revenues support the congress budget, the exhibits are a learning resource for the delegates and provide an opportunity for exhibitors to make valuable contacts with potential customers.

Another type of satellite event might be a tradeshow or exhibition occurring concurrently, usually in the same city, in which congress delegates have an interest. It may be an event related to their field or one of general interest to meeting participants. As with other satellite events, program planners need to allow free time for interested parties to attend and, where interest is high, provide transportation. From a marketing standpoint, an exhibition that generates a high degree of interest for the delegates can be a significant factor in their attendance. The mutual benefits of such congruent events afford both parties unique opportunities for promotion.

Although surrounded by the myriad details of logistics, technology, and communications, meeting professionals must never lose sight of the importance of the program to both attendee and sponsor. It is, after all, the adhesive that binds all the other elements into a dynamic event.

▌KEY POINTS

To assist with time zone changes, avoid business or formal functions on arrival day and avoid over-programming the entire program to give attendees a chance to experience the country and its culture.

Provide substantial time for delegates to network, share experiences, attend social events, and have free time to explore the culture for a value-added experience.

Using technology such as interpreters and visual aids ensures better communication and comprehension for multinational audiences.

Interpretation may be necessary at multilingual congresses. Depending on different meeting sizes and situations, use simultaneous, consecutive, or whisper interpretation.

Based on the attendees' nationalities, translate printed materials and provide interpretation at presentations.

Carefully interview experienced speakers by utilizing your DMC or PCO and review the content of their speeches for relevancy.

Prepare the speaker for an international audience by sharing the history and culture of the host country and cutting out language nuances.

Choose music and entertainment in good taste that is easily understood by all cultures and does not distract from mingling at social events.

Seek sponsorships, tradeshow exhibitors, and satellite meetings for the mutual benefit of both the organization and the attendees.

▌PASSPORT

Books

Axtell, Roger E., *Do's and Taboos of Public Speaking,* John Wiley & Sons, New York, 1992.

Carey, Tony, CMM, ed., *Professional Meeting Management: A European Handbook,* Meeting Professionals International, London, 1999.

Internet

Association Intérnationale de Interprètes des Conference (AIIC): www.aiic.net.

National Speakers Association (NSA): www.nsaspeaker.org.

Chapter 7

CULTURAL CONSIDERATIONS

In only 10% of 191 nations are the people ethnically or racially homogeneous. Never before in humanity's history have there been so many people traveling beyond their homelands.
—G.F. Simons, R. Abramms, L.A. Hopkins, and O.J. Johnson, eds.,
Cultural Diversity Fieldbook, Peterson's/Pacesetter Books,
Princeton, NJ, 1996.

IN THIS CHAPTER

We will explore:

- How to become culturally competent as a meeting, convention, and exhibition manager.
- Proper forms of address for global colleagues.
- How other cultures think.
- Ways to recognize and respond to other cultural styles.
- How different cultures learn.
- The basics of effective cross-cultural communication.
- Culturally sensitive seating and staging arrangements.
- How to arrange proper protocol for honored persons.

Meeting planners who are not experienced in international gatherings often make the mistake of trying to transplant their domestic events to other countries without recognizing the differences in cultural attitudes, business practices, and basic communications. Confused, bewildered, and frustrated by their inability to control new situations, they often become judgmental and critical, bemoaning the fact that everything does not work exactly the way it does at home.

By contrast, their more seasoned colleagues acknowledge the unique challenges inherent in transnational, cross-cultural event planning. They have learned that *different* does not mean better or worse—it just means different. In fact, the excitement and satisfaction they obtain from their work come from embracing the differences and being able to work comfortably and successfully anywhere in the world.

Let us be very clear about this important and fundamental perspective on international event planning: *If you want everything to be just the way it is at home, stay home.* If your attendees want everything to be just as it is at home and you are unable or unwilling to educate and motivate them to enjoy the richness of another country and culture, you probably should not take your meeting abroad. If, however, you are able to open your mind and expand your professional horizons to encompass different ways of working with a variety of professional colleagues, by all means plan your events abroad and enjoy it.

People involved in planning and managing international events have an obligation to develop an understanding of the components of other cultures (see Figure 7-1) and gain competence in cross-cultural communications.

Cultural competence must begin with an attitude adjustment. Not only must you understand what is different, you must accept and respect the differences you encounter. Do not think of people of other cultures as alien or foreign. Eliminate those terms from your vocabulary and remember that to those with whom you will be dealing, you are the foreigner. You and your attendees will be the guests in their countries, and you have a responsibility to act appropriately and graciously within the existing norms. To do this, you must make a commitment to learn as much as possible about the people and culture of the country you will be visiting.

- Research the geography of the country with which you will be dealing.
- Before interacting with other nationals, study their history, culture, customs, and religions, if the latter is significant.

Accepted ways of behaving
Arts and artifacts
Beliefs
Ceremonies
Concept of self
Customs
Ideas and thought patterns
Ideals
Knowledge
Language
Laws
Manners
Morals
Myths and legends
Religious beliefs
Rituals
Values

Figure 7-1 Components of Culture

- Ascertain the degree of formality expected in attire for various occasions and the customary manner of address. The first-name basis favored by North Americans is appropriate only after a close acquaintance in most cultures, and never in some.
- Learn the proper form and use it when addressing people you meet. Keep in mind also that in most countries in Europe and Latin America, it is customary to use titles such as Doctor and Professor.
- By all means, study the country's taboos so that you avoid committing social blunders (see the Passport at the end of this chapter).

▌CULTURAL STYLES

Can good communication be achieved without understanding how other people think, what their cultural background is, and what their customs are? Conference organizers who specialize in international meetings would answer with a resounding *no.* The problem goes beyond researching and understanding cultural protocol and business etiquette. Successful globally oriented people try to anticipate how their counterparts will act.

According to Dr. George Borden, an American authority on cross-cultural communications, this requires insight into how people of other cultures think, what he calls their cognitive styles. According to Borden, all cultures have distinctive cognitive styles: the way individuals receive, process, and store information. These characteristics are by no means homogeneous within cultures; individual differences exist, molded by each person's experiences, biases, and personality traits. Cognitive style can be either associative—that is, associated with other information received in similar circumstances—or abstractive.

The abstractive style organizes information around relationship among other pieces of information. Take the phrase "an expensive gift." A Japanese will associate expensive with the recipient, his or her status, and the circumstance under which it is given. An American tends to look at the gift in the abstract, comparing it with other gifts of similar quality and price. About 10 percent of the world, including North and Central Europeans and North Americans, tend toward the abstractive. The other 90 percent, including Latin cultures, use an associative method.

Another interesting and useful cultural framework is that developed by Edward T. Hall and Mildred Reed Hall, which compares "high-context versus low-context" and "monochronic versus polychronic" cultures. Figure 7-2 summarizes the characteristics of these groups and the differences between them that can have a profound effect on negotiations, team building, and interpersonal dynamics.

If there are differences between cultures, there are also similarities. A wise communicator or negotiator plays to the similarities but is aware of the differences. Associative, high-context cultures, particularly Latin, Middle Eastern, and Asian cultures, value relationships. They seek to establish rapport

LOW-CONTEXT CULTURES
Information must be provided explicitly, usually in words
- Less aware of nonverbal cues, environment, and situation
- Lack well-developed networks
- Need detailed background information
- Tend to segment and compartmentalize information
- Control information on need-to-know basis
- Prefer explicit and careful directions from someone who "knows"
- Knowledge is a commodity

HIGH-CONTEXT CULTURES
Much information drawn from surroundings; very little must be transferred explicitly
- Nonverbal important
- Information flows freely
- Physical contact relied on for information
- Environment, situation, gestures, and mood all taken into account
- Maintain extensive information networks
- Accustomed to interruptions
- Do not always adhere to schedules

MONOCHRONIC PEOPLE
- Do one thing at a time
- Concentrate on the job
- Take time commitments (deadlines, schedules) seriously
- Are low-context and need information
- Adhere religiously to plans
- Are concerned about not disturbing conversations
- Emphasize promptness

POLYCHRONIC PEOPLE
- Do many things at once
- Are highly distractible and subject to interruptions
- Consider time commitments an objective to be achieved
- Are high-context and already have information
- Are committed to people and human relationships
- Change plans often and easily

Source: Edward T. Hall and Mildred Reed Hall, *Understanding Cultural Differences*

Figure 7-2 How People from Different Cultures Learn

before business is discussed. Family, schooling, cultural pursuits, and sports are areas of interest in all cultures and serve as ideal topics for building a relationship.

Attitudes toward time vary greatly from one culture to another. Low-context, monochronic cultures tend to value punctuality, whereas high-context, polychronic cultures are less concerned about adhering to schedules.

It would appear that as one travels from north to south, time sensitivity becomes less important. In China, Germany, and Japan, if a luncheon appointment is set for noon, you can expect your guests to be there at 12 sharp. In Taiwan, the Philippines, and Italy your guest may arrive around 12:15, whereas in Egypt and most South American countries it's not unusual for them to arrive at 12:30 or later.

DEVELOPING CULTURAL COMPETENCE

Perhaps the most important lesson in achieving cultural competence is to avoid stereotypical judgments. Each country is a mélange of regional, ethnic, and socioeconomic subgroups, and no international city has a totally homogeneous population. For instance, we tend to associate lederhosen, knockwurst, and oompah-pah music with Germany, but anyone who has been there can tell you that these are Bavarian traits; it's quite different in Berlin or Hamburg. To a Westerner, Chinese people may look alike, yet there is considerable variety in stature, dialect, and social customs among the Han, the Cantonese, and the Manchu. In all countries you will find differences in behavior, values, perception, and attitudes between urban and rural people and among those embracing various religious creeds or political ideologies. Understand the cultural characteristics of the country but learn to read people and treat them as individuals.

Learn the capital and major cities, cultural attractions, and places of historical interest of the country in which you will be working so that you will appear knowledgeable. The people with whom you come into contact will be flattered by your effort and impressed with your knowledge. By the same token, take time to acquire a few phrases in their language. They will be surprised and pleased when you say "pleased to meet you," "thank you," and "good-bye" in their language. Be sure to learn the customary toasts and expressions of appreciation at a meal. When it comes time to prepare your attendees, management, and speakers, pass along what you have learned.

GENERAL LANGUAGE CONSIDERATIONS

English is the globally recognized first language of business, and so it is easy for inexperienced international planners to assume that they will not have serious language issues in the major cities and tourist areas in which they will be working. Certainly everyone from the local CVB, the sales contacts at the hotel, people at the convention center, and the DMC will be fluent in English since they want to secure your business. However, these upper-level hospitality industry managers, along with the "front line"—reception, concierge, and bell staff at hotels—may be the only English speakers you will encounter.

Back of the house personnel—the maids, maintenance workers, meeting/function room set up staff, and audiovisual technicians—are often immigrants who may not speak the language of the host country, much less English. For this reason, a project team member, accountable to you, who speaks the host country language fluently and understands the local culture is an absolute requirement on any job.

This person may work for your company, be an independent planning colleague hired in your home country, or be someone provided by your DMC or PCO on-site. Whoever it is, you should consider that person your eyes and ears on-site and involve him or her from the outset.

Whether in writing or in speech, if you are addressing people whose native tongue is not English, you need to follow certain guidelines to ensure rapport and effective communication of your message. Even if listeners are fluent in your language, certain nuances may elude them, resulting in misunderstanding or noncomprehension.

Communicating with people for whom English is not the first language requires understanding and patience. For some reason, most of us have a tendency to raise our voices and take on the tone of a parent or primary school teacher even when we are speaking with adults. The key is to speak slower, not louder, and to enunciate clearly, keeping sentences short and simple whenever possible. Pause between sentences to give your listener time to think and answer.

Do not assume that you are being understood even if your listener appears to be following you with no problem. In some cultures it would be impolite or embarrassing to ask you to speak more slowly, explain a word or phrase, or admit that the listener does not understand you completely. For this reason, it is important to ascertain comprehension periodically during your conversation by asking a question that requires more than a yes or no answer.

Here are some other guidelines to follow and to pass along to colleagues and especially presenters at multicultural events:

- In writing and speech, avoid the use of colloquialism and idiomatic or slang expressions, including analogies to sports that are not popular outside the United States "Slam dunk," "home run," and "the whole nine yards" have no context in most of the world.
- Similarly, jargon ("geek"), buzzwords ("chief honcho"), acronyms (ACCME), and monocultural references ("as genuine as Mom's apple pie") should be avoided.
- Use basic words that have cognates in other languages rather than euphemisms. If you give directions to the toilet—the W.C. in some countries—most people will know what that is and will be clear about its function. Terms such as *restroom* and *powder room* may be confusing to a person translating the phrase literally. Are people actually resting in a restroom? Do people come out of powder rooms covered with powder?
- Resist the temptation to demonstrate your vocabulary prowess with arcane and esoteric words such as *arcane* and *esoteric*.

- Recognize that even among English-speaking people—Australians, Canadians, Americans, and Britons—there are different nuances and connotations, not to mention variations in vocabulary. A boot in the United States is footwear. A boot in the United Kingdom is the trunk of a car.
- When giving examples or using analogies, don't be provincial. Illustrate your comments with references to international cities such as London, Vienna, Tokyo, and Rio rather than Chicago or Los Angeles. Don't assume your listeners are familiar with North American geography, though most will be.
- If your topic is a technical one, ascertain your audience's level of understanding and familiarity with the subject without appearing to be condescending. Provide handouts to ensure comprehension.
- Make use of visual aids, diagrams, and charts if possible. Pictures are universal and aid understanding.
- Develop a working knowledge of the metric system, at least with respect to distance (kilometers), dimensions (meters), area (square meters), and temperature (Celsius). Most of the world uses the metric system, and the sooner you get comfortable with it, the easier your communications with suppliers will be.
- Conclude your presentations with a summary of the key points you covered. Ask for questions on any point that may not be clear but understand that in some cultures people will be reluctant to be considered ignorant by their peers by asking questions before an audience.
- Document all important business discussions in a written contact report as soon as possible after they occur and request verification of your summary by the recipients.

PROTOCOL FOR INTERNATIONAL MEETINGS

Interaction and dialogue at meetings among delegates of different, often divergent cultures has never been greater. Gregarious Australians, Americans, and Canadians often are taken aback when their casual bonhomie is not reciprocated in other cultures. The venerable adage "When in Rome . . ." applies equally to Kyoto, Koblenz, and Katmandu, perhaps even more so. Knowing what is appropriate behavior in other cultures is the foundation of protocol and business etiquette.

Many people confuse protocol with etiquette or use the terms interchangeably. In fact, they are different, though they are related in the sense that both delineate acceptable behavior in specific situations. Protocol generally refers to formal rules of custom, rank, and behavior established by governments or organizations and applied mainly to governmental, diplomatic, and military situations, both domestic and international. Etiquette concerns generally prescribed or accepted rules of behavior in social, business, and interpersonal situations.

At any gathering of people from various cultures and nationalities, proper behavior and decorum are essential to avoid embarrassment or affront. The customs governing such behavior vary with culture and usage, but certain rules of protocol apply to most international events. For those responsible for organizing such gatherings, understanding those rules is essential.

Meeting planners new to international events often approach the matter of protocol with trepidation or leave it to others. *Protocol* comes from the Greek words meaning "the first glue," and it functions as a social lubricant that permits people and organizations of disparate cultural backgrounds to interact in an atmosphere of understanding and mutual respect. It is not an arcane ritual but a means to minimize friction and maximize efficiency among people from disparate governments and organizations who must interact. As a meeting professional, you have an obligation to be aware of protocol requirements. There are excellent resources available (see the Passport section below), and you can avoid gaffes and embarrassing incidents if you prepare yourself, your officers, and the attendees by reading up on customs and business etiquette in various cultures.

LANGUAGE

If the audience is multinational and attendees from different language groups will be there, protocol demands that the meeting organizers arrange for translation and interpretive services. This is appropriate even if the conference language is English, as it often is. Whereas French, German, Italian, and Spanish once were considered standard, today's meetings may call for Arabic, Japanese, Russian, and even more exotic tongues. Some associations, anticipating a minimal number of delegates not from the primary language groups, offer interpretation at a nominal add-on to the registration fee.

The language team works closely with the program committee. It usually consists of the meeting planner or PCO, a representative of the language service, and a technician who is familiar with the interpretation system to be employed. The team meets early to assess the event's requirements, logistics, and costs; arranges for the appropriate number of interpreters and/or translators; and prepares the language annex to the staging guide. A memorandum is prepared and distributed to speakers, session chairpersons, and officers, advising them of the interpreters assigned to each event, social as well as business-related.

FORMS OF ADDRESS

Any person's name is very important to him or her. Be sure that all your people who will be in contact with visitors and dignitaries learn the proper pronunciation of names and the use of titles, if any. Instruct your staff, officials, and attendees that the use of titles is customary when addressing doctors and other professionals and particularly dignitaries. Verify the appropriate form of address for high-ranking participants and advise all officers and members who will be interacting with them of this form. Also inform media representatives if interviews are to be granted.

Throughout Asian countries as well as in Hungary, the family name precedes the given name. Thus, Janos Arany from Budapest would introduce himself as Arany Janos. Some officials in frequent contact with Westerners have rearranged the traditional order, thus exacerbating the problem. To avoid confusion, design registration forms that call for "surname" or "family name" rather than "last name" and provide a space for the person to indicate "your name as you wish it to appear on your name badge." To be sure that you are clear about whether registrants are male or female, you may want to check with a native of their country or someone familiar enough with the language and culture to be able to ascertain gender. For example, is Doctor Han Lei Ming a man or a woman?

It is also important to be aware that Spanish-speaking Latin Americans (that is, everyone except Brazilians, whose official language is Portuguese) have two family names—the paternal and maternal—and are addressed by the paternal, which comes first. Thus, Fernando Garcia Moreno would be addressed as Fernando Garcia. In Brazil and Portugal, however, the paternal name is placed last, so that Fernando Garcia Moreno in Rio de Janeiro would be addressed as Fernando Moreno.

But what if Fernando is a Fernanda? If she is unmarried, her name follows the same rules in both Spanish and Portuguese. However, if she is married, she adds *de* followed by her husband's last name. If Fernanda Garcia Moreno is from Bogotá and is married to José Vargas Perrera from Caracas, her name badge would read Fernanda Garcia de Vargas. What would her name badge read if she and her husband were both from São Paulo? Fernanda Moreno de Perrera—right! We will leave you to figure out what her name badge would read if she was from São Paulo and her husband was from Buenos Aires.

SEATING AND STAGING

When honored personages (HPs) such as high-ranking government officials are participating in a meeting, one of the most important considerations is order of precedence by rank. Specific rules govern the manner in which dignitaries enter the meeting room or dining facility, how they are seated, when and where they address the meeting and how they depart. Typically, the presiding officer greets the HP at the entrance to the facility if the HP is arriving by car or in the prefunction area if the HP is already in-house. They enter the function room with the ranking HP on the right of the presiding officer, followed by other HPs, in order of rank, escorted by other host officers. The audience rises and remains standing until the entourage is seated. The HP is seated to the right of the presiding officer and other dignitaries, in order of rank, to his or her right, alternating with escorts. If he or she is seated on stage or at a head table, the presiding officer is seated at the center or to the right of the lectern (if one is used). The ranking HP sits at his or her right, and the next highest ranking guest at his or her left. The others alternate with their escorts from right to left. If spouses are seated at the head table, they are seated next to their husbands or wives.

Guest dignitaries are introduced by the presiding officer and address the audience from the lectern. If twin standing lecterns are used, the one at stage right is the position of honor. Introductions are made from the lectern at stage left.

Departure follows the same pattern. The HP may depart after the opening ceremonies or at the first break or remain for the entire session. The audience again rises and remains in place until the guests and their entourage have exited. These procedure should be explained to the audience before the HP's party arrives.

FLAGS

At international meetings it is customary to display the host nation's flag and the flags of the countries represented by delegates. On the podium or dais, the host country's colors are positioned at stage right and the others are placed to their left in alphabetical order (according to the country's name in English). If the host national colors are displayed at center stage, they are placed higher than the others, which are displayed in alphabetical order alternating from the host flag's right and left (as it faces the audience) successively.

If you are uncertain about proper display, don't guess; seek counsel from the protocol officer of the host country's consulate. Personal standards are displayed when royalty, heads of state, nobility, and high-ranking military officers or church officials participate. To ensure proper flag etiquette and arrange delivery of standards, contact the HP's aide or a consular officer.

HONORS

The rendering of honors for arriving heads of state and other HPs may include salutes, anthems, processions, honor guards, greeting, escorts, or all of these. Such formalities are quite exacting, and any departure from the norm is considered a breach of etiquette at best and a diplomatic incident at worst. Failing to follow proper protocol is an affront to the HP, his or her office, and the government he or she represents and reflects poorly on the sponsoring organization. The same consideration should be shown to leading corporate officers and persons of achievement. Although diplomatic rules govern rank universally, each country may have variations.

▌ KEY POINTS

To achieve good cross-cultural communication, one must understand how different cultures think and learn.

Take the time to learn phrases, cultural and historical sites, and customary mealtime behavior and share this information with your attendees.

Work closely with a personal interpreter who speaks the host country's language fluently and understands the culture.

When speaking, avoid colloquialism, slang, and jargon; speak clearly; and give people time to respond and ask questions.

Follow the rules of protocol and etiquette in the culture you are in to avoid embarrassment and appearing offensive.

Learn and follow the proper ways to introduce people and use their correct titles and first and family names.

Learn how to greet, introduce, and seat or stage an honored personage as well as the proper usage of flags and the protocol for bestowing honors.

PASSPORT

Books

Axtell, Roger E., *Do's and Taboos around the World: A Guide to International Behavior,* 3rd ed., John Wiley & Sons, New York, 1993.

Axtell, Roger E., *Gestures: Do's and Taboos of Body Language around the World,* John Wiley & Sons, New York, 1991.

Borden, George A. *Cultural Orientation: An Approach to Understanding Intercultural Communication,* Prentice Hall College Division, Englewood Cliffs, NJ, 1991.

Bosrock, Mary Murray, *Put Your Best Foot Forward: Asia,* International Education Systems, 1997.

Bosrock, Mary Murray, *Put Your Best Foot Forward: Europe,* International Education Systems, 1995.

Bosrock, Mary Murray, *Put Your Best Foot Forward: South America,* International Education Systems, 1997.

Dresser, Norine, *Multicultural Manners: New Rules of Etiquette for a Changing Society,* John Wiley & Sons, New York, 1996.

McCaffree, Mary Jane, and Pauline Innis, *Protocol: The Complete Handbook of Diplomatic, Official, and Social Usage,* Devon Publishing Company, Washington, DC, 1989.

Morrison, Terri, Wayne A. Conway, and George A. Borden, *Kiss, Bow, or Shake Hands: How To Do Business in Sixty Countries,* B. Adams, Holbrook, MA, 1994.

Pachter, Barbara, and Marjorie Brody, *Prentice-Hall Complete Business Etiquette Handbook,* Prentice-Hall, Englewood Cliffs, NJ, 1995.

Internet

International Association of Protocol Consultants: www.protocolconsultants.org.

Individual country overviews and reports: www.culturegrams.com.

Chapter 8

MARKETING THE EVENT

The same market data we collect at home are important overseas. The difference is that we must take a fresh look at factors that we might take for granted at home. . . . There is never just one culture.

—Lewis Griggs and Lennie Copeland

IN THIS CHAPTER

We will explore:

- How to apply principles of mass communication to marketing.
- Utilizing the elements of mass communication to create a dynamic marketing plan.
- Steps in selecting and budgeting for promotional media.
- Sources of funding for promoting events.
- Cultural considerations in directing a promotional message.
- Effective methods for publicizing events.
- Enhancing marketing efficacy through industry partners.

Whether an event takes place across the country or across the world, organizations recognize that it needs to be introduced suitably and, as marketers are fond of saying, "attractively packaged." Even corporate event organizers find that employees need somewhat more motivation to be there than the rubric "attendance is mandatory." When it comes to independent dealers, representatives, affiliates, and association members who can decide for themselves whether taking time to go to the meeting is worthwhile, a vigorous motivational marketing program is essential.

Communicating the particulars of an event to multicultural prospects entails somewhat more than the customary four-page, single-fold coated stock mailer. Even if your organization is known to the target audience, your message needs to convey a more emphatic reason to attend than is the case with domestic meetings. It may have to be in several languages and should reflect an awareness of cultural differences and attitudes. Marketing entails the selection of specific media, the design and production of elements, the compilation of mailing lists, and identification of other promotional resources. The task involves getting people to attend by appealing to as many motivating elements as possible (for a list, see Figure 8-1). A proper marketing program

DELEGATES' MOTIVATIONS
  Professional development
  Advancement
  Cultural interaction
  New contacts
  Information sharing
  Social
  Recreational

ASSOCIATION SPONSOR'S MOTIVATIONS
  Member interaction
  Conduct association business
  Educate members
  Recruit new members
  Produce nondues revenue
  Provide exhibitor exposure

CORPORATE SPONSOR'S MOTIVATIONS
  Inform and motivate employees
  Introduce products and or services
  Establish new markets
  Inform or acquire global affiliates
  Conduct shareholder meeting

EXHIBITORS' MOTIVATIONS
  Exposure to new markets
  Lead generation
  Product introduction
  Social interaction

Figure 8-1 The Motivations to Attend Your Meeting

creates a sense of anticipation and delivers an audience that is prepared, in-formed, and receptive to the sponsor's message. A well-designed program of promotion and publicity gives participants everything they need to know about getting to the meeting from home and back, some details on the venue, and what they can expect as well as what is expected of them.

An effective marketing plan not only reflects the event, the venue, and the meeting content, but also must reflect the motivation of all stakeholders: potential attendees, sponsors, and, if applicable, exhibitors as reflected in Figure 8-1.

MARKETING STRATEGIES

Because locales, objectives, agendas, and audiences often change from one event to another, there is no such thing as an omnibus strategy for marketing. There is, however, one guiding principle that applies to all event promotions: Seek competent, professional counsel to help you target and schedule the marketing budget to achieve maximum impact. An MPI study titled "Trends in Event Marketing Research" traces current information on marketing practices in the United States, Canada, the Asia-Pacific region, the United Kingdom, and Germany. See the Passport at end of this chapter.

Marketing an international event may be entirely a function of the meetings department or secretariat or may be shared with committees for registration and marketing. Procedures entail the selection of foreign and domestic media, compilation of mailing lists, and identification of available promotional resources such as related events, publications, and tradeshows. Although they recognize the appeal and effectiveness of Web marketing, many show organizers regard Web-based promotion as an accessory to print and mail.

As with any promotion, the following mass communications guidelines apply:

- Analyze market demographics and the perceived needs of the target audience. Design a marketing program that addresses those needs.
- Assess cultural differences and what motivates prospective attendees to respond. Program content? Speakers? Interaction with peers? Venue? Time of year? Concurrent or adjacent events?
- Consider potential deterrents to attendance: cost; distance; destination factors such as safety, climate, political stability; and attitude toward the host organization or nation.
- Research available media to include Web site, e-mail, direct mail, trade publications, publicity, cooperative advertising, trade-outs, and participation in preceding events. Aim for multiple impressions and budget accordingly.
- Reach out with a multimedia program that packages online resources such as e-mail blogs and chat rooms with print elements and visual media recorded on CDs.
- Promotional materials should be produced in multiple languages to reflect the main language groups if they are aimed at a multicultural audience.
- Create a dynamic theme. Select a graphic style with universal appeal and text that translates readily.
- A multinational audience is not a homogeneous group. Emphasize benefits according to cultural values.
- Market throughout the year, not just in the months before the event. Promote the next event at ones currently in progress.

"Suppose you gave a meeting and your carefully chosen speakers looked out on a half-empty room or spoke to a multicultural audience that had a problem understanding or relating to the speakers' remarks," asks Sara Torrence, CMP. "A solidly thought-out, effective marketing effort is key to ensuring the right audience attends." Torrence, a meetings industry leader, and author, and the head of a respected meeting and event management firm, offers these additional pointers for a dynamic event promotion plan:

- Plan a program that features topics and speakers that will attract attendees as well as media attention.

PROMOTIONAL TOOLS

Mass media
Trade journals
Society journals and newsletters
Current event (for future meeting)
Tie-in events, shows, exhibitions
Web sites email
Direct mail:
   Mail lists
   Mailing services
Affiliate promotion—CVBs, NTOs
Telemarketing
Scholarships
Word of mouth

Figure 8-2 Typical Conference Marketing Tools

- In developing the meeting timetable, consider a marketing plan and a schedule to publicize the event effectively.
- Budget for funds to support a varied promotional effort—advertisement, e-marketing, flyers, brochures, translation, and so on—to attract the desired audience.
- If the anticipated attendance suggests, budget for a media campaign, newsroom equipment and staffing, press kits, and related elements.
- Include in the meeting evaluation criteria for measuring marketing efficacy.

See Figure 8-2 for a list of useful promotional tools.

MARKETING BUDGET

Whether you are marketing stretch jeans, breakfast cereals, or meetings, these principles apply. If the "product" is an international event, pay special attention to costs.

The Internet can be the most cost-effective medium whether it involves e-mail, a dedicated Web site, or both. Direct mail advertising to other countries can be economical when the printed materials are sent as a bulk shipment and subsequently mailed abroad. Most airlines provide this service, and if an official airline has been named, it may offer special rates. A foreign mailing service, a local convention bureau, a counterpart organization, affiliate offices, or allied members in other countries also can handle the mailing. Shipping camera-ready art and having the printing done locally may be advisable if there are tariffs on print materials or if the mailing is extensive.

Business, trade, and professional publications and association journals offer the most effective media for display advertising to a targeted audience. They will insert registration forms for an additional cost and are a reliable conduit for publicity releases. Promotion at related tradeshows, exhibitions, and allied events is one of the most cost-effective ways to disseminate news of a meeting to a well-defined audience.

SOURCES OF FUNDING

Organizations often find that effective attendance marketing on a global scale is beyond their budget, especially with rising costs and less than favorable exchange rates. Younger audiences in particular, which are accustomed to Web conferencing and electronic communication media, are skeptical about attending meetings. They need to be convinced of the benefits of face-to-face communication, John Naisbitt's implied need for "high touch" notwithstanding. To help fund their marketing efforts, more creative meeting organizers seek out sources of sponsorship.

Recognizing the economic impact of a substantial number of visitors, convention bureaus and the venues they represent have a significant stake in building attendance. As early as the 1980s the Netherlands Convention Bureau introduced "bridge funding" for associations that contracted to meet in Dutch cities. This was an offer of funds to be used for marketing purposes aimed at building attendance. Their stakeholders—local businesses, institutions, and facilities—contributed to the fund. Other destination marketers, recognizing the economic impact of a large number of convention visitors on the local economy, followed suit.

The Destination Marketing Association International (formerly the International Association of Convention and Visitors Bureaus) emphasizes to its membership that CVBs need to offer a variety of attendance-building strategies and incentives to remain competitive. Many such organizations offer in-kind services such as digital marketing campaigns and direct mail to help the association build attendance once their venue is designated as the convention site.

▌ CULTURAL ISSUES

Language influences marketing to multinational audiences. It is customary to produce brochures, ads, and announcements in multiple languages, depending on the regions that are involved. For European audiences, English, French, German, and Italian are customary. For Asia, Japanese and Mandarin Chinese may be advisable. Although programs normally are published in the conference language, proceedings, handouts, and press releases may need to be translated. Be sure to have the translation verified by persons who are current in the language. Foreign residents in North America, even though fluent, may not be up on current idiom and usage. The safest method is to use a translation service in each country. The alternative is to use a professional translation service at home but have the copy verified before it goes to press.

If an exhibition is part of the conference and exhibitors from other countries are invited, they should be afforded the same considerations as attendees vis-à-vis language for printed materials. Floor plans and contracts need not be translated, but weights, measurements, and dimensions should be expressed in metric as well as the Imperial equivalent.

PUBLICITY

Press releases to the foreign trade, business, or technical press provide a low-cost means of promoting meetings. Many of these publications will include a registration form for a nominal charge.

At the event itself, special provisions should be made for accrediting and accommodating the foreign trade press. Press kits in the conference language but containing copies of translated materials should be sent to assignment editors in advance and provided to accredited press on-site. During the event, schedule regular press conferences featuring noteworthy speakers, visiting dignitaries, and your most articulate organizational officers and members.

INTERNET PROMOTION

"Your organization's Web site can be the most effective marketing medium for your meeting," says Jim Daggett, CAE, CMP. "The key objective is to drive traffic to the site. Make sure that people can find it with search engine optimization, banner ads on related sites, news release distribution, and other off-line marketing. There are various ways to ensure that it is effective and supports the organization's objectives." Daggett's strategies are shown in Figure 8-3.

- Integrate registration, housing, and travel booking capabilities for one-stop shopping.
- Incorporate personalization wherever possible by prepopulating fields and greetings.
- Include capabilities for speaker and/or abstract management on the site.
- Feature related Webcasts, real-time or on-demand pay-per-view.
- Enable visitors to purchase merchandise.
- Make topical chat rooms/message boards/discussion lists available.
- Provide other types of Web-based educational opportunities.
- Include booth (stand) assignments and show facilitation capabilities (if applicable).
- Incorporate online business exchange opportunities.
- Provide electronic versions of newsletters, surveys, evaluations, and questionnaires.

Figure 8-3 Meeting Web Site as a Marketing Tool

WEBLOGS

Blogs and blogcasts are rapidly influencing how events are marketed.

A blog is basically an online journal that is created and maintained by an individual. The activity of updating a blog is *blogging,* and someone who keeps a blog is a *blogger.* Blogs are typically updated daily with software that allows people with little or no technical background to use it. Postings on a blog are almost always arranged in chronological order, with the most recent additions featured prominently.

In the meetings industry there are thousands of blogs worldwide, which enable members to post opinions, evaluate events attended, seek input from colleagues, and add another communications tool to e-mail. Organizations encourage their meeting participants to create personal blogs in order to understand their needs and concerns, They also serve as valuable adjuncts to post-event evaluation.

A podcast is an Internet broadcast that enables individuals to transmit information, opinions, questions and reactions before, during, and after an event (see "Passport").

DIRECT MAIL

Despite the wonders of e-mail and the Internet, direct mail offers benefits that electronic communication may not. Visualize a typical meeting promotion pamphlet. The cover has a theme graphic, the conference name, the venue, and dates. Inside is a message from an organization executive or celebrity telling readers why they must not miss this event. This is followed by several pages of program content, including business agenda—with speakers' pictures and topic summaries—social and recreational events, registration data, the registration form, and transportation and housing information—all of interest to potential attendees. Of course all that can be accessed on a Web site, but does the viewer have the patience to read it all? E-mail and Web-based communications are suitable for short, specific data, but most viewers don't have the patience to sit before a monitor and take in all the particulars. With printed pieces they can absorb the information at their leisure.

Ideally, for recurring events, the promotional package begins with an audiovisual presentation at the current meeting and a printed flyer announcing the dates, venue, and conference theme. In subsequent months, e-mails and Web site reminders keep the momentum going until the program begins to take shape. At that point a detailed flyer or brochure is mailed.

When one is marketing to other countries, direct mail materials sent in bulk shipments and subsequently mailed using a remail service can be cost-effective.

The U.S. Postal Service offers International Surface Air Lift (ISAL) for shipments of 50 or more pounds. Alternately, they suggest a service called Global Direct in which mail is bulk shipped but locally postmarked and carries a local return address.

One year out	Announce the dates and site of next year's meeting at the current one. Establish Web site. Evaluate audience demographics and language fluency. Solicit exhibitors.
Eighth month	Decide on theme and design graphics. Determine preliminary agenda. Analyze prospective audience and prepare marketing plan. Draft announcement letter and text for promotional pieces. Obtain draft and design approval. Submit for translation if applicable.
Seventh month	Verify translation. Design registration forms and systems or contract for electronic registration services. Prepare mailing labels and/or order lists. Alert mailing service. Obtain bids on printing and Web hosting. Submit first mailer elements to printer. Mailing labels produced.
Sixth month	Deliver mailers to mailing service. First mailing out. Prepare second mailing elements. Establish registration controls. Design and produce ads for trade publications. Contract for space. Prepare news releases.
Fifth month	Fine-tune business and social agendas. Design second mailing elements and obtain approvals. Contract Web services. Second mailing to printer. Include registration forms. Submit ads, insertion orders, and initial news releases to trade media and Web sites.
Fourth month	Second mailing out. Continue news releases. Track registrations. Design final mailing and registration kits. Fine-tune program.
Third month	Track registrations. First ads appear. Final releases to trade media. Determine need for additional mailings based on registration. Finalize program. Mailing elements to printer.
Second month	Confirm speakers. Final mailing out. Program book to printer. Prepare press kits. Contact talk show producers.
Last month	Contact assignment editors and follow up. Order staff and equipment for press room. Generate signage and name badges; assemble registration kits. Schedule press conference. Officers and spokesmen arrive early for talk show appearances.

Figure 8-4 A Typical Conference Marketing Plan

For mailings of less than 50 pounds, Deutche Post World Net provides ISAL mailing through its exclusive distribution network. It tracks mailings and provide confirmation of deliveries. DPGM does not have a minimum weight restriction. Great Britain's Royal Mail has a similar program serving European Union (EU) countries, Australia, and New Zealand. (See the Passport at the end of this chapter for contact information.)

Shipping camera-ready art and having the printing done locally may be advisable if there are high tariffs on printed material or if the mailing list has over a thousand names.

MARKETING PARTNERS

Once the venue is determined, destination marketers such as the convention bureau or national tourist offices (NTOs) can provide a wide range of promotional support. Given adequate lead time, many organizations announce a subsequent meeting venue at their current conventions. Tourist boards often assist in promoting attendance with a wide range of support materials featuring the benefits of the chosen destination for the upcoming event.

Depending on the perceived value of the meeting, support resources may include the following:

- Official guides and maps showing places of interest, museums, and attractions.
- Brochures featuring leisure attractions, beaches, restaurants, shopping, and so forth.
- Printed shells with color photographs of the area suitable for customizing.
- Professionally produced videos and DVDs highlighting destination features.
- Souvenirs characteristic of the region for distribution with promotional elements.

For larger or more prestigious organizations, destination marketers often provide speakers and entertainers to promote the venue. Singapore's famous lion dancers, Bavarian musical groups, Britain's colorful Coldstream Guards, and a Mexican mariachi band and dancers are a few of the assets available as promotional entertainment.

The majority of NTOs that depend on meeting business have elaborate Web sites illustrating a country's attractions, history, and culture. They can be a valuable reference for attendees who want to familiarize themselves with the meeting venue in advance.

Affiliate organizations such as corporate branch offices, suppliers or affiliates, local association chapters, and allied organizations can be invaluable marketing assets if they are included early in the planning cycle and given a prominent role in the event's operations. Other strategic marketing partners include support services and entities that can benefit from increased attendance at the event. When provided with the target audience's names and contact information, they can utilize e-mail, Web site publicity, direct mail, and ads or articles in their publications. These supporting promotional alliances include:

- Exhibitors who have a vested interest in promoting attendance.
- The host hotel, especially if it is part of an international hotel chain.
- Airlines designated as recommended or official carriers.
- A PCO if one has been contracted to manage or support the event.

- DMCs and, through them, the services and attractions they contract for on behalf of the group.
- Exhibit services in connection with exhibitions or when exhibits are part of the event.

MARKETING TIMETABLE

Like all activities related to international events, effective marketing requires more lead time than it does with domestic meetings. Working with audiences and services in other countries takes longer, even with e-mail and fax communications. Translation and verification are time-consuming but essential, and postal services are not equally efficient in all countries. A good rule is to double both the lead time and the marketing budget and then add an additional percentage for contingencies. Figure 8-4 illustrates a marketing schedule for an average-size meeting.

KEY POINTS

MARKETING STRATEGIES

In your marketing efforts, stress to your audience the multicultural benefits they will receive and demonstrate sensitivity to each culture on which you are focusing your marketing.

MARKETING BUDGET

Be cost-sensitive with printed promotional materials. Make heavy use of the Internet and Web sites as well as professional publications to market your meeting to a wide range of people.

Utilize CVB incentives and sponsorships to deal with budget constraints.

PUBLICITY

Utilize press releases, the Internet, and Web sites as well as the direct mailing services offered in many countries.

Make use of promotional materials offered by tourist offices, exhibitors, airlines, and hotels that have marketing materials that showcase cultural and historical draws to the international site.

PASSPORT

Books

Copeland, Lennie, and Lewis Griggs, *Going International: How to Make Friends and Deal Effectively in the Global Marketplace,* Random House, New York, 1985.

Torrence, Sara R., CMP, *How to Run Scientific and Technical Meetings,* Van Nostrand Reinhold, New York, London 1991.

Internet

American Marketing Association: www.marketing-power.com.

Association of Convention Marketing Executives (ACME): www.acmenet.org.

Deutche Post Global Mail: www.mailglobal.com.

International Surface Air Lift, *USPS Publication 51:* www.uspa.gov.

J.R. Daggett & Associates: www.jrdaggett.com.

Meeting Professionals International, *Trends in Event Marketing Research:* www.mpiweb.org.

Royal Mail (USA): www.royalmailus.com.

www.podcastalley.com (to search for Blogs)

www.blogger.com (to establish a Blog)

Chapter 9

INTERNATIONAL CONTRACTS AND LEGALITIES

A verbal agreement is not worth the paper it is printed on.
—**Attributed to movie producer Samuel Goldwyn**

IN THIS CHAPTER

We will explore:

- How international contracts differ from those in the United States.
- How U.S. tax laws affect international events.
- What you need to know about host country legal matters and regulations.
- How local law enforcement can affect an event and its participants.
- How health regulations differ and their impact on attendees.
- Major differences in how contracts are written and how they apply to an event.
- Negotiation strategies for dealing with other cultures.

Contracts often are defined by attorneys as blueprints or road maps, providing a precise definition of what has been agreed on and guidance in the event of a dispute. It has been said that the best contracts are those written as if the people drafting the agreement would not be around to implement it. That is, nothing is assumed, everything agreed to is noted in detail, and the expectations and responsibilities of both parties are clear even to someone who was not present during the initial discussions and negotiations.

Contracts are considered to be binding when the following criteria are met:

- An offer is made.
- The offer is accepted.
- "Consideration" is provided (i.e., something is done, given, or promised).
- The document is in writing when this is required by law.
- The people signing the contract are legally authorized to do so.

Basic provisions of both domestic and international meeting contracts include the following:

- Names of the contracting parties
- Dates of the event
- Sleeping room requirements
- Meeting space requirements
- Function space requirements
- Food and beverage requirements
- Sleeping room rates (including surcharges and/or taxes)
- Meeting and function space rates (including surcharges and taxes)
- Complimentary accommodations, services, and amenities
- Payment terms
- Force majeure
- Attrition
- Cancellation and/or termination
- Dispute resolution

However, it is important to note that although these basic contract components are similar at home and abroad, the definitions and expectations attached to some of them can be very different. For example, hotel sleeping rooms in North America are generally uniform in size, and a group rate is the same whether one or two people occupy a room. In many European hotels, single rooms are smaller than double rooms and rates are quoted per person rather than per room. Thus, when contracting for sleeping rooms overseas, the planner must specify what type of room as well as how many rooms. If it is important for everyone to have the same size room, the contract must specify "double rooms for single occupancy."

Similarly, the expectation of what constitutes a coffee break can surprise an unsuspecting planner contracting for this food function overseas. Unlike the standard North American refreshment break, with hot and cold beverages and a variety of food items, a coffee break in Latin America is exactly that: a break for coffee. Food, when served, is usually no more elaborate than a plate of cookies or finger sandwiches. An elaborate coffee break would include fruit juice and more than one type of cookie. European breaks are equally simple and not congruent with the expectations of a planner from the United States who expects fresh fruit and granola bars, smoothies, ice cream sundaes, or freshly popped popcorn to be available.

Jonathan Howe, a leading industry attorney and the general counsel to Meeting Professionals International, gives the following example of the importance of defining terms precisely when one is communicating needs and requirements to suppliers overseas:

The director of sales and the meeting planner are sitting there together talking, and the planner asks, "Do you have a freight elevator?" and the sales director says, "Yes, we do!" and they go on talking. Well, they were both accurate—the question was a good question, and the answer was an accurate description. The hotel did have an elevator that was used for freight, but it was actually just one of the passenger elevators with a load capacity of 2000 pounds that was designated "freight elevator." The planner's tradeshow was going to take place on the second floor of the building with heavy equipment that weighed far in excess of 2000 pounds. The net effect was that they couldn't use the elevator to get what they needed up to the tradeshow. Question asked, question answered, but no one bothered to clearly define the requirements for the freight elevator or determine whether it had the capacity to do the job that had to be done.

In addition to defining terms and aligning expectations carefully, it is important to remember that although many of the contract components are similar, the laws of the host country governing the contracts may be very different. You can avoid legal problems by following a few basic rules and understanding how a meeting may be affected by local law. That doesn't mean you have to pass a bar examination in that country. Simply accept the fact that the laws may be different and follow these guidelines:

- Consult the national tourist office for advice on legal considerations.
- In some cultures, one's word is held in high esteem and contracts carry a perception of distrust. Inquire about the local protocol.
- Determine whether contracts are governed by civil law ("Napoleonic" code) or by common law. The distinction will influence contract provisions.
- Find out under what conditions contracts may be terminated.
- Inquire about alternatives to deposits paid to a hotel or service, especially if you are contracting for a long term and there is a question of stability.
- If delegates from several countries are attending, investigate visa requirements and restrictions for various nationals.
- For extranational meetings, in which an American group travels to another country, look into U.S. tax laws governing offshore travel.
- Consider the services of a PCO to represent you in negotiations and contracts.

Cultural considerations and business protocol govern the process of negotiations and vary greatly from one country to another. In certain cultures, some parts of a written contract may be superseded by generally accepted practice, custom, and tradition. In others, insisting on a written contract is seen as implying distrust and therefore is bad manners. As was noted in Chapter 7, people from Asia, the Middle East, and Latin America place greater value on a person's integrity and reputation than on contracts. Experienced international organizers recommend an understanding of business practices in other cultures and a willingness to be flexible, patient, and resourceful.

"Keep a comprehensive paper trail and document what has been agreed. If it comes to litigation, lawyers demand the production of all relevant documents," advises Jonathan Howe. He points out that with today's global communications, documents include e-mails, computer hard drives, faxes, recordings, phone logs, and phone bills as well as handwritten notes.

Paper trail notwithstanding, it is important to remember that all your contracts will be of little use on-site if you do not establish a successful working relationship with your suppliers that is based on honesty, respect, and trust. Taking someone to court after the fact is small consolation after a disastrous event, especially when the cost of an international lawsuit is added to the losses incurred.

CONTRACT PROVISIONS

Contracts in North America can be long and extremely detailed and may contain attrition, termination, and cancellation clauses that enable the organization to avoid penalties in certain circumstances. Strikes, war, natural disasters, and acts of God are some of the grounds for canceling a meeting. Rebooking at a later date or another hotel in the same chain also may mitigate claims for liquidated damages. Asian and European contracts most often lack such remedies and are more demanding of performance. In fact, in some countries a contract can be no more than a one-page letter outlining the dates, rate, space, food and beverage requirements, and penalties for cancellation.

There is also the issue of the language in which the contract is written. Although most contracts are written in English and you can certainly ask for this, many times contracts are written in the host country's language with an English translation provided. Peter Haigh, former director of sales operations in Europe for Le Meridien Hotels and Resorts, offers this useful caveat:

"As a rule, the contractual language of the host country takes precedence over that of any translation in case of a dispute. Therefore, a contract written in Portuguese for facilities or services in Rio de Janeiro has precedence over its English translation." For this reason, it is wise to ask for a certified translation and read it carefully.

When contracting for services or facilities in another country, you can avoid problems and conflicts by following these guidelines:

- Retain the services of counsel familiar with contract laws of both countries.
- Ensure that contract provisions are enforceable under that country's laws.
- Determine when the contract is in force and when it is considered satisfied by both parties.
- Know which country's laws are binding and under which one's jurisdiction disputes may be settled.
- Investigate alternative dispute resolution methods such as mediation and arbitration since going to court in a foreign country can be very expensive. Mediation requires that for the dispute to be settled, both parties have to agree to the settlement. In arbitration, the parties agree to be bound by the decision rendered by the arbitrators.

DEPOSIT AND CANCELLATION OR TERMINATION

Be prepared to provide deposits for all services and facilities abroad. Unlike many U.S. suppliers, who will accept payment of a balance due after the meeting occurs, most offshore suppliers will require 100 percent payment in advance of the meeting for all services contracted. This is especially true of hotels and DMCs that have to subcontract other independent businesses and pay them in advance. To protect your organization against the possibility of the provider's insolvency, arrange for deposits in the form of interest-bearing escrow accounts or irrevocable standby letters of credit. The latter place the deposits in a bank acceptable to both parties, with instructions to release funds once the letter's conditions have been fulfilled.

Many people use the terms *termination* and *cancellation* interchangeably, but their legal definitions and consequences are quite different. When a contract is terminated, both parties are excused from performance of their obligations without liability. Termination clauses generally cover situations such as disasters (see "Force Majeure," below), change in facility management, unsatisfactory conditions at the facility, or if one of the other contracting party becomes insolvent or files for bankruptcy.

Cancellation occurs when one party does not perform under the contract, and when this occurs, that party generally has to pay damages. *Actual damages* usually are calculated as a combination of lost profits and additional expenses caused by the breach of contract. The party claiming the damages not only has to prove the extent of the loss incurred but also must take steps to reduce ("mitigate") that loss, for example, in the case of a hotel, show a good faith effort to resell the canceled space.

Since the definition of what constitutes lost profit can be highly variable, subjective, and difficult to confirm, many meeting professionals prefer to include a *liquidated damages* clause as a compromise to reduce the risk to both parties. In this case, they agree at the outset on an amount and a method for calculating the damages that will be paid if there is a breach of contract. This enables the parties to know exactly what the cost of cancellation will be and releases the party receiving payment for the damages from having to prove either the actual loss or an attempt to reduce it. Given all the other variables with which the planner must contend when negotiating international contracts, a cancellation clause based on liquidated rather than actual damages is usually the most desirable.

FORCE MAJEURE

Force majeure loosely translated means "great force" in French and refers to the occurrence of something unexpected and/or so overwhelming that one party or both parties are unable to perform their contracted obligations. Acts of God, which are natural disasters such as hurricanes, earthquakes, blizzards, and floods, as well as acts of war, civil unrest, labor disputes, and terrorism, are included in force majeure clauses. Since the definition of force majeure and acts of God varies not only from country to country but also from locality to locality, it is very important to define precisely what will excuse performance and what obligations both parties will have if something unexpected and/or cataclysmic occurs. For example, when all commercial airline flights into and out of the United States were halted for several days after the 9/11 terrorist attacks, meetings booked around the world had to be canceled since the attendees were physically unable to get to where they needed to go. In this case, since attending the meeting was literally impossible, force majeure applied. In contrast, during times when U.S. citizens are not prohibited from traveling abroad but simply feel concerned or uncomfortable about doing so (such as during the Gulf War in 1990), force majeure does not apply.

U.S. TAX IMPLICATIONS

For the meeting organizer or planner, the key element here is the tax deductibility of participant expenses. The Internal Revenue Service (IRS) guidelines for deductibility require that the meeting and its deductible expenses be directly related to the attendee's profession or trade; that the deduction be reasonable and appropriate, not "lavish" or "extravagant"; and that the days for which the deduction is claimed be devoted primarily to a business purpose. The Internal Revenue Code further demands that the sponsoring organization's choice of a foreign venue be "as reasonable" as one in North America and select "beneficiary countries." See Figure 9-1 for the current listing. In applying the reasonability test, the following factors are relevant:

- The nature, purpose, and activities of the sponsoring organization.
- The meeting objectives and the activities that take place during the event.
- Countries of residence of the organization's membership and venues where meetings have been or will be held.

American Samoa
Barbados
Bermuda
Canada
Guam
Marshall Islands
Micronesia
Mexico
Pacific Trust Territory
Puerto Rico
Virgin Islands

Figure 9-1 IRS "beneficiary countries" with respect to meetings

Other tax legislation affects organizational reports as it pertains to international meetings. Effective in 2004, *all* publicly traded companies are required to submit an annual report of the effectiveness of their internal accounting controls to the Securities and Exchange Commission (SEC). The major provisions of the Sarbanes-Oxley Act (SOX) include criminal and civil penalties for noncompliance violations, certification of internal auditing by external auditors, and increased disclosure regarding all financial statements. Officials of publicly traded companies are now directly legally culpable for any reporting omissions or errors, and the penalties include fines and imprisonment. The international impact of this law is enormous for multinational public corporations. Those doing business with U.S. companies may now have further reporting responsibilities, and so accurate record keeping is even more critical.

Associations have not been affected yet, but it is expected that the trickle-down effect will soon embrace them as well. Whatever the organization, whether public or private, your responsibility remains the same: you must accurately and honestly account for and record all funds over which you have control. This includes payables, receivables, and everything associated with the events you plan for which you have budget responsibility.

HOST GOVERNMENT REGULATIONS

All countries tend to guard their frontiers to ensure that visitors, goods, and materials entering the country conform to government regulations. Within the meetings industry, imported materials, equipment, and supplies that may be consumed or transported to another country are usually exempt from duty. Yet another set of rules apply to passenger baggage, gifts, and goods for personal consumption (see Chapter 13). How these items are treated varies according to category, use, and country. All countries, however, accept an ATA Carnet, a document that guarantees that imported materials will be reexported. The ATA Carnet permits duty-free and tax-free temporary import of good for up to one year. The initials ATA are an acronym of the French and English words "Admission Temporaire/Temporary Admission."

You are well advised to contract the services of a transportation coordinator, customs broker, or forwarding agent who will handle all the documentation and transportation required to get your materials from the point of origin to the meeting site and back. The nominal fees are well worth the savings in problems, delays, and unforeseen expenses.

The other side of the coin is clearing customs on the return home. Obtain and disseminate to your travelers current regulations governing the following:

- Amount of gifts and purchases that may be brought home duty-free
- What items should be declared and listed individually
- What items carry a quantity limit or are prohibited altogether

PASSPORTS AND VISAS

Attendees should be advised well in advance of departure to apply for a passport or, if they have one, ensure that it is current. Some travel organizers include passport applications with the initial mailing. It is a good idea to have travelers make a photocopy of the inside cover and first page of the passport. This speeds replacement in case of loss and serves as identification. Visa regulations vary from one country to another. Research visa requirements and assist attendees in making applications. For groups traveling together, it is possible to arrange for group visas. Be aware that countries may require visas of certain nationals but not others. Even if all passengers originate from one country, determine whether the group includes resident foreign nationals, who may be subject to different visa regulations. Keep in mind that even countries that do not require visas for individual travelers or convention delegates may demand that paid staff and speakers apply for business visas. Clarify these points with your travel counselor or the NTO representative. Chapter 13 goes into more detail about acquiring and safeguarding passports and visas.

LAW ENFORCEMENT

Occasionally attendees run afoul of the host country's laws by intent or ignorance. This can arise from a dispute, an omission or commission, or an altercation in which the delegate is held culpable. Joshua Grimes, Counsel for the Professional Convention Management Association (PCMA), notes, "Travelers who are arrested in a foreign country are subject to the laws of that country and will not normally be granted any special privileges because they are foreigners."

The local consulate of the lawbreaking attendee's country of domicile should be contacted, but bear in mind that embassies and consulates will provide assistance only in cases in which a citizen has not been given proper legal protection by the courts of the host country. Even then, it will not provide legal assistance or assist in obtaining local legal counsel. In cases of arrest by local law enforcement, Grimes suggests that the organization's attorney be consulted for advice on retaining foreign counsel.

Violations of the law are resolved under the criminal code of the country in which they occur. Travelers should be advised that the guarantees in American jurisprudence—right to counsel, a bail hearing, presumption of innocence, and protection from self-incrimination—may not be relevant in other countries.

HEALTH REGULATIONS

There are some countries for which inoculations are required or advised. Some areas are known to have a high incidence of malaria, amoebic dysentery, hemorrhagic fever, and other exotic diseases. Travelers to those regions should obtain inoculations or be prepared to show a record indicating current immunization. Caution your attendees on this point. Health authorities can detain, inoculate, and isolate travelers who are not properly immunized. Chapter 13 discusses compliance with these regulations and preparing attendees for healthy travel in more detail.

▌NEGOTIATIONS

Keep in mind that in many cultures one's word and commitment may be more binding than a contract. Furthermore, it is important to understand that you may be dealing with people whose business philosophy differs substantially from what is accepted as the norm in the United States. Therefore, it is essential to develop and nurture relationships. Learn the customs of the country as they apply to negotiations. In Arab countries, China, and Latin America, negotiation is a fine art and you are expected to bargain for the best price. In other places, such as Japan, Northern Europe, and the United Kingdom, bargaining may be considered an affront.

Peter Haigh cites differences in Europeans' motivation to negotiate: "Due to lower room inventories, generally high occupancy, elevated transient demand, and a culture that heretofore had no need to negotiate, rooms and services were provided for a given price. To the degree that there is meeting space, it is dedicated to social functions such as weddings, dinners, receptions, and other such events."

In many European venues, hotels tend to be smaller and there are fewer of them. Occupancy rates tend to be relatively high, and meeting space is a definite revenue generator in terms of both rental fees and the profit margin on functions. Haigh also points out that other services, such as ground transportation, can be more expensive in some destinations: "The smaller economies of scale mean high costs to produce automobiles and motor coaches, resulting in higher prices and thus a higher cost to lease them. Labor costs are high, the taxes are extraordinary, and don't forget the higher cost of petrol." Audiovisual (AV) equipment and services tend to be contracted externally and generally are more expensive in Europe than in North America, particularly for high-tech items such as video cameras, computers, and multiscreen and large-screen projection.

Getting this kind of information about standard costs is very important, since it will determine your negotiating stance. There is a difference between being asked to pay more because someone is gouging you and being asked to pay more because the baseline cost is higher than what you are used to paying. You can still negotiate for the best possible price, but you must judge the extent of your bargain against the local cost, not the cost you are accustomed to at home.

When all is said and done, the key to successful negotiating and contracting overseas lies in one's ability to adapt to the local customs, laws, and business practices. We are the visitors, and the burden is on us to work within the constraints of the host country. As Jonathan Howe reminds us, "We've got to play the game by their rules. They are not going to play the game by our rules. Our traditional way of doing business is not the way they do business, and they will be doing it their way whether we like it or not."

KEY POINTS

Contracts must meet several criteria in order to be valid, binding documents.

In addition to terms and conditions, the laws of the host country governing contracts may be very different.

Cultural considerations and business protocol affect the process of negotiations and vary from one country to another. Business philosophy, and local practices may differ substantially from what is accepted as the standard in North America.

When contracting for services or facilities in another country it may be advisable to retain the services of and attorney who is familiar with contract laws of both countries.

It is important to understand the tax impact of both the host country and attendees' country of origin.

Organizers need to be familiar with immigration procedures and customs regulations so as to advise attendees of their specific requirements and restrictions.

PASSPORT

Books

Brake, Terence, Danielle Medina Walker, and Thomas Walker, *Doing Business Internationally,* Irwin, New York, 1995.

Goldberg, James M., *The Meeting Planner's Legal Handbook,* Meeting Professionals International, 1996.

Internet

Prism Business Media (articles on international contracts): www.meetingsnet.com.

Worldlink (international network of lawyers): www.worldlink-law.com.

Chapter 10

IMPLEMENTING THE MEETING PLAN

Consider the postage stamp. It secures success through its ability to stick to one thing until it gets there.

—Jack Billings

IN THIS CHAPTER

We will explore:

- Best practices for developing and implementing effective registration procedures.
- Automating the registration process.
- How to develop PC-based and Internet-based registration systems.
- Techniques for processing registrations and coordinating housing.
- Managing online booking for housing.
- Room block attrition and how it affects a meeting.
- Developing and coordinating systems for name badges.
- Follow-up site visits and their function.
- Food and beverage planning in other cultures.

The initial planning, organization, and announcement of the event have been completed. The dates are set, the venue has been chosen and contracted for, and the program is in place. Now begins the point in the sequence that implements the detailed planning and coordination that has gone on continuously since the initial decision to meet.

This stage varies in terms of time and activity according to the size, duration, and location of the meeting. It consists of the following phases:

- Registration and coordination
- Housing attendees

- Coordination visits
- Premeeting tasks

The implementation phase flows logically into the operations stage, which begins when staff arrives at the site. It includes:

- Working with in-house staff
- Preconference meeting
- On-site operations and logistics
- Postevent duties

The operations stage will be discussed in detail in Chapter 12.

▍REGISTRATION

Soliciting, receiving, and processing registrations for an event and for the attendees' accommodations call for diligent planning, monitoring, coordination, and follow-up. A wide variety of registration software and hosted Web sites are available to simplify the task (see Appendix 2).

No matter how efficient the software or how detailed the promotional information, much of the task cannot be left to computers. Questions arise and demand people time to answer phones, write responses, give advice, and prevent misunderstanding. These tasks call for knowledgeable, intelligent people with good communication skills and a fair amount of diplomacy. Those traits avert potential problems that if left unattended can work against even the best promotion and program.

REGISTRATION PROCEDURES

Presumably, the organization conducting the meeting has a system for registering attendees who respond to the marketing messages. This may be a manual system in which the registrant submits a registration form mailed out with the meeting announcement, published in the organization's journal, or downloaded from its Web site. Because meetings can involve large numbers of people, meeting professionals prepare clear, concise, and complete registration instructions and meeting information. They utilize readily available registration software or design simplified forms and systems to make the process convenient for the registrant and convey the information the organization requires. The end result should be a well-informed registrant and a precise record of all attendees.

Recognizing that registration for international events requires greater sensitivity to cultural perceptions, meeting professionals plan their methodology to reflect that concern. Procedures address two distinct functions: advance and on-site registration. Advance registration involves an announcement of the date and place of the meeting and other pertinent details.

THE MEETING ANNOUNCEMENT

It is customary to utilize e-mail, a Web site, and occasionally postal delivery for all communications. Generally, the main announcement will include the following elements:

- An attractive, thematic graphic with the name of the meeting, dates, location, organization's logo or name or both, and link to a Web site. The meeting's purpose, the benefits of attending, and eligibility for attendance, if any, also are included. This may be toned down considerably for internal corporate meetings, where everyone invited is required to attend. In fact, for the majority of these meetings, an e-mail with the agenda attached usually constitutes the announcement.
- Site information, map, and hotel brochure or hotel Web page. Headquarters hotel if applicable.
- Conference lodging rates, availability for early arrival or stay-over, check-in and check-out times. Hotel's telephone, fax, and e-mail address.
- Registration fees according to category for attendees and guests. Early registration discount and late penalties. Cost of optional events. Cancellation penalties and refund policies, currency and methods of remittance. (This component would not be included for a corporate meeting.)
- Program details. Description of speaker topics by date, breakout sessions, and special seminars requiring advance registration. Program elements, materials, and functions included in the fee.
- Tentative social and recreational agenda with guidelines for appropriate attire to follow.
- Exhibition information, if applicable, including exhibitor list and hours.
- Registration data and forms. (For an example of a typical registration form, see Figure 10-1.)
- Travel arrangements. Official airline if designated, group code, special fares, and toll-free number.
- Airport reception (if offered). Ground transportation, transfers, and car rental information. Brochure with information about the country, its culture, and its history. Banking hours, currency exchange rate, and a phrase book are always welcome.
- Information provided by the participant is much the same as it is for domestic events. It includes membership status (if applicable), arrival and departure, contact information, badge preferences, dietary or special needs, and other details the organization requires. These items are incorporated in a registration form to be returned by the participant electronically or by fax, although for the most part online registration or e-mail registration is the rule.
- On-site registration entails the processing of attendees at the meeting venue either by registrars or at work stations. The sponsor establishes procedures for verification of credentials and registration status. Collection of fees and related administrative details are carried out by the staff. Further details of on-site registration are given in Chapter 12.

World Congress of Engineering
www.wce.org
Registration Form
July 1–5, 2006
Chicago, Illinois

Deadline for receipt of registration form: June 15, 2005. If you cannot register by this date please register on site at the meeting.

1. REGISTRATION INFORMATION:

Family name or surname   Given name   Initial   Title

Mailing address

City   State   Zip/Postal Code

Do you require any special accommodations? (check one)

☐ Yes (Please describe below).

☐ No

2. REGISTRATION CATEGORIES AND FEES (in U.S. Dollars) (Check one)

CATEGORY	REGISTRATION DEADLINE	INVESTMENT/FEE
☐ MEMBERS Full Early Bird (Discounted, save $100)	By April 1	$595.00
☐ MEMBERS Exhibit only (Discounted, save $100)	By April 1	$195.00
☐ NONMEMBERS Full Early Bird Registration (Discounted, Save $100)	By April 1	$995.00*
☐ NONMEMBERS Exhibit Only (Discounted, Save $100)	By April 1	$295.00*
☐ MEMBERS Daily registration Full Early Bird Registration (Discounted, Save $100	By April 1	$195.00
☐ NONMEMBERS Daily registration		$395.00
Sub total		$_____

*Includes one-year membership.

Figure 10-1 Sample Registration Form

3. SPECIAL EVENTS (Check all that apply)

SPECIAL EVENT	DATE AND TIME	INVESTMENT/FEE
Pre-event City Tour	July 1, 2006 1pm–5pm	$49.95
Off-site industry tours	July 2–3, 2006 3pm–5pm	$29.95
Awards Banquet	July 5, 2006	$99.95
Subtotal		$_____

TOTAL PAYMENT ENCLOSED (Add sections 2 and 3) $_____

4. PAYMENT INFORMATION (Check one)
☐ Check enclosed (Make payable to WCE Association)
☐ Credit card (Complete information below)
☐ Bill me at address above

Credit card type and number (Check one)
☐ MasterCard
☐ Visa

— — — — — — — — — — — — — — — — —

Expiration date:

‾‾‾‾   ‾‾‾‾
Date   Year

Remit payment and registration form to:
The World Congress of Engineers
International Congress Division
1111 Massachusetts Avenue N.W.
Washington, DC 20053
Or Fax to:
Country code: 1, Area code: 202, Phone number: 454-2345
Visit us Online at
www.wce.org

Figure 10-1 *(Continued)*

REGISTRATION SYSTEMS

There is a wide range of software and systems for processing registrations, collecting fees (if appropriate), and providing data needed by the organizers.

Developing a registration system begins with establishing the information needed from registrants. In its simplest form, this may include no more than name, address, and date of arrival. The nature of the event also influences system design and procedure. That may fall into one of the following categories:

- Corporate meetings for which management determines who is to attend and all expenses are borne by the company.
- Sales meetings involving corporate staff as well as independent dealers bearing some expenses.
- An association convention or a seminar for which attendees pay a registration fee and all expenses.
- Government-sponsored events involving legislators, department heads, and affected citizen groups.
- An exhibition attended by both exhibitors and invited guests or the general public.

Those are some of the more common categories. There also are seminars, reunions, symposia, and a profusion of special events attended by a wide range of demographic groups. Each type of meeting is different, and the information needed fluctuates. In the first example, there may be only an announcement and a rooming list.

The following components emphasize registration at events for which fees are charged. Many of the guidelines presented apply to fully sponsored events as well.

REGISTRATION FORMS

Registration form design plays a key role in multinational events, and professionals know that an efficient, trouble-free system is dependent on proper documents. These forms must be clear, easy to complete, and designed for efficient and accurate processing whether this is automated or done manually. The key elements of a comprehensive form are:

- Event name, sponsor, theme, dates, and venue.
- Registrant data: name, title, affiliation, address to which correspondence is to be sent, daytime telephone number, membership category or credentials, name badge data, and preferred form of address (especially important for delegates from other cultures who may choose to be called by surname and title; see "Forms of Address" in Chapter 7).
- Accompanying persons: a potentially delicate area requiring diplomacy. Avoid imposing moral values on attendees' guests. Name and badge data are sufficient.
- Registration fees according to category of attendee: member, nonmember, guest.
- Currencies accepted for payment.
- Fees for early registration with cutoff date, full or partial registration for accompanying persons, cancellation and refund policy, currency and methods of payment, credit card number and authorization, if applicable.

- Telephone and fax numbers and e-mail address for inquiries or emergency notification.
- Processing data for registration staff.

In addition to these basic elements, the form may include the following:

- Housing information: name of the conference hotels and rates, system for selection by attendee, arrival and departure dates, special room preferences, credit information or reservation deposit (see "Housing Meeting Attendees," below).
- Ticket policies and prices for special sessions, functions, and other ticketed events with check-off boxes for designating selected options.
- Listing of special sessions requiring advance reservations. Request that attendees indicate first and second choices.
- Medical or special dietary information.
- Airline, flight and arrival time if an airport reception is planned.
- On-site registration location and hours.

Some organizations use a different form for on-site registration. Whatever the format, certain design criteria apply. The form, with the conference logo, should provide the needed information without looking cluttered. A clean typeface is advised, with boldface or color type used for critical information. Be certain that there is adequate space for the data. Nothing is more frustrating for a delegate from Al Garrobo del Aquilla (Argentina) than to have to cram his or her hometown into a line designed for Peoria.

It's amazing how many supposedly intelligent people act like fifth-grade dropouts when completing a form. To ensure legibility, use boxes instead of lines and, wherever possible, provide multiple choices in place of write-in spaces. Line and pitch dimensions should be suitable for handwritten, typewriter, or computer generation. Tabulate the various fees and acceptable currencies so that the preparer can add them readily and the staff can verify the sum. If registration forms for more than one event are processed together, color-code them for easy identification and sorting. This is where registration software can be most effective.

MULTISITE REGISTRATION

Organizations soliciting registration from widely dispersed participants may offer decentralized registration through national association chapters, global affiliates, local NTO offices, PCOs, or travel agencies. As a rule, this method is reserved for attendees who lack Internet access and requires close coordination between the local registration entity and the central secretariat.

The benefits for registrants include one-stop travel reservations, ease of communications, and payment in the local currency. The system, however, is subject to miscommunication, especially when changes in registration or housing are needed.

█ AUTOMATING THE REGISTRATION PROCESS

If e-mailing and site and vendor research are the meeting professional's most commonly used technology tools, registration management runs a close second. As software and Web-based options proliferate, a substantial majority of meeting applications are utilizing these multiple-benefit tools.

Specific usage varies, however. Many users have chosen to create an internal program. Custom applications fill the need but have added maintenance and support costs due to rapid and significant changes in technology.

Current methods used for both international and domestic events include the following:

- Creative use of suite-based applications such as Microsoft Office or Sun Star Office.
- PC-based registration software.
- Web-based registration systems ranging from simple forms to secure themed event Web sites.
- Integrated enterprisewide applications.

As a rule, a blend of the first three methods is required to handle the myriad details involved in registration management. There are considerable cost efficiencies in applying relevant technology to the meeting registration process. The more registration transactions, including travel and housing and all their peripheral products, the greater the potential savings.

PC-BASED REGISTRATION SOFTWARE

During the 1980s—meeting technology's gestation period—techno-savvy meeting planners' hot button was software designed for use on PCs. Registration software led the way, enabling users to automate the burdensome task of processing reams of paper registration forms. Software developers rose to the task, and names such as Peopleware and PC Nametag became meeting management icons. The fact that they survived and others, such as Meeting Trak, Plansoft, and Event Solutions, entered the fray and prospered proved that even with the onset of Web-based programs, there was a need for such planning tools. PC solutions tend to be more stable and offer greater security than do Web-based registration systems. Consequently, many product vendors now provide front-end Web interfaces to compete with dedicated Web-based applications.

PC-based registration software has many ancillary benefits, including session tracking, presentation graphics, badge and ticket generation, spreadsheets, budgeting, and signage. Other applications that benefit from PC software are meeting room scheduling, floor plan design, and attendee evaluation. However, as in all applications, there is a caveat: Most programs lack the facility for real-time updates of registration and housing data.

WEB-BASED REGISTRATION

Online applications such as RegOnline are replacing registration software because of their flexibility and cost savings. They require no extensive training for registration staff and offer attendees accustomed to Internet benefits comfort and convenience. Other advantages of Web-based systems include the following:

- Registrant familiarity and comfort using Internet tools.
- Tiered registration fees that motivate attendees to sign up early.
- Longer lead time. Web-based registration kiosks at the current event permit attendees to sign up for subsequent events.
- Availability of translation tools to reach a multilingual audience.
- Simplified customization from one event to another.
- Reduced production and printing with personalized e-mail marketing.
- Dramatic savings on international postage costs.
- Lateral marketing by which attendees can forward event data to colleagues and co-workers.
- Potential reduction in no-shows by using personalized online reminders in place of repeat mailings.
- Added ability for exhibitors to extend their reach and identify prospective clients.
- A single integrated database with greater flexibility in outputs for data collection.
- A wide range of planner and registrant options such as task lists, special needs, event calendar, attendee rosters, session selection, and evaluations.

As meeting professionals become familiar with the benefits and mechanics of online registration functionality to their organizations, they find ways to extend meeting registration data to other applications. Thus, they enhance the benefits of computing while providing ease of use for attendees. A note of caution applies to offshore events, however. Once the meeting goes abroad, a PC-based system can provide access to the database regardless of the location (assuming it has electricity). This is not the case with Web-based systems, which depend on ready and continuous access to the Internet. If the chosen venue provides unstable, slow, or limited Internet connection or levies unreasonable charges for it, accessing the database on-site can be a problem. Add that to your site-inspection checklist.

▋ HOUSING MEETING ATTENDEES

Beginning in the second half of the twentieth century, as business meetings and association conventions in North America proliferated, the meetings industry observed a relatively new phenomenon: the "convention hotel." With construction approaching a high point in the 1970s and 1980s, large, 600- to 1,000-room chain hotels with tens of thousands of square feet of meeting space were constructed.

That was not the case, however, in major Asian, European and Latin American cities where space for newer hotel construction was limited and building costs were high. There were also problematic restrictions on what could be built and where without disturbing the historical ambiance of Old World metropolitan centers. Opportunely for organizations meeting abroad, this began to change as municipal authorities recognized the tax revenue potential of large meetings and major hotel chains used their economic influence to build new or expand existing facilities.

Today, however, they may have to compete with tourism in the more popular venues. Nevertheless, depending on the season, meeting organizers have a wide choice of venues with substantial capacity and state-of-the-art meeting facilities.

HOUSING RESOURCES

Unless attendees are totally responsible for their own accommodations, the meeting manager will be involved with some aspects of housing coordination. For large multihotel conventions, it is customary to use the services of the local convention or tourism bureau. Many of those organizations provide housing coordination at a nominal cost or no cost. Use of these bureaus, however, does not relieve the meeting professional of the responsibility of supervision. After all, the information is essential for determining room pickups and adjusting room blocks to avoid penalties. Accurate arrival data also can be useful in determining guarantees for various functions.

Whether one is working directly with the hotel's front office or with a housing bureau, it is important that form data conform to the system used for processing housing requests. The following are traditional methods:

1. Incorporate the housing request in the registration form. The entire form is received by the registration staff, which sends the housing data or a copy of the form to the hotel online or by mail. To avoid excessive handling of funds, a separate deposit check payable to the hotel or a credit card guarantee is requested with the reservation.

2. Enclose a hotel reservation form with registration documents. Most hotels can provide self-addressed cards or multiple-copy reservation forms that contain deposit information. The registrant fills out the form, encloses the required deposit or credit card guarantee, and mails it to the hotel. The hotel rooms staff confirms reservations directly to each guest and submits periodic rooming lists to the organizer. These lists include room blocks, pickups, cancellations, and related data. This, however, entails postage costs.

3. If a housing bureau is used, the planner may incorporate the housing information into the registration form and forward housing requests to the bureau or use the bureau's own form, which is returned to it as in

the last example. The bureau then notifies the hotel, confirms the reservation to the guest, and submits periodic reports to the event manager.

The sponsoring organization's policy on suite assignments should be stated clearly on the housing form. Room allocations may be made by the hotel, but most organizers reserve the right to assign suites designated for their use.

ROOM BLOCK ATTRITION

The Convention Industry Council's APEX glossary defines Attrition as the difference between the actual number of sleeping rooms picked up and the number or formulas agreed to in the terms of the facility's contract. Usually there is an allowable shortfall before damages are assessed.

Failure to fill the contracted room block because of cancellations or no-shows can be a significant drain on the meeting budget. In many countries and foreign hotels, there is no attrition clause in the contract to protect the buyer. Generally, the organization has the option to reduce its room block at various cutoff dates before the meeting (according to its review of confirmed registrations). However, after the last cutoff date, the sponsor is responsible for the full block, including unoccupied rooms. Most organizations point out to their attendees that they will be charged for an unoccupied room in the event of late cancellation or a no-show.

WEB-BASED HOUSING OPTIONS

Processing of housing data has made significant strides as a result of Internet access and the open architecture of information systems. With more varied applications designed to manage complex elements, meeting professionals have more options for contracted room inventories.

Conference housing continues to improve in terms of the scope of services available and real-time access to inventory. As with all elements involving technology, ease of use, speed, security, and flexibility, along with maintaining a range of data inputs and formats, are essential elements of housing management.

Unfortunately, the comfort level in supplying credit card information and other personal data online requires wider use and acceptance for an online system to be the sole data conduit. Any housing solution must provide alternative vehicles for processing this type of information, whether serviced through a calling center or through fax or mail processing.

Not everyone has a personal digital assistant (PDA), a handheld computer, or easy computing access, nor do all people have the same comfort in using the newer technologies often required in the online transaction process. As a result, meeting professionals need to find a technology solution that meets the core requirements of their market. Corporations have a clear advantage in that they can set companywide policy and provide funding for projects that can show a positive ROI within an 18-month period, whereas association management are limited to the support of the sponsors and member responsiveness.

Over the last few years, the major players in the online housing market have merged with or made their application protocols available to several online registration companies, providing meeting professionals with the option of offering both housing and conference registration to their end users. The integration of these processes is clearly a benefit to the online user, who can access streamlined data entry and enjoy one-stop shopping.

It is ironic that regardless of convenience, the criteria for conference housing are the same as they always have been: location, price, and brand identity of the lodging venue. In short, if lodging options don't meet users' needs, the technology will be circumvented.

ONLINE BOOKING

With Internet giants such as Travelocity and Expedia looking to expand their operations to meetings, the question arises whether the future may see a meeting attendee register online for the conference and concurrently reserve a hotel room, flight, and ground transportation all in one transaction. Travelocity's rationale is that this kind of packaging offers travelers greater savings as well as speed and convenience.

That may come about as some international meeting prospects avail themselves of those advantages, but, like leisure travel, it benefits only the individual traveler, not the meeting staff. There are factors particular to meeting-related group travel that are not well served by such services. Organizing meetings entail more than booking hotel rooms and travel. The process involves negotiations, site inspection, meeting room evaluation, suite assignments, registration and in-depth logistics. Much of this process requires a face-to-face relationship that cannot be fulfilled by a computer interface.

Online booking can be a valuable customer convenience for some attendees. However, it is not a labor-saving solution for meeting professionals.

PREMEETING PROCEDURES

This phase of operations varies in duration with the size and complexity of the event. It is a point at which the organization is committed and, barring unforeseen or catastrophic circumstances, the meeting is a definite go. It is also a time of intense activity on the part of the meeting staff. Earlier, the meeting manager will have decided which staff members will travel to the meeting site and will have made arrangements for their transportation and accommodations.

PROCESSING REGISTRATIONS

As with all other elements of the meeting, the efficiency, or lack of it, with which registrations are handled influences attendees' perception of the organization. A misspelled name on a badge is a small thing, but it is an embarrassment to the person who's stuck with it. A delayed acknowledgment or incomplete registration information that necessitates a phone call can leave a negative impression before the registrant arrives at the site.

It is important that advance registrants receive prompt acknowledgment. It may be no more than a simple e-mail, letter, or postcard confirming their registration and, if appropriate, the sessions to which they have been assigned. A welcome letter from the CEO or conference chairman is always appreciated.

Organizations that mail advance meeting announcements in a higher volume than the anticipated attendance will hold much of the meeting materials for this follow-up mailing to confirmed registrants. The packet also may contain special airfares, the airline reservation telephone number, information on the destination and hotel, airport reception arrangements, ground transportation fares, and the latest details on business and social programs. Invoices reflecting payment or balance due in case of underpayment may be enclosed or be part of the confirmation notice.

For paper registration, the processing system should be designed so that all data on the registration forms can be recorded and retrieved readily. Some organizations assign a control number or utilize membership numbers; others use names. Control numbers, which are preferred for computerized registration systems, seem to be better for recording registration and payment, generating receipts or invoices, and maintaining individual account status. They are also useful for recording changes, cancellations, and subsequent computation of refunds.

A key byproduct of the processing system is an attendance roster that can be outputted in several permutations. Its primary function is to provide a master registration list for the event organizer and the registration staff. Information on the master list varies with the input and the various functions the list is to perform.

One advantage of an automated registration system is the ability to supply many different reports from the same data. One of these reports would be an advance registration roster that is reproduced and distributed to attendees in advance or on arrival. It informs people who else will be attending the conference and thus facilitates interaction among participants. Because final registration can be substantially different, it's customary to produce a supplement during the meeting.

BADGES

Badges are to meetings what kilts are to Scots. They distinguish members of a group and, like the distinctive patterns of a Scottish tartan, provide a sense of belonging. Besides identifying the wearer and his or her affiliation and hometown, badges facilitate greetings and introductions. They help avoid that embarrassing and awkward moment when one recognizes the face but draws a total mental block on the name. When color-coded and under observation of trained personnel, badges are a useful control device for restricting access to certain functions or sessions.

A badge can reflect the quality of the meeting. One bearing the meeting theme in color, with a bold name clearly printed or computer-generated and a durable badge holder, does far more for the sponsor's image than an adhesive label with felt-tip lettering. Not that there is anything wrong with felt-tip lettering when it is done by an expert calligrapher.

In addition to the attendee's name, title, affiliation, and domicile, badges often display, in larger bold letters, a given name or nickname. Keep in mind that this custom is peculiar to North Americans, Australians, and, increasingly, Britons and some Europeans, although many are reluctant to display such familiarity. In much of Europe, Latin America, the Middle East, and Asia, the practice may be inappropriate.

The badge holder should be the clutch-back type rather than the pin-back, which tends to leave holes in clothing. Women are particularly reluctant to wear the latter; most prefer a lanyard. The format may be vertical or horizontal.

Many computer software programs have the ability to generate attractive, distinctive badges by using ink-jet or laser-jet printers. There are also a number of vendors, such as PC Nametag, that specialize in printing badges at a nominal cost. For recognition of officers, directors, press, and others receiving a special distinction, colored ribbons gradually are being replaced by color-coded badge holders with the designation printed on the badge or the holder.

With the rapid development of meeting technology, badges today have the capacity to fulfill functions beyond name recognition. Thanks to advances such as microchips, bar codes, infrared, and wireless communications, a new generation of "smart badges" has matured into exotic communication devices whose applications are limited only by the organizer's imagination and the sponsor's budget. Some of these marvels are described in Chapter 15.

▌SITE COORDINATION VISITS

Organizing meetings abroad entails more than booking hotel rooms and travel. It includes a wide range of face-to-face activities such as negotiations, site inspection, meeting room evaluation, suite assignments, registration, and in-depth logistics. Much of this process demands a relationship that cannot be fulfilled by a computer interface.

Because of the complexity of conducting business abroad, even with the benefits of e-mail and high-speed access, preevent site visits tend to be more frequent. Contracting the services of a local PCO or destination manager does not eliminate that need. The number of trips varies with the meeting parameters and the resources available on-site.

During these visits, the following details are addressed and finalized:

- Interview and engage staff for registration, security, and conference aides or volunteers.
- If not previously done, open an account with a local commercial bank. Deposit a letter of credit.

- Contract for audiovisual and other technical services and equipment.
- Verify the cost and effectiveness of Internet access.
- Interview and contract interpreters. This usually is done through a language service.
- Arrange for the production and printing of program materials, signs, tickets, and related graphics.
- Investigate and purchase awards, room gifts, and meeting supplies. Include electrical power adapters and one or more currency converters if relevant.
- Interview and engage an exhibit service contractor if applicable. Arrange for shipping services.
- Finalize arrangements with the DMC for airport reception, ground transportation, special events, and pre- or postmeeting tours. Ask to be driven between the airport and the hotel or from hotel to scheduled sites to verify travel time and conditions.
- Conduct a walk-through of all meeting rooms contracted to assure their suitability for the final program. Check acoustics and the condition of furnishings, carpeting, lighting, and equipment.
- Meet with the facility staff to review master account procedures, event orders, guest room pickups, suite assignments, hospitality suites, security plans, meeting room setups, storage of shipments, on-site communications, and food and beverage requirements. Set the date and time and specify attendance for the preconference meeting.
- Arrange for postconference services, activities, and procedures.
- The information, impressions, and insights gained in advance during these visits, along with the relationships established, will benefit the event organizer and the event as the transition is made from preparation to implementation.

FOOD AND BEVERAGE

In many countries, especially in Europe, Latin America, and the Middle East, hotels were built to meet the needs of their clientele: the local populace and leisure travelers. The emphasis was on social events such as weddings, receptions, dinners, and other celebrations. The meeting rooms were designed to provide an ambience consistent with food and beverage service. They boasted ornate chandeliers, wall sconces, mirrors, and pillars (the bane of audiovisual technicians).

Peter Haigh points out that these rooms were not meeting-friendly, tending to be banquet-driven, as opposed to properties in North America, most of which are rooms-driven. "This helps explain to the embattled American meeting planner the European hotel's perceived obsession with food," says Haigh. "The quality tends to be excellent, the service superior, and one can all but forget the standard North American one-hour lunch (and forget the rubber chicken as well!). A typical two-hour convention luncheon at a meeting on the

Côte D'Azur progressed from appetizer, to fish course, to meat course, to salad, to dessert, and then coffee."

For most cultures outside the United States, mealtime is more than an opportunity to grab some food from the buffet table and get back to business. In most of the world it is a time to enjoy dining, linger, and exchange pleasantries—not do business—with one's table companions. The working lunch that often characterizes domestic meetings is frowned on in some cultures and disdained in most. As an illustration, look at some of the variations within Europe, using lunch as an example.

Austrians don't mind a light lunch during a meeting program. A typical menu at a Salzburg event would be soup, salad, a meat or fish course, coffee, and dessert. However, no meal is complete without a fabulous Austrian pastry such as a sensational Salzburger nockerln. Their German cousins enjoy a simple three-course meal or a light buffet with pastries and fruit. Of course in Bavaria, beer is a standard lunch menu item.

By contrast, Italians expect a hearty, multicourse lunch that may include wine, soup, pasta, and a meat dish, followed by salad and dessert. Spain and Portugal serve filling lunches, and wine is customary. The British are not so averse to the working lunch, possibly because of their frequent exposure to Americans. Three courses are usually adequate, and buffets are popular. In fact, some meetings in the United Kingdom feature stand-up buffets, a typically British practice much like a cocktail reception without the cocktails.

Writing in M&C magazine, Lisa Grimaldi illustrates cultural differences in other parts of the world:

In Asia, the F&B contact at the hotel is not always the convention services manager; it is often someone in group sales who probably speaks English. Many chefs do not speak English, however, so an interpreter might be necessary. Most meeting- and incentive-caliber hotels in the East have two kitchens, Asian and Western, manned by two separate chefs. The Asian kitchen is set up to accommodate industrial-size woks and often live fish tanks. For most meals, U.S. planners work with the Western chef and kitchen staff. Food is generally priced on a per-person basis and a deposit of 30 to 50 percent of the event is required in advance for F&B functions. In China, unless Western service is requested, hotels typically serve food family-style—normally 10 people to a table, with no individual portioning, except for formal banquets. Planners should specify whether they prefer Asian or Western service, because the styles—including elements such as utensils, table settings and service—are so different.

In Latin America, a major concern of U.S. planners is the safety of water, ice and local produce. Planners should find out if the property and/or facilities they select have their own water purification systems and if produce is treated to kill bacteria and potentially harmful pesticides.

When ordering F&B, planners generally work with a group and convention sales manager, rather than a banquet manager. Advance or partial payments are not always required.*

To the hapless meeting professional attempting to balance such cultural anomalies with the need for adequate program time, and in some cases exhibit hours, the task may seem insurmountable. Consulting the banquet manager and the executive chef during premeeting site visits is the best way to avoid problems. Ask about creative cuisine options, such as buffet luncheons, that are not so time-consuming and keep in mind the admonition against overprogramming the participants.

It is also important, especially when there is multicultural attendance, to be sensitive to diets, medical needs, and the dietary restriction of members of various faiths.

Earlier, it was suggested that you gain at least a passing knowledge of the metric system. Ordering beverages requires the understanding that liquid measures are expressed in liters and milliliters. Specifying fruit and some snack items means ordering in kilos; specifying serving sizes calls for grams. Since it's unlikely that you will be stipulating the temperature of the meat or the atmosphere in the ballroom, you need not worry about the conversion of Celsius to Fahrenheit or vice versa.

Themed functions abound in Asia, Latin America, and Europe and can be an added dimension in any gathering. Cultural and folkloric shows are in great favor. They also tend to be less expensive to stage in some venues due to lower labor costs. At a management conference in Sharm el Sheik, Egypt, participants arriving for dinner were amazed to find the ballroom had been converted into a scene from the land of the Pharaohs. They entered a native market where camels, sheep, and goats mingled with costumed staff offering drinks and hors d'oeuvres. Waiters in traditional Bedouin garb and waitresses in harem costume meandered through the marketplace while merchant stalls offered a variety of exotic fare.

Theme dinners and local folklore shows have one potential drawback that can be avoided if the event and entertainment are previewed during the site visit. There are components of folklore shows that, though authentic, may have elements that are disturbing to nonlocals. For example, the classic Mexican folklore show includes dances from a variety of regions, mariachi music, a *charro* (Mexican cowboy) on horseback doing rope tricks with his lasso, and a mock cockfight in which two roosters are made to poke at each other and flap their wings. In real cockfights, the roosters have sharp spurs attached to their feet so that in a short period of time one slashes the other to death. This obviously does not occur during the show; however, just the concept of a cockfight and a reenactment, albeit a safe one, is enough to upset many North

*Excerpt reprinted with permission from *Meetings & Conventions* magazine, a publication of Northstar Travel Media, LLC.

American spectators. Nothing deflates a celebratory mood at an event more than an attendee who is verbally outraged unless it is an attendee who bursts into tears and claims nausea from the emotional distress of the entertainment.

This kind of situation can be avoided by a culturally sensitive meeting professional who knows his or her attendee group. With tact and diplomacy, the local supplier or host committee can be requested to shorten the program and remove whatever may be misinterpreted by some people and disturbing to others.

If exhibits are part of the event, their planning coordination and operations are an essential part of the meeting plan. This topic is covered in detail in Chapter 11.

KEY POINTS

Registration is a complicated event even when one is utilizing high-technology systems and advance registration. Be sure to have the correct amount of people to ensure smooth registration.

Use a checklist to make sure registration forms are clear and easy to read to ensure efficient processing.

Registration management software allows attendees to register online and staff to access information quickly and efficiently.

To coordinate housing, many resources are available, including working with the hotel's front office or the local convention bureau.

Managing housing data by utilizing the Internet can save time, but not everyone is comfortable utilizing this technology. It is necessary to provide other options for registration.

Take care to provide high-quality badges, as badges reflect the quality of the meeting and give exhibitors, attendees, and security valuable information at a glance.

Don't rely on the Internet or the PCO to take the place of personally inspecting each site and interviewing each hotel contact.

Cater your food planning, especially in relationship to meeting timelines according to the culture you are in and the nationality of the people present.

Themed functions can add culture and flavor to any event if the entertainment is carefully screened for parts that may be misinterpreted or insulting to a certain culture.

PASSPORT

Books

The Convention Industry Council Manual, 7th ed., Convention Industry Council, McLean, VA, 2004.

Professional Meeting Management, 4th ed., Professional Convention Management Association, Chicago, 2002.

Shock, Patti J., and John M. Stefanelli, *Hotel Catering, A Handbook for Sales and Operations,* John Wiley & Sons, New York, 1992.

Wigger, Eugene, *Themes, Dreams, and Schemes: Banquet Menu Ideas, Concepts, and Thematic Experiences,* John Wiley & Sons, New York, 1997.

Internet

Convention Industry Council: www.convention-industry.org.

Chapter 11

EXHIBITING ABROAD

Expositions are the timekeepers of progress. They record the world's advancement.

—U.S. President William McKinley

IN THIS CHAPTER

We will explore:

- Global exhibitions.
- How to find qualified service and general contractors for an exhibition.
- The similarities and differences between domestic and international exhibitions.
- Guidelines for exhibiting abroad.
- Why expanding the lead time is important.
- How to communicate in multiple languages to reach many different audiences.
- Coordination with customs and customs brokers.
- Anticipating taxes and other fees.
- On-site activities and services.
- High-tech electronic accreditation for tracking attendee data.

The dramatic growth of meetings throughout the world has been accompanied by a parallel increase in exhibitions as countries have evolved from a collection of regional economies to a worldwide marketplace. Fairs and tradeshows—the successors to the age-old marketplace—are gaining greater prominence as buyers and manufacturers recognize their value in doing business on a global scale.

The dynamics of this segment of the industry have had a ripple effect as organizations have spread out from the familiar markets of their domicile countries to bring their products and services to the global bazaar. Exhibitions and tradeshows, which once moved from city to city in the home market, now span continents in a dynamic escalation of international commerce. Despite the distances involved in intercontinental travel, these events are perceived by buyers and sellers as being cost- and time-effective. On a broader scale, exhibitions such as the semiannual Canton Fair, the Berlin Trade Fair, and the Paris Air Show attract exhibitors from all over the world and are attended by tens of thousands of visitors. Many events are sold out years in advance and require timely planning.

To meet the increased demand, convention cities have been building convention and exhibition centers at an accelerated pace. Hong Kong's massive Convention & Exhibition Centre, Taipei's International Convention Center, the Nippon Convention Center on the outskirts of Tokyo, and most recently Singapore's Suntec Convention & Exhibition Center, the largest in Asia, host global events almost daily. Congress Centrum Hamburg, Amsterdam's RAI Congress Centre, ICC Berlin, and the NICE Acropolis Centre are among the largest in Europe. Other complexes throughout the world are geared for conventions and exhibitions of any size with state-of-the-art facilities and professional services.

MEETINGS AND EXHIBITIONS

More and more meetings are being combined with exhibitions, resulting in a substantial increase in frequency and attendance as associations venture abroad for their conventions and corporations recognize a strategic need to interact with employees and clients worldwide. Organizations with branch offices or counterparts in the host venue find that the problems associated with foreign exhibitions are lessened. Nevertheless, for any group contemplating sponsorship or participation in a show abroad, it is best to conduct a thorough analysis of attendee benefits, competing events, and the availability of services.

FINDING QUALIFIED HELP

As in any exhibition, the services of a competent exhibit contractor can affect the success of the event. These services are valuable in domestic shows, but they are absolutely indispensable for international exhibitions. International exhibition contractors such as Cahners Expo Group organize and service exhibitions throughout Asia, Europe, and the Americas. These multinational companies provide a wider scope of services than do their domestic counterparts, offering full management in addition to basic decoration and drayage. Their services may include marketing assistance, translation and interpretation, customs assistance, and currency transactions. The last item can be especially helpful since payment for services is usually made in the local currency. Most exhibition contractors can function as fiscal agents, collecting and banking revenues and disbursing funds as well as handling tax payment and accounting for all financial transactions.

SIMILAR BUT DIFFERENT

Although major centers cater to the needs of international shows, organizers who are contemplating exhibiting at overseas venues need to understand some of their differences. Exhibit managers who have not had experience in a region should seek counsel from their colleagues who have. Above all, it is advisable to research foreign exhibition sites thoroughly, with particular emphasis on labor laws, local customs, and codes regulating the design, construction, and operation of exhibit "stands" (the term for *booths* in much of the world).

Here are some typical differences: The pipe-and-drape shows North Americans favor seldom are seen in most of the world; hard-sided and modular stands are preferred. Hotel hospitality suites popular in the United States are relatively unknown elsewhere. Most entertaining is done in the exhibit hall,

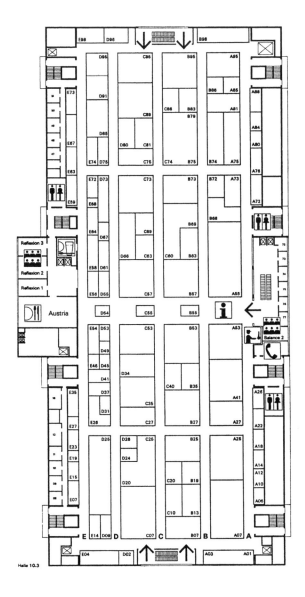

Figure 11-1 Typical European Exhibit Floor Plan

necessitating special conference areas incorporated in the stand design or in adjacent areas. Utility access has to be checked in advance. Some cities do not allow lines to be laid under carpets. This may call for raised platforms that must be incorporated in the design whether stands are built at home and shipped or built on-site.

It is common to custom build exhibits on-site, especially when long setup times (months in some cases) are available. Setup on the floor of a European exhibition hall looks more like an exhibit builder's shop with table saws, drill presses, sawdust, and even pneumatic paint sprayers—everything needed to create an exhibit. The high demand results in smaller hall footprints that translate into multistoried exhibits. It is also common to build elevated flooring, which allows cables and wires to run underneath. Exhibit stands abroad are more than environments for displaying products or graphics. They often encompass conference seating, increased storage, and refreshments. The primary on-site resource for support services is not the exhibition contractor but the contractor/builder.

Exhibitors who participate in shows in Europe and other overseas venues also find that stand grouping differs. Whereas at North American shows booths are assigned in random locations throughout the hall, Europeans tend to group their stands according to similar products or services. Thus, at a travel show, for instance, one might find separate groupings for hotels, airlines, luggage, car rentals, and so on. There are also variations in stand configurations, unlike the customary rectangular or square shapes one is accustomed to seeing (see Figure 11-1). They may be deep with a short aisle frontage or shallow and long. Based on space allocations, a 12-square-meter stand may be 6 meters wide and only 2 meters deep, or it can even be L-shaped as at aisle intersections.

GUIDELINES FOR EXHIBITING ABROAD

Allowing for these differences and some of the complexities of operating beyond their borders, exhibition organizers and exhibitors recognize that a different set of rules applies. Here are some useful suggestions:

- Increase the lead time. Two years is not unreasonable.
- Supplement the promotion budget to allow for translation and multilingual printing, along with increased mailing costs.
- Allow additional time for mailing and responses.
- Investigate having translation and printing done abroad.
- Increase the operating budget by 100 to 200 percent over that for domestic shows. Then add a budget line item for contingencies.
- Check with the convention bureau for competitive events, national holidays, and other factors that may interfere.
- Make provisions for the collection and disbursement of funds and for filing and paying local taxes.

- Select a freight forwarder experienced with overseas shipments.
- Ascertain the legal distinction between exhibit materials to be trans-shipped and promotional and advertising materials or souvenirs to be left behind and learn what duties are applicable. Are prizes and trophies subject to duty?
- Have the customs broker advise on booth equipment and audiovisual and office equipment. What bonds or carnets are required?
- If you are bringing entertainers, ask about waivers or work permits and weigh that against hiring locally. What union regulations apply?
- Most European and some Asian countries charge a value-added tax (see Chapter 5) on purchases, transportation, accommodations, food, and services. Ascertain what VAT percentage is charged and how much of it is refundable.

PLANNING CONSIDERATIONS

After the facility has been selected, certain decisions must be based on the nature of the event. If it is a closed exhibition that is limited to meeting registrants, the process is relatively simple. If it is a public show held in conjunction with a convention or conference, the planning becomes more complex. Some factors to consider at this point may include the following:

- Coordination of exhibit hours with the meeting program, which is often a source of conflict. The exhibitors need to be assured that sufficient time and attendance will justify their expenses. The program committee, however, is reluctant to surrender program time. The meeting professional, knowing that exhibitions are as much an educational resource as presentations and workshops, usually mediates to arrive at a fair balance.
- Are the program and exhibits held at the same facility or in close proximity? If not, how much transit time will be allowed? Will transportation be needed? What are the costs and turnaround times?
- Can the exhibit hall accommodate all the anticipated stands, or will overflow space be required? A safe rule for computing required gross space is to total the net square meters required for booths and double it.
- If overflow areas are utilized, what type of traffic pattern is needed to assure balance and proper flow? Will exhibitors who cannot be accommodated in the main hall be offered reduced rates for booth rental?
- Recognize that the host country may make a distinction between conference attendees and those conducting business, including exhibitors, thus requiring business visas.
- How you will develop a list of prospects to exhibit in your exhibition (see Figure 11-2) and how you will implement the selling phase for closing exhibit sales.

- Previous exhibitors at your exhibition or related industry exhibitions
- Allied/supplier members of your industry (association allied members)
- Organizations suggested to you by your members or members of your exhibitors advisory commitee
- Companies that have responded positively with interest after your mailer
- Companies that advertise in industry publications
- Your vendors

Figure 11-2 Prospects for Your Exhibition

THE EXHIBIT PROSPECTUS

When details about the exhibition (space, hours, rates, etc.) are determined, exhibitors are invited to contract for booth space. The exhibition is promoted in a series of mailings that include the exhibit prospectus and culminate in the complete information kit for interested exhibitors. Contracts are executed, and space is assigned during the months that follow the initial promotion. The exhibitor's prospectus and kit include the following:

- Information about the date, location, and nature of the show; anticipated attendance; and market demographics.
- Exhibitor eligibility requirements if restrictions are imposed by sponsors.
- The marketing plan, which includes publicity, the advertising schedule, and attendance promotion measures.
- Exhibit hours and a floor plan with booth dimensions, booth number, utility access, obstructions, and variations.
- Data on available utilities, floor loads, ceiling height, door sizes, freight elevators, and docking as well as crate removal, storage, and return.
- Shipping and drayage information, including the name of the freight forwarder, preprinted labels, and assigned PRO numbers for each exhibitor.
- The contract for space, specifying fees, deposits, discounts, payment schedules, and conditions governing cancellations and refunds.
- Information, price lists, and order forms from the exhibit service contractor regarding labor, signage, booth furnishings, rentals, cleaning, and decorator services.
- Hours for installation, rigging, and dismantling. Most contracts stipulate the date and time when dismantling may begin.
- Registration procedures for exhibitor personnel and attendees.
- Restrictions imposed by the facility or municipality governing exclusive contracts, union rules, and safety ordinances such as limiting the use of toxic or flammable materials in booth construction and display materials.

- Specifications for exhibit booths, including items such as carpeting, drapes, and lighting provided by the organizer.
- Restrictions on signage and sound amplification limits for demonstrations and/or entertainment.
- Security procedures governing ingress and egress for exhibitors and the public as well as badge control and package removal policy.
- Insurance coverage, including limits of liability, bonding requirements, and disclaimers, also a form for exhibitor listing in the exhibition directory, including directory advertising rates.
- Information and order forms for special services such as pagers and telephones, photography, computer, video and audiovisual rental, floral and plant decorations, and temporary help such as demonstrators and models.

SHIPPING AND CUSTOMS

International shipments are subject to multifaceted import procedures, complex documentation, and, depending on the product, special permits. The most commonly used document in transnational shipping of exhibit materials is the commercial invoice. It includes a list of the items shipped and their description, value, and, where applicable, serial numbers. The value is required to establish a temporary import bond, called a carnet, that ensures that the material is reexported at the termination of the event.

Because of such complexities, it is advisable in all cases when exhibiting abroad to retain the services of a reputable customs broker. That broker will assist in preparing documentation, advise on packing and freight limitations, and generally help ensure that all shipments arrive on time at the exhibition hall.

As was pointed out previously, in most countries exhibit stands are constructed on-site. That results in some savings in shipping volume and cost. However, any saving is offset by the added cost of time, labor, and materials at the site.

WHAT TO EXPECT ON-SITE

Exhibitors participating in such events avoid problems by anticipating them. They find it advisable to arrive at the site three or four days before the show's opening to verify that shipments have arrived on time and in good condition and to oversee their unpacking. They make it a point to consult with the exhibition management to review ordered equipment and services and to observe progress and the accuracy of the stand's construction. If interpreters have been retained, exhibitors meet with them to ascertain their understanding of advance information on the organization's background, products, services, and policies. This is also a good time to walk the hall and see what other exhibitors are offering, make contact with friends and colleagues, and identify potential allies.

Americans exhibiting at or attending an exhibition abroad often are surprised at the differences they encounter. For one thing, exhibit hours tend to be longer. It is not unusual for a show to last five or six days and run for eight or more hours per day. This often demands increased staffing for exhibitors to provide relief for their personnel. That should be taken into consideration when one is budgeting.

Appropriate attire for exhibitor staff tends to be more formal in Europe and Asia. Unless the exhibitor's product is a resort, sportswear, or a leisure activity, it is unusual to find personnel dressed in anything casual. The trend is trousers, shirt, and tie for men and skirt, blouse, and scarf for women, with footwear to match. Sport jackets are fairly common, and business suits are appropriate for executives. The exception to the rule pertains to models. In much of Europe and Latin America, female models are as scantly clad as they are in Las Vegas.

Because of the multicultural nature of exhibitions abroad, considerable attention is paid to language requirements. Directional signs are in three or four languages, as is the exhibit directory. Multilingual service and security staff wear flag pins to indicate their language fluency. Announcements usually are made in two or three different tongues, and multilingual telephone operators staff the exhibition hall switchboards.

Security tends to be even more prevalent abroad than it is in the United States. The use of security checkpoints with screening equipment is common, and in some countries there is a continuous police or armed forces presence in addition to the internal security staff. Most venues also have emergency medical personnel on duty during show hours. The cost for these services may be built in to the exhibit fee or charged as a separate line item.

▌WEARABLE TECHNOLOGY

Rapidly replacing traditional badges, Smart Cards make use of bar codes or, in a more advanced technology, embedded chips to store a variety of essential data about a visitor. Smart badges can hold demographic information, buying interests, contact data, and company or product information. When they are read by an on-site reader, information can be sent automatically via e-mail or page. A thank you note or product information can be sent electronically to the attendee.

Smart Card technology also can be used for maintaining high-level security. Holographic images and embedded chips can store a wealth of information while emitting radio signals for tracking the whereabouts of an individual or for transmitting data to PDAs and handheld computers.

Introduced in 2003, a new product called nTag functions as both an identification device and a communication medium. Using infrared technology and an LCD screen the size of a conventional name badge, nTag records, displays, and communicates data entered by the wearer. Like Smart Cards, it can receive data from the show's sponsor, event changes, messages, and the like, or it can display wearer-generated communications. Its built-in radio facilitates its use as a communicator or feedback device at program sessions.

Organizations that hold annual exhibitions as part of their meetings can project exhibit sales based on past history and expect an increase as the event grows. Organizers of a first-time event do not have that luxury and must project participation on the basis of industry characteristics and the perception on the part of potential exhibitors of the exhibition's value as a marketing medium. In such circumstances, planning must include a decision to cancel if booth sales do not meet expectations. The exception would be a meeting at which the exhibits' educational value justifies their inclusion regardless of the economic consequences. Show managers, knowing the high cost of excess baggage, offer to ship literature packets for visitors from other countries to their home cities, a service subsidized by export exhibitors.

In conclusion, exhibitions can be a valuable adjunct to any meeting, whether managed by the meeting sponsor or part of a satellite event in close proximity. The additional cost in terms of time and expense often is offset by their perceived value to attendees, who view the exhibition as a beneficial adjunct to their global experience.

KEY POINTS

Exhibitions evolved from the ancient markets that were common in towns and cities. These events have grown to huge events, many of them global in their reach. There has been considerable growth of exhibitions held as part of a convention, or in conjuction with one.

Exhibitions held in other countries have unique characteristics and differ substantially from domestic shows. For that reason, it is advisable to seek help and advice from qualified sources.

Because of distance and complexity, lead time and the budget need to be increased. It is advisable to retain a customs broker for shipments and to get advice on taxes and legal matters.

If exhibits are held in conjunction with a meeting, it is important to balance exhibit hours with program hours. Both should be made clear to participants and exhibitors to avoid conflicts. That information, along with specifics on exhibit operations, is distributed to exhibitors in the prospectus.

At the exhibition venue, participants are advised to arrive at the exhibit site early to supervise the many logistic details involved in construction and operations. They can expect substantial differences in duration, show hours, attire, and language.

Today's exhibitions feature many high-tech advances unknown a few years ago. One such development—the so-called smart badge—enables two-way data interchange and communication between exhibitor and visitor.

PASSPORT

Books

Convention Industry Manual, 7th ed., Convention Industry Council, McLean, VA, 2004.

Morrow, S. L. (1997) *The Art of the Show: An Introduction to the Study of Exposition Management,* IAEM Foundation, Dallas, 2002.

Internet

International Association for Exhibition Management: www.iaem.org.

Trade Show Exhibitors Association: www.tsae.org.

U.S. Department of Commerce Country Desks: www.commerce.gov.

Chapter 12

ON-SITE OPERATIONS

The excitement of the hospitality industry is never more evident than when the doors to the grand ballroom are swung open to reveal a magnificent event. The ambience of the room, its lighting, theme props, music, sound, temperature, table décor, and place settings combine to create memories for the guest that will leave positive impressions for years to come.

—Patti Shock

IN THIS CHAPTER

We will explore:

- How to work effectively with meeting, convention, and exhibition support staff.
- Organizing and coordinating preconference activities.
- Coordinating setup and daily tasks such as hotel reception, event registration, and the message center.
- Pointers on organizing and conducting staff meetings.
- Coordinating and implementing event logistics.
- How to establish and operate the media center.
- Guest programs and their role in the agenda.
- Tickets, name badges, and other credentials and admission documents.
- Coordinating housing for speakers, staff, and participants.
- How to anticipate, mitigate, and resolve on-site problems.
- Organizing meeting room setups.
- The role of volunteers in chairing individual rooms and events.
- Speaker support: ready rooms, briefing, rehearsals.
- Monitoring and managing the hotel master account.
- Postevent activities and responsibilities.

The last three decades have seen an accelerated proliferation of convention hotels and conference centers. The trend started in North America and has continued throughout Europe, Latin America, and the Asia-Pacific region, not only at leading convention venues such as London, Hong Kong, Rome, Rio de Janeiro, Singapore, and Sydney but at many emerging destinations as well. Whereas 4000 square meters of meeting space once was considered adequate for hotels, it is not unusual to see facilities being built with double and triple that capacity.

Keeping pace with the construction of purpose-built conference facilities is a new emphasis on competent, trained support staff and supervision. It is not unusual in places such as Munich and Mexico City to see the title "Director of Convention Services and Catering" on a business card.

WORKING WITH SUPPORT STAFF

In Europe, North America, Latin America, and parts of Asia, there has been a manifest development of skill and professionalism in an area that meeting professionals consider critical to the successful execution of their events. This is the individual employed by hotels and conference centers and variously called the conference manager, convention coordinator, or, most commonly, convention services manager (CSM). A sense of comfort that results from being able to arrive at a strange hotel and interact with such trained specialists. Accordingly, for the purpose of clarity (and in hopes of a self-fulfilling prophecy), the key meeting services contact will henceforth be called the CSM in this text regardless of the actual job title.

The availability of such trained individuals is rare in much of the developed world. Compared with their North American counterparts, not many overseas hotels have a CSM on staff, and even when they do, such as at the larger convention hotels, event coordination and support are initially the responsibility of the sales staff. Thus, the staff member responsible for servicing meetings was, and in many overseas venues still is, a facilitator in the sales or catering department. However, in newer hotels and congress centers designed to facilitate meetings, this staff position has gained increased stature. The result is that throughout the world, at venues committed to and oriented toward meetings and exhibitions, the situation is changing in response to demand. At the more progressive convention facilities, the CSM is now an essential member of the management team. These specialized department heads, whose primary responsibility is event support, seek to master the same body of knowledge and achieve the same level of competence as their clients and are entitled to be called meeting professionals.

When you are planning events in facilities abroad, ascertain which staff member has the authority and the training to facilitate your meeting requirements. Your goal is to work with a competent professional facilitator who understands your needs and is responsive to your requests.

In recognition of the fact that language proficiency and cultural diversity often influence communications between clients and hotel staff, the following guidelines help ensure a successful relationship and trouble-free events:

- Avoid complex, lengthy instructions. Keep communications clear, specific, and brief.

- Sophisticated high-tech equipment may not be readily available except in primary meeting venues. Verify the availability of suitable audiovisual apparatus and trained technicians.
- Overall, hotel and convention center staff in Asia have a great desire to please. However "face," culture and religion are very much a part of their life, so be sensitive to local business etiquette.
- Check holidays, festivals, international sporting events, and religious observances to ensure that they do not interfere with your program (see Figure 11-1).

PRECONFERENCE ACTIVITIES

When one is working with a transnational venue for the first time, the precon meeting takes on even greater importance than it does at domestic meetings. Some meeting professionals even schedule it during one of their site coordination visits or as much as a week before the conference dates.

In addition to the customary logistic items covered at the precon, there are topics that are specific to meeting in another country:

- *Language.* Determine the degree of English fluency on the part of the staff, especially key personnel such as the convention services representative, banquet captains, engineers, telephone operators, security staff, setup crew, front desk personnel, and cashiers. If a local PCO is not employed on-site, a reliable interpreter is essential. It may be economical to hire a local interpreter fluent in English to serve on the meeting staff. Temporary registration staff should consist of persons whose language skills cover those of attendees from other countries.
- *Event orders.* The contents of these vital documents and their function and distribution vary from those used in North America and from one country to another. To avoid having confusing data reach the house staff, defer to the format commonly used at the venue. This avoids errors and misunderstandings due to language lost in translation.
- *Special needs accommodations.* The concern for persons with disabilities is not universal, and the Americans with Disabilities Act (ADA) neither applies nor is enforceable overseas. Few countries provide for disabled access, although newer hotels in large international chains are more likely to provide adequate facilities. Study the facility's architecture, especially public space, and ascertain what can be done to facilitate access for the disabled.
- *Shipment load-in and load-out.* Ascertain how shipments are received and stored on-site and whether there are charges for delivering them from the storage site (this is not uncommon). Ask how packages should be labeled. If a customs broker is used, provide the broker with the name of the shipping department head or the convention services manager.

- *Communications.* Request a list of names of key department contacts, their working hours, and their telephone numbers or radio contact information. Provide the facility with the same information for the planning staff.
- *Verify on-site currency exchange.* Hotels in most countries routinely provide this service, but their exchange rates may not be competitive. Check on nearby banks and ATM machines and inform attendees.
- *Ask about charges for telephone calls* (local and international), facsimile service, Internet access, copying services, and the surcharges for each one. Those charges may be negotiable.
- *Find out what other groups will be meeting at the same time* and ask to be kept advised of bookings to avoid conflicts.
- *Inquire about plans for construction or renovation* during the meeting dates.

SET-UP AND DAILY TASKS

HOTEL RECEPTION

To avoid congestion and delay when large numbers of registrants arrive at the same time, knowledgeable meeting professionals arrange in advance to have additional staff at the reception counters and/or set up a separate group reservation area. Other strategies to avoid overcrowding or speed up the procedure include preregistration on the hotel's Web site and doing hotel and event registration in the same area. In both methods, key cards are given out on arrival, thus confirming occupancy. A feature available at some hotels is the use of self-service kiosks that allow guests to avoid long lines, complete the registration procedure, and receive their key cards. The same system can accommodate checkout.

EVENT REGISTRATION

Advance planning before arrival and a thorough review during the precon meeting will expedite the setup of equipment and furnishings for event registration. Once the physical setup is complete, registration personnel are briefed and rehearsed on their key responsibilities:

- Registration requirements on eligibility, classification, fees, and charges.
- Materials to be distributed and their location.
- Reports and documents.
- Fee collection procedures.
- Acceptable currencies.

Some organizers provide a "trouble desk" to handle problems that arise during registration. This keeps the lines flowing and allows one staff member with convenient access to key supervisors to concentrate on problem solving.

A hospitality desk manned by DMC staff and/or tourist office personnel is a convenient way to supply information on area attractions as well as maps and brochures. This desk also can provide restaurant and tour reservations, transportation, and personal and business service recommendations.

MESSAGE CENTER

A centrally located message center is a vital part of the conference communications system, serving both the meeting staff and the participants. It allows attendees to keep in touch with colleagues, their families, and their offices and serves as a communications focal point.

A variety of systems are available. The basic message center has a staff member equipped with all the necessary meeting and area information to take messages and post them on an electronic message system using video monitors or work stations or on a bulletin board divided into alphabetical groupings. Messages are taken over the phone by arrangement with the switchboard or are left by individuals. Each posted message is flagged for the attention of the intended recipient and posted in the appropriate alphabetical section of the display.

If the facility does not provide messaging systems, monitors and electronic message boards can be rented from local suppliers. Other systems range from a simple overhead projector message display to sophisticated computerized message retrieval and personal data assistants. Each system requires that the recipient check in by phone, on the Net, or by stopping by the center. Policies need to be established for expedited messages such as emergency telephone calls and procedures for locating or paging recipients. A new generation of smart badges, as described in Chapter 11, facilitates instantaneous notification of wearers.

Adequate space is needed for equipment layout. Telephones may be equipped with visual light ring indicators if audible rings might be disturbing. Preprinted message forms provide uniformity of information and can be either stock pads or specially designed forms that incorporate the organization logo or conference theme. Telephone directories or disks are helpful to have on hand, and envelopes should be supplied to allow for sealed messages.

MEETING LOGISTICS

Once the conference is under way, the meeting professional must stay on top of the many logistical details already planned, confirming and reconfirming them, as well as monitoring events from start to finish. Day-to-day activities during the conference encompass participants, the meeting staff, the facility staff, and suppliers. To ensure that responsibilities are met even when they have been delegated to other staff members, a checklist is essential:

- Review each day's schedule of events at morning or evening staff meetings and brief the staff for the following day.
- Monitor the master account and review the current and following day's events with the CSM.

- Verify registration and room pickups.
- Inspect meeting room setups.
- Meet the major speakers at the session location.
- Monitor events for participants' reactions.
- Maintain frequent contact with interpreters.
- Observe restaurants, lounges, and facilities for service and attendee use.
- Be prepared for impromptu press interviews, if applicable.
- Work closely with the media for proper meeting coverage.
- Take the opportunity to rest whenever possible. Don't overeat or over-drink.

RESOLVING PROBLEMS

"Nothing is as easy as it looks. Everything takes longer than anticipated. Anything that can go wrong will go wrong, and at the worst possible moment!" Every meeting veteran is aware of Murphy's law. It seems that Murphy must have been a meeting planner, his law fits the industry so well. With so many plans, people, and variables coming together at one time in one place, the possibility of error is substantial no matter how well planned the meeting is. But a professional who prepares for the worst and anticipates the unforeseen at least will avoid being surprised and can cope better with the problems that inevitably arise.

Lack of communication and miscommunication are the most common causes of mistakes and problems. In arranging for services from facilities or vendors, satisfactory results depend on the quality and timeliness of the information communicated. When it comes to obtaining essential information, meeting professionals are often at the mercy of the sponsoring organization and its management. Conversely, they must ensure that management and participants understand the importance of timely, accurate input. "Guestimates" from an ill-informed staff member are invitations to disaster.

Expect some problems to occur in the field and establish contingency plans to handle them. Typical problems that may arise include the following:

- A speaker who is late or doesn't show up at all.
- A meeting or banquet setup that is wrong or late.
- Materials lost in shipment.
- Strikes at hotel, airlines, ground transportation, or restaurants.
- Remodeling or construction at the hotel.
- Medical emergencies.
- Transportation schedule changes or disruptions.
- Slow or poor food service.
- Slow check-in or checkout causing congestion and missed flights.
- Key meeting personnel unavailable.
- Inclement weather and storms.
- Civil disturbances and strikes.

These and other meeting emergencies are covered in depth in Chapter 14.

The effects of conflict, miscalculations, and problems can be ameliorated by anticipating them. Review the staging guide and ask "what if?" For example, what if:

- AV or hotel equipment breaks down or electricity fails?
- Services are delayed or not provided according to contract?
- An attendee becomes unruly?
- A VIP is mistreated or perceives that?
- Meeting rooms are unavailable at contracted times?
- Meeting rooms are noisy or overcrowded?

Considering such questions prepares the meeting professional for contingencies. If problems arise, be willing to accept the recommendations of the facility staff. They are professionals too and have a wide range of experiences from past meetings. If problems occur that are not being solved satisfactorily, go to the top. Here are some other helpful hints:

- Keep an ear out for scuttlebutt at the meeting. Rumors, whether they involve staff, attendees, or facility personnel, should not be ignored. Analyze them, make contingency plans, and hope the plans won't be needed.
- Knowledge of local laws, customs, and holidays, offshore as well as domestic, will reduce the number of surprises.
- Inquire about unions, their importance in the various service categories, and whether contract negotiations are pending.
- Obtain AV requirements and specifications well in advance. See that equipment is tested with the actual program elements (this is especially critical with videos and DVDs).

When errors occur, as they invariably will, keep a record of the problem, the cause, and the solution. These can be invaluable tools in planning the next meeting. The only mistake to regret is the mistake that is repeated.

MEDIA RELATIONS

Recognizing the value of good public relations, most organizations assign that responsibility to a trained senior staff member or outsource it to a professional media consultant. For meetings abroad, it is advisable to retain the services of a local public relations firm. In some venues, if the prestige of the event justifies it, the convention bureau may assign a staff media specialist to fill that function. Coverage by local and trade media is an important aspect of the meeting. It not only showcases the event, the organization, and its issues but also builds anticipation for future meetings. Inviting the press to the conference and expediting its registration and housing is just the beginning. Throughout the conference, press representatives need special attention and service to get their interest and support and ensure that the event generates the exposure it deserves.

If the media activities are outsourced, a knowledgeable staff member should be assigned to serve as media liaison. This is not a public relations executive but a member of the meeting staff charged with logistic support of media activities. This individual must be knowledgeable about the organization and the issues of the conference and have some familiarity with press operations. In some organizations that have no permanent public relations staff, this person or a publicist retained for the occasion may originate contact with the trade press and local assignment editors. This entails advance planning to ensure that a spokesperson is designated and appropriate media representatives are notified, invited, and accredited.

Before contacting local media, the media liaison investigates the newspapers, business publications, and television and radio stations in the host city. He or she finds out the kinds of stories local editors and news directors run on their slow days, especially weekends, and provides a schedule of noteworthy events, including a press conference with the meeting's news makers. The news media respond favorably to professionally prepared story ideas and background on a conference and its participants. This will stimulate interest, especially with the local media, which will want to know how the conference affects their audience or readers.

Press kits with releases on the conference and the organization are prepared and made available. If the press packets are complete and properly compiled, even media that are not represented will have material to use as fillers and spot news items. The packets should consist of the following:

- An attractive folder with the logo and/or conference theme.
- Demographic data on attendees.
- Releases covering provocative issues or newsworthy activities or people.
- Event information and program as well as noteworthy speakers or guests, with a synopsis of speakers' text, particularly the keynote.
- Organization history, background, and statistics.
- Photographs and biographies of officers and speakers.

Make sure the press packet reads well. It must hold the attention of a busy editor or news director, informing without swamping with detail.

During the meeting, the duties of the media representative include supplying all required information to the media people; arranging interviews with executives, exhibitors, and VIPs; and answering questions ranging from program content to the location of restrooms. This person should be fluent in the local language and should be given the authority to manage media activities and act independently.

MEDIA CENTER

When contacting media representatives, let them know that a fully staffed and equipped media center will be available. This will provide further inducement to cover the event. A well-equipped media room facilitates the tasks of correspondents by supplying needed equipment and communications, and serving as a clearinghouse for all announcements and appointments. The center is managed by the staff media liaison assisted by clerical personnel to aid in registration and message center services. A highly appreciated perk is coffee or tea service, snack items, and soft drinks (contrary to the stereotype of hard-drinking reporters). Provide sandwiches and fruit for the correspondents, who often miss meals while covering a story, an occupational hazard in their field. Newsroom setup requirements include the following:

- Sufficient electrical outlets to accommodate equipment needs.
- Good lighting with access to windows if possible.
- Adequate desk space and chairs.
- Several multiline telephones, preferably with outside lines and data ports.
- High-speed Internet access.
- Computers with word processing software and a network printer.
- A copier and enough copy paper.
- Paper and other clerical supplies.
- Amenities, including refreshments, a message board, a wall clock, and a coat rack.
- Information resources: organization background and data, annual reports, industry statistics, biographies, histories, photographs, copies of speakers' texts, and contact name and phone number on all forms.
- If exhibits are part of the conference, exhibitor product literature.

A space should be set aside as a news conference area either as an extension of the newsroom or in a separate room. This area also can serve as interview space and should be equipped with comfortable furniture in conversational groupings. A wall hanging featuring the conference theme can serve as a photographic background. When arranging appointments, establish ground rules covering topic and duration. Find out the purpose of the interview and who will be conducting it and prepare respondents with ground rules and subjects to be covered.

It is customary for the newsroom to be set up and open before the beginning of the conference and remain open each day during conference hours. During off hours, security staff should be instructed to open the room for properly credentialed media representatives if they require access.

STAFF MEETINGS

In light of the fluid nature of meetings, particularly those convened in another country, periodic meetings are needed to keep staff informed of changes, solve problems, and disseminate new information. Even though all facets of the conference have been reviewed during the preconference meeting, daily staff meetings provide a forum for continued communications and clarification. Some meeting professionals schedule staff meetings in the evening to cover the following day and to critique the one just ending. Others prefer a morning breakfast meeting so that the staff is well rested. Whenever the meeting is scheduled, it should be stressed that the staff is encouraged to communicate their problems and concerns openly, though confrontation should be avoided. This is not a time for a gripe session but rather for encouragement of teamwork and mutual support.

The meetings are held in an area free of distractions, allowing sufficient time to cover all the elements in the day's schedule and any questions that may arise. Event orders and other meeting documents are reviewed, and time is allowed for alterations to be implemented smoothly.

TICKETS AND BADGE CONTROL

If tickets are used for program sessions and functions, they should be numbered consecutively, color-coded for each event, and properly accounted for. Printing the time and location of the event on each ticket will prevent confusion and simplify record keeping. It also assists attendees who do not have their program schedules handy. Designate in advance the applicable currency.

For ease of accounting and fiscal procedures, where applicable, keep ticket prices in whole numbers and provide preprinted receipts (for attendee tax and expense purposes) that can be filled out quickly. For major functions included in the registration fee, provide coupons to be exchanged for tickets in advance by those planning to attend. Although this adds a step to the process, substantial savings can be realized through more accurate meal guarantees. A count of tickets sold, unsold, complimentary, and unaccounted for will provide a record of the function. This can be extremely valuable during postconference accounting.

BADGES

The exotic high-tech, multifunction badges described previously serve a wide variety of specialized functions. However, for most events, printed paper badges are still the norm.

Badges come in a variety of designs but generally fall into three categories: self-adhesive, plastic-encased, and laminated. Adhesive badges may work for small one-day events, but they do not last long and are not aesthetically pleasing. Plastic-encased badges and the laminated type are more versatile and durable. They utilize various fastening devices, the most functional being clip fasteners and lanyards.

Preprinting badge stock with the conference name and theme has become an almost universal practice, leaving only the attendee name and affiliation to be printed. Minimize further information to avoid crowding the badge. Bold type should be used and should be standardized for all badges. Registrars responsible for typing badges on-site should be briefed on the cultural name variations described in Chapter 7. The use of different colored borders to denote special status or position gradually is taking the place of ribbons. Still, many organizations prefer ribbons attached to the badge holder to denote the attendee's status or office.

A broad range of computer graphics programs, peripherals, and services specializing in badge preparation enable organizers to offer attractive preprinted badges in highly visible typefaces. They also simplify on-site badge preparation and offer many creative options.

Knowledgeable registration supervisors keep an extra supply of blank badges and holders on hand to replace lost or incorrect badges or to issue badges to unplanned walk-in registrants, guests, or personnel. Stress to attendees that their badges are the identification that gives them access to the meeting events and should be worn at all times.

MONITORING MASTER ACCOUNTS

A daily review of master account charges will help prevent surprises during the postmeeting review session. Daily statements should be required, with detailed backup of all charges available for inspection. This policy encourages the hotel to exercise care in identifying and documenting all master account charges. At each session, approve correct charges and identify any disputed ones or delayed and missing items. A periodic check with the front office will help clear up discrepancies, as the office often receives charges not covered by the master account billing instructions. Some meeting managers contact the night auditor just before retiring each night to inquire about billing questions that have arisen since the last review session.

PROGRAM MANAGEMENT

Program management refers to the activities and procedures related to the support and proper conduct of the meeting program: the business agenda, functions, exhibits, (if part of the event), and social activities. These are probably the most critical meeting elements since they have the greatest influence on attendees' perception of the event.

MEETING ROOM SETUPS

Among the most significant gauges of a meeting professional's competence is the ability to estimate the number of people attending a session or function, accommodate those who arrive, and adapt to variations between the estimate and the reality. Proper planning and controls certainly help minimize surprises, but true professionals still anticipate changes and incorporate contingencies in their planning. For theater-style seating, for instance, it is customary to leave rear and side aisles for standing room if an overflow crowd is anticipated. (Be sure to check local fire regulations on this point.) In class-room setups, it is good planning to add a few rows of theater-style seating in case of overflow; this also encourages early arrivals to sit forward in the room.

Although it is assumed that the reader is familiar with various seating formats for meeting rooms, it may be valuable to touch briefly on the major setups, their advantages, and their limitations. (For a visual example of types of meeting room arrangements, see Figure 12-1.)

Theater style. Permits maximum capacity seating and rapid setup or reset; directs attention to a speaker or a single focal point. Because of the row seating, this setup restricts interaction, limits notetaking, and is not conducive to extended sessions. (*Note:* Unless otherwise directed, the house staff will set chairs one behind another and butting side to side. For better sight lines, ask that seating be staggered and, if capacity permits, specify that there be a minimum of four inches between chairs.)

Classroom or schoolroom. Considerably more comfortable for extended periods. Directs attention to the speaker and offers better sight lines. Suitable for writing and positioning of program materials and beverage service at tables. Interaction is possible but requires rearranging the chairs. A modified classroom setup in which participants can make eye contact can be achieved by arranging the tables and chairs in an arc or semicircle.

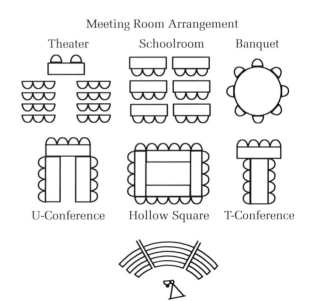

Meeting Room Arrangement

Figure 12.1 Typical Room Setups

Conference. This designation encompasses u-shape, t-shape, hollow square, and variations of them. They are appropriate for smaller groups and are characterized by the fact that participants face each other, facilitating interaction. Attention is still directed to the speaker or panel, and contact is more intimate. Effective for use of data projector or whiteboard.

Rounds. Tables two meters in diameter, which are standard for meals, also may be designated for educational sessions. They offer maximum intimacy and interaction among participants and accommodate note taking and beverage service. Ideal for case studies and the nominal group technique. A limitation is that there is no clear focal point, thus restricting speaker contact. This setup hampers the use of visual aids unless tables are set as "crescent rounds" with no more than six chairs set in a semicircle on the side of the table facing the speaker or screen. Setting crescent rounds also requires a larger meeting space and can reduce capacity. Nevertheless, it is currently one of the most popular and preferred setups for internal corporate general sessions and interactive breakouts at association meetings.

Having communicated the setup for each session by means of event orders, vigilant organizers try to be present when setup begins. If that is not practical, it is essential that the setup be observed by a staff member early enough before the session begins to make minor changes. At this point the following points should be checked:

Room Entrance and Exits

- Signage identifying session properly posted.
- Table for literature, if called for.
- Front door capable of being propped open for attendees' entrance and exit.
- Exit doors clearly marked, unlocked, and clear of barriers.
- If the weather is inclement and attendees are arriving from outdoors, provisions for coat check or coat racks.

Seating Area

- Chairs and tables set to specifications, with ample space between chairs, enough distance between rows, and adequate aisles.
- Proper sight lines for audiovisual projection. Front row no closer than 2H and last row no farther than 8H (H = image height).
- Lighting and climate controls set to comfortable levels. The room should be cooler than normal since body heat tends to increase room temperature.
- Water pitchers or bottled water and glasses properly placed.
- Telephone and public address turned off. (Music may be desired during the entrance but should be muted before the session starts.)
- Projectors properly set up, connected, and focused; appropriate size screen placed for optimum height and viewing angle.

- If projectors are not behind the screen or dropped from the ceiling, stands positioned not to interfere with traffic flow. All exposed cables taped.
- Handouts available for distribution, if called for.
- Floor microphones (or wireless mikes) set, turned on, and adjusted for sound level.

Presentation Area

- Lectern set according to plan. Reading light working. Ceiling or stage light focused on lectern. Water carafe and glasses available.
- Screen positioned away from lectern so that the speaker can see visuals. Front overhead lights turned off to prevent light bleed on the screen.
- Lectern and/or lavaliere microphone working and set at the proper level. With a wired lavaliere, the cord should be long enough for freedom of movement.
- Table for laptop computer with power extension and cable to the data projector, if called for.
- Draped table for panel or speaker materials set close to lectern. If set for panel, check table microphones (minimum of one microphone for two panelists).
- Podium (platform) properly set, specified height and size, draped, and with stairs as needed.
- Flags, banners, and other stage decorations properly placed according to protocol.
- If a rear-projection format is used, the screen should be draped to the full width of the stage; lectern should be positioned to avoid light spilling on screen.
- Projectors connected and focused. Screen properly positioned for optimum viewing. Other visual aids as requested: flipchart, whiteboard, eraser, laser pointer, marking pens, and so on.

SPEAKER SUPPORT

Chapter 6 outlined in detail the designation and handling of speakers. In the operation phase, the planner's primary concern is to see that speakers are properly briefed, given an opportunity to rehearse, and provided the support they require for an effective presentation. There is also the need to ensure that the principal speaker arrives at the site early, is introduced to interpreters (if applicable), and is present for his or her session before it begins.

RECEPTION AND HOUSING

With travel arrangements established in advance and arrival time confirmed before the meeting, it may be necessary for certain speakers to be met at the airport and transported to the meeting site. Some organizations assign this responsibility to a speaker host, usually a member of the program committee. Others delegate this function to a receptive operator or convention bureau greeter. For celebrities, high government officials, and security-sensitive individuals, protocol and security considerations govern the extent of the reception and escort. The general rule is that VIPs be met by officers of equal rank. Occasionally, government officials may need to be involved in the reception committee and police escorts or other honors may be appropriate.

There is sometimes a conflict between speakers and hotel staff regarding room accounts. Regardless of the policy, clear instructions must be given to the hotel to avoid embarrassing the speaker.

Not all presenters need to be housed in suites, but they should be provided with upgraded rooms. Accommodations must reflect speakers' rank or stature, and speakers are entitled to VIP status on the rooming list. The concierge, telephone supervisor, and duty manager, plus, in select cases, the head of security, need to be aware of their presence. In some instances, the general manager may want to be on hand to greet a prominent guest. Little courteous touches such as expedited registration, an upgraded room, and a bowl of fruit or another arrival amenity are appreciated and manifested in the subsequent performance.

Speakers routinely are invited to attend all hospitality and social functions. They are seated with the organization's leadership, not merely for prestige but also to give them an opportunity to discuss and understand the nature of their hosts, their objectives, and their special needs. Receptions and less formal gatherings give speakers opportunities to mingle with the audience, gauge their private agendas, and gain valuable insights into the nature of the group they will be addressing. Some speakers take this opportunity to build a camaraderie that permits them to address their remarks to specific individuals during the presentation, achieving greater rapport with the audience.

SPEAKERS' LOUNGE

It is customary to set up a speakers' lounge in the vicinity of the conference area. This facility allows the speakers to rehearse their presentations, view and cue audiovisuals, or relax before and between sessions. If staff allocations permit or volunteers are available, the lounge should be manned during conference hours by individuals who have been briefed properly. They should be introduced to the audiovisual supplier in case last-minute equipment is needed by speakers. The room is equipped with an overhead projector and an LCD projector and screens at a minimum. If called for, other audio and video equipment may be added. Refreshments are optional, although bottled water, soft drinks, and coffee and tea are basic for most meetings. A sewing kit, steam iron, and ironing board are helpful for last-minute wardrobe adjustments, and presenters appreciate a full-length mirror.

SPEAKER BRIEFING

However detailed the speaker information kit may be, most meeting professionals consider it essential to hold a briefing, particularly when a number of presenters and session leaders are involved. It should be held the day before, though some program managers find that a breakfast meeting on the day of the presentations works well. (Some executives who serve as conference chairpersons invite speakers to dinner the night before.)

At this meeting, the program host reviews the meeting's objective and conducts a verbal walk-through of the agenda, emphasizing points that involve or affect speakers. Simultaneous interpretation, special announcements, introductions, session formats, and AV support are detailed. If room captains have been designated, they are introduced to their presenters. Both are encouraged to check their meeting rooms before the sessions begin if they have not done so already.

ROOM CAPTAINS AND SESSION CHAIRMEN

Proper program planning calls for a coordinator for each session. Most organizations designate a room captain whose function includes duties such as speaker introduction and time monitoring. Generally, the room captain serves in a logistic support capacity, whereas a session chairman is part of the program. The session chair also may act as a moderator when a panel discussion is involved. The role of the chair is similar to that of a master of ceremonies, guiding the audience and presenters through the program, keeping presenters on time, and acting as a continuity link between several presenters in a session. Occasionally, when the discussion gets heated, the chairman may have to become a referee or master-at-arms, controlling the more outspoken and keeping the program on track and the participants' behavior consistent with decorum.

When the chairmen act, as a moderator, there is the additional responsibility of ensuring that speakers' comments are understood by the audience and asking for elaboration when that is not the case. The moderator guides the discussion, oversees or poses questions from the audience, and monitors responses to ensure that they are clear, concise, and relevant. As a timekeeper, the moderator has the difficult task of getting verbose speakers to limit their presentations to the prescribed time frame and ensuring that the session begins and ends on time.

A chairman's brief or a room captain's instructions may contain the following elements:

- Session title and outline or text of presentations.
- Speaker introductions.
- Copies of papers, handouts, and instructions for dissemination.
- Attendee roster, if available and applicable.
- Interpreters' names
- Badge or ticket control instructions if attendance is restricted.

- Copy of event order designating room setup, staging, AV, and so on.
- Diagram of prompter signals for communicating with the speaker.
- Instructions on timer controls or lights, if available.
- General instructions on duties, timing, and announcements.

REHEARSALS

Major presentations, particularly those involving complex productions, are rehearsed, preferably in the room in which they are to take place. Live cast productions, special effects, and programmed AV elements such as multimedia and multi-image presentations may require one or more technical rehearsals as well as a final dress rehearsal. If computer-supported sessions are part of the program, as they usually are, check the bandwidth capacity of data ports and encourage presenters to rehearse that aspect of the program.

To ensure availability of the site for staging, setup, and rehearsal, it is best to reserve the room in advance and have that activity on the event order. Meeting professionals and CSMs practice space economy, however, so that space that is not needed can be released for other functions, effecting considerable cost savings.

The actual conduct of speaker rehearsals is a matter of individual or management choice. Some presenters want to rehearse their materials verbatim, and some may require the services of a speech coach. Others merely rehearse cue lines or, if accompanied by visuals, "jump cue" their lines, by going rapidly through the script and reading only the cue lines for the benefit of the technical crew and to verify the correct sequence of visuals. If timing is critical, however, it is best to rehearse all audiovisuals, presentations, bridges, and continuity in real time.

GUEST PROGRAMS

In transnational meetings there is a far greater likelihood of participants having a spouse, children, a relative, or another companion accompany them than is the case at domestic events. The opportunity to share the experience of other lands and cultures is a powerful influence. Accordingly, organizers anticipate and provide for such accompanying persons by arranging guest programs, usually through a DMC.

For a meeting professional, this added dimension calls for imaginative programming that maximizes the benefits of overseas travel and integrates it into the business agenda. Aside from the need to plan innovative guest programs, budgeting for them, contracting for services, and providing logistic support, there is an added element of uncertainty in planning meal functions, providing guarantees, and estimating seating capacities. Many companies and most associations feel it is beneficial to have an attendee's guest attend business sessions. Thus, in estimating room setups, most corporate planners factor in a percentage of guests to ensure adequate seating. Associations generally restrict guest attendance—except at general sessions—unless a guest pays the full registration fee.

During the operations phase, one of the meeting organizer's concerns is balancing the guest programs with the business agenda. Some let their enthusiasm for innovative guest agendas carry them away, to the detriment of the educational sessions. It is important to understand that participants who bring their spouses or guests to an overseas meeting site want to participate in sightseeing excursions and recreational events. A fine balance must be maintained in designing a program that is stimulating but does not interfere with the business agenda. Nothing is more distressing to a meeting professional than to have a highly paid speaker address half the registered delegates while the rest are shooting the rapids on a scenic river with their significant others.

A competent DMC can be a tremendous help in planning and managing guest and joint programs. DMCs are familiar with local attractions and resources and can relieve organizers of much of the burden of supervising and administering the program, allowing them to devote their attention to the business agenda.

POSTEVENT RESPONSIBILITIES

Your responsibilities do not end when the final gavel falls or when the exhibit stands are dismantled. There are a number of postmeeting logistic and operational details that must be attended to, and most of them need to be arranged before the event ends, some even before it begins:

- Consult the DMC and review group and staff departure. Implement the departure plan and ensure that no one is left behind (unless this has been arranged in advance).
- Notify the customs broker or freight forwarder of return shipments.
- Activate VAT reclaim if and where applicable.
- Review the master account, resolve conflicts, and arrange for settlement of charges.
- Settle accounts with the PCO, the DMC, and suppliers or arrange for billing.
- Collect attendee evaluations for later review and tabulation.
- Compare event objectives and outcomes. Rate staff performance.
- Conduct a postconference staff meeting and review problems encountered as well as benefits gained.
- Write letters of commendation for exceptional service and distribute gratuities.

Finally, if at all possible, plan to stay after the postevent tasks are completed. Many meeting professionals who manage international events, the authors included, are unable or unwilling to take advantage of the destinations in which they find themselves. This is a shame, since the opportunity to enjoy the location in which you have been working so hard may not occur again for a while—if ever. Part of the excitement and pleasure of global event planning is the ability to practice your profession in places you never thought you would get to go as well as places you have dreamed about visiting. Whenever possible, try to take a day or two, after all the hard work is done, to enjoy your surroundings and recharge your batteries for the next project.

KEY POINTS

A preconference meeting should be done up to a week in advance at the property to ensure that no difficulties will arise concerning the event orders, translation, currency, and many other important issues.

To expedite registration and anticipate problems, online as well as on-site registration is used, as well as a help desk and message center.

Use a checklist and have daily briefing meetings with your staff to stay organized and ensure that the event runs as smoothly as possible.

Receiving press notice is extremely beneficial to the organization. Have glossy press kits available as well as a press business center.

Favorable perception of an event depends on proper planning, Be sure meeting rooms are set up according to the nature of the event and the number of people expected to attend.

Meeting Room Inspection

Check signage, entrances and exits, seating areas, and presentation areas for each meeting room.

Handling Speakers

To get the best from speakers, treat them as guests and provide organized transportation and housing. Arrange for briefing, introductions, rehearsals, and a private speakers lounge for preparation and relaxation.

Guests

Guest programs, if included, should be memorable and creative. Utilize creative marketing to publicize speakers, events, and the benefits of attending the meeting.

Postmeeting Responsibilities

Arrange for return shipments and settlement of accounts. Write thank you letters and distribute gratuities. By all means, take the opportunity to see the country.

PASSPORT

Books

Morrow, S. L., *The Art of the Show*, Education Foundation, International Association for Exhibition Management, Dallas, TX, 1997.

Moxley, Jan, *The AC Manual*, Zone Interactive Communications, Boulder, CO, 1991.

Shock, Patti J., and John M. Stefanelli, *Hotel Catering: A Handbook for Sales and Operations*, John Wiley & Sons, New York, 1992.

Internet

Arranger: A Comfort Calculator (seating calculator), MPI Bookstore: www.mpiweb.org.

International Association for Exhibition Management: www.tradeshowstore.com.

Chapter 13

PREPARING FOR TRAVEL ABROAD

The great thing in this world is not so much where we are, but in what direction we are going.

—O. W. Holmes

IN THIS CHAPTER

We will explore:

- How to select an official airline for an international meeting, convention, or exhibition.
- How to negotiate airline fares and services.
- How to coordinate with immigration and customs agencies.
- Obtaining proper passports and visas.
- How to determine appropriate immunizations.
- Managing travel security for the participants.
- What issues to cover in the on-site briefing meeting.

There may be some nominal exceptions to airlines as the chosen form of travel to an international meeting venue. To attend a meeting in, say, Geneva, some European attendees may drive or go by train if the site is within convenient travel distance. However, it is primarily air transportation that concerns an organizer planning international group travel. It is rare to find a corporate meeting sponsor who takes a "let them get to the meeting on their own" attitude, even for domestic meetings. Most corporate meeting travel is now subject to the travel management policies of the particular company, and travel to meetings is no exception. Depending on the presence or absence of in-house or outsourced travel managers and preexisting corporate contracts with certain airlines, a corporate meeting planner may or may not be involved with air transportation decisions or negotiations.

However, associations and other organizations that must attract attendees to their events continue to charge meeting professionals with the responsibility of researching, negotiating, and disseminating information on convenient, economical air travel. Association planners looking for ways to reduce costs for attendees often designate an official airline. Before booking flights on Internet travel sites became common, group fares negotiated for specific events were usually the least expensive alternative. This is no longer the case, since some airlines have done away with group fares altogether and others post their lowest fares on the Internet. Nevertheless, the combination of lower fares and additional services makes group contracts a cost-effective option, and many meeting organizers continue to choose an official carrier.

SELECTING AN AIRLINE

The first step in travel planning is to know what the originating points are for all travelers attending a meeting. This information may be available from travel patterns of past meetings or the organization's geographic extent. In the case of corporate meetings, the list of invited attendees is known in advance, and so the distribution pattern of primary originating points can be developed easily.

A designated official airline is chosen for its reputation for service and safety, frequency of flights, scheduling, and lift capacity. Security considerations also may influence the choice. Price is also a factor; however, price breaks for international travel are more difficult to obtain than for domestic travel. Compared with domestic air travel, it is more important for a planner to understand how international airlines operate and how concessions often outweigh reduced fares. That is not to say reduced fares should be overlooked. Indeed, many foreign carriers that are subsidized by their governments can be very competitive in fare pricing. However, in the final analysis, foreign carriers, like their domestic counterparts, are dependent on revenue passenger miles for their profitability.

NEGOTIATING FARES AND SERVICES

Within their prescribed limitations, airlines have some degree of flexibility in quoting guaranteed fares, usually with an advance deposit. This can be particularly helpful in the face of long lead times and currency fluctuations. Cancellation penalties and cutoff dates are also subject to negotiations. Many airlines have instituted nonrefundable tickets and change fees, making it difficult and expensive for travelers to accommodate to changes in their travel plans. In the authors' experience, a one-day change to connect with an international flight ended up more than doubling the cost of the connecting flight. Today planners and travel managers carefully weigh the costs and benefits of early ticketing against later itinerary changes.

Aside from serving a vital role in transporting participants to the event, an airline can be a useful resource for site research and selection, information on and liaison with program support elements, and overall promotional assistance.

Periodic updated passenger manifests provide valuable data for planning ground arrangements and verifying room blocks. National airlines, especially those which are government-owned, have a vested interest in promoting their destinations. As a planning strategy, this suggests negotiating air travel *before* the final decision is made on the destination. It is important for organizers to understand what is negotiable and how concessions can outweigh reductions

| [MEETING NAME] [LOCATION] | ARRIVAL/DEPARTURE MANIFEST | Page ____ of ____ |

LAST NAME	FIRST NAME	ARR DATE	ARR FLT	ARR TIME	DEP DATE	DEP FLT	DEP TIME	COMMENTS

Figure 13-1 Sample Travel Manifest

in fares. There are many valuable services an air carrier can provide to assist you in planning an international event, including the following:

- Assistance with customs clearances for passengers and freight.
- Advance group seat selection, which might include blocking off one or more cabins, with the organizer given the option of seat assignment.
- Subsidies or special rates on accommodations at stopover cities during long-haul flights. These rates may be applied to hotel rooms used to relax and refresh during a long daytime layover or to rooms used overnight.
- On-site assistance with conference trips, ticketing, and flight changes.

As in all negotiations, there is a quid pro quo. In return for concessions granted, you agree to designate the airline as official carrier and, if travel is paid by a company, ticket all or most passengers on that airline. When participants pay their own way, you can show good faith by publicizing the special fares Web site and the telephone number of the airline's or designated travel agency's group department to the attendees.

Finally, seek out the air travel professionals at industry events and solicit their counsel. Maintain contact with the various regional and national meeting and incentive specialists. Negotiation strategies should not be based on adversarial roles but should be a cooperative effort toward a common objective. Airline representatives are as eager as you are to ensure the comfort and safety of the attendees and contribute to the success of the event.

Producing a travel manifest enables the ground team to plan for the many arrivals you will expect before and during the meeting, convention, or exhibition. Figure 13-1 provides an example of this document.

CUSTOMS AND IMMIGRATION

Compared with domestic travel, crossing international borders can seem intimidating to an inexperienced planner. Government regulations, visa requirements, customs forms, and taxation can be daunting the first time around. The key to navigating this bureaucratic minefield lies with the national tourist office, consulate, or convention bureau of the destination you will be visiting. They can provide you with specific information and even assist in clearing some of the obstacles. Although government regulations vary greatly from one country to another, some general rules apply. The first one is that anything associated with government regulations cannot be left until the last minute.

PASSPORTS AND VISAS

Attendees must be advised well in advance of departure to apply for a passport or, if they already have one, ensure that it is current. Some countries will not issue a visa if a passport is within six months of expiration. The advent of passport services over the Internet has expedited the process considerably, and although this involves a service charge, the time saved in getting the passport may be worth the additional expense to many people.

Many of the same agencies also assist with visa acquisition. These services are particularly helpful, since visa regulations vary from one country to another and can change at any time. In addition, some countries may require visas of certain nationals but not others. Even if all the attendees originate from the United States, this does not mean that they all hold U.S. passports. Determine whether the group includes resident foreign nationals, who may be subject to different visa regulations.

Keep in mind that even a country that does not require visas for individual travelers or convention delegates may demand that paid staff and speakers apply for business visas. Clarify these points with your travel counselor or the NTO representative well ahead of time and stay current on any changes in requirements. Airlines are also a good source of up-to-date information since they have a financial interest in knowing what the regulations are at any given time. They are fined by destination governments when they allow passengers to leave the United States without the proper documents. Since they neither want to pay a fine nor fly passengers home for free when they are denied entry, airlines will deny boarding to anyone who checks in without a visa when one is necessary.

Once obtained, a passport and the requisite visas stamped or attached to its pages should be protected at all times, since replacing a lost or stolen passport overseas can be a difficult, time-consuming, and frustrating exercise for both the attendee and the organizing staff providing support. U.S. consulates abroad are extensions of the U.S. Department of State and function like every other government office. Contrary to popular belief (or perhaps wishful thinking), U.S. embassies and consulates abroad do not offer round-the-clock service and support to distressed citizens in their location. If your passport is lost or stolen on a Friday night and you are supposed to fly home the next day, you should change your return flight, since you will have to wait until Monday morning to appear at the consulate during regular business hours to report the loss or theft and apply for a replacement. Regular business hours for passport replacement may be only during certain times in the morning and then again in the afternoon, worsening an already stressful situation.

There is also no guarantee that you will receive a replacement passport the same day unless you can prove that you have a ticket home within 24 hours and have everything the consulate requires when you arrive to report the loss. The following recommendations will help expedite the process. Consider them the core of your emergency passport replacement kit and share this information with your attendees in advance:

- In case of a stolen passport, a police report is mandatory and must be obtained before making a report to the U.S. authorities. Although one's inclination is to go to the consulate for help immediately, this is not the correct first action. Many unknowing and unfortunate people have spent hours waiting to talk to a consular official, only to be told to come back with a police report.

- Bring a photocopy of the lost or stolen passport, showing the pages with your name, photo, and issue and expiration dates. This is the single most useful document as it proves that you had a passport, provides its number, and verifies your identity.

- Bring an additional photo identification and/or credit card with your signature to verify that you are who you say you are. If everything has been lost or stolen and you have no ID, including no photocopy of your old passport, you will have to bring along someone who will affirm that he or she knows you personally and knows you are a U.S. citizen.

- Bring two regulation passport pictures: one for the application and another for the actual replacement passport. Most people do not think to bring extra pictures even if they remember to bring a copy of their passports. Bringing two passport photos on every trip will prevent having to waste hours in a strange city finding a photography store to take passport pictures.

- Complete the application, which can be obtained at the consulate or downloaded from the Internet.

- Bring the necessary amount of money for the processing fee in whatever form is required. This is usually cash or traveler's checks, rarely a credit card or personal check, but it is best to obtain this information from your travel counselor, your local contacts, or the Web site of either the U.S. State Department or a passport/visa service agency.

- Bring written confirmation from the airline or travel agency of your return flight home. If you are due to leave that day or within 48 hours, this information will help get you a higher priority for expedited replacement.

Needless to say, although it is good to know what proactive steps can be taken to replace important documents, it is much better not to have to replace them at all. To reduce the risk of passport loss or theft, your predeparture materials to attendees should include a strong statement about the importance of keeping all travel documents, especially the passport, safe at all times. Since it is much easier to replace a passport if the number is known, registration questions should include the person's country of origin, citizenship, date of birth, passport number, date of issue, and date of expiration.

Underscoring the importance of having a photocopy made of the first two pages of the passport showing the bearer's picture and giving all the information just mentioned, it is advised that two copies be made. One should be kept by the attendee in a place other than the passport, and the other should be turned in at registration so that travelers and the organizing team have a record of everyone's passport. In the event of loss or theft, even if some attendees cannot find their copies, they will be on file. As a final precaution, ask attendees to bring two extra passport photos along just in case.

HOSTING INTERNATIONAL VISITORS IN THE UNITED STATES

International events also occur in domestic venues, requiring travel by delegates from other countries. Recognizing that those travelers are affected by significantly more restrictive immigration laws enacted in the wake of 9/11, specific information needs to be disseminated. The most effective medium is the event Web site.

Advise potential travelers of the heightened security procedures at U.S. points of entry. This includes information on early visa application (six or more months). The U.S. State Department recommends personalized letters of invitation, but they should not be issued by you or anyone in your organization who does not actually know the person filling out the application. If the applicant is unknown, the invitation letter should be an open or general invitation to any interested parties. Although letters of invitation may be required by U.S. consulates as a condition for issuing visas, you should be very careful to clarify that the invitation to attend the meeting does not include any financial support to travel to the United States and that you or your organization will not be responsible for the person while he or she is in the country. The invitation letter should simply state the dates and location of the meeting and the purpose of the meeting and emphasize its educational program.

Alert travelers to possible delays on arrival due to heightened security. This may involve detailed questioning, photography, fingerprinting, and body scans. The tone of this communication should be given considerable thought so that it appears factual without frightening the reader. Since 9/11, the United States has been much less friendly to foreigners seeking visitors' visas, and the impact on the meetings industry has been enormous. Organizers must walk a fine line between attracting as many overseas attendees as possible and not exposing their organizations to liability.

IMMUNIZATIONS

In addition to passports and visas, there are some countries for which immunizations are required for entry or at the very least advised. Some areas are known to have high incidences of malaria, amoebic dysentery, and other infectious diseases. Travelers to those regions should obtain the necessary inoculations or be prepared to show a record indicating that their immunizations are up-to-date. Caution your attendees on this point. Health authorities can detain, inoculate, and isolate travelers who are not properly immunized. Contact the Centers for Disease Control, the World Health Organization, or you destination country's NTO for information on required and/or recommended immunizations. Figure 13-2 lists the most common immunizations for

- Diphtheria and tetanus (DT)
- Hepatitis A
- Hepatitis B (destination- and activities-specific)
- Malaria (destination- and activities-specific)
- Measles, mumps, and rubella (MMR)
- Typhoid (destination- and activities-specific)
- Yellow fever (destination-specific)

Figure 13-2 Basic Travel Immunizations and Vaccines

international travelers suggested by health authorities. Attendees should be instructed to talk with their personal physicians about the upcoming trip and take the appropriate precautions.

SHIPPING EQUIPMENT AND MATERIALS

Shipping goods overseas is another area where you want to work with a specialized professional from the very beginning, especially if you are shipping large quantities of materials for an exhibition, for example. You will want the services of a freight forwarder who will get your shipment from your origin point to the destination, a customs broker who will clear your shipment through customs at the destination, and possibly a transportation or drayage company to transport your materials from the customs depot to your hotel, convention center, or other facility.

Fortunately, these people often work together so that when you identify an appropriate freight forwarding company, it will already have a corresponding customs broker and transportation company available. Whenever possible, you want to hire a freight forwarder with these relationships already in place, since it will make tracking your shipment easier and your communications more efficient.

The most astute global planners know that the myriad regulations and reams of paperwork involved in international shipping and customs clearance are too complicated and specialized to deal with unassisted. One mistake on a manifest can hold up meeting materials for days or even weeks. Professional international freight forwarders and customs brokers will handle all the documentation and transportation required to get your materials from the point of origin to the meeting site and back. Their nominal fees are well worth the savings in problems, delays, and unforeseen expenses. Although they arrange all documentation, including carnets, bonds, and manifests, the shipper can help assure trouble-free transportation by following these guidelines:

ASIA
- Chinese New Year
- Buddha's Birthday
- Moon Festival

EUROPE
- Ascot (United Kingdom)
- Bastille Day (France)
- Dusseldorf Shoe Fair (Germany)
- Farborough Air Show (United Kingdom)
- Frankfurt Auto Show (Germany)
- Geneva Car Salon (Switzerland)
- Milan Fashion Show (Italy)
- Paris Air Show (France)
- Whit Monday (Northern Europe)
- Wimbledon (United Kingdom)
- World Football Cup (Europe)

LATIN AMERICA
- Carnival in Brazil (Brazil)
- Semana Santa (Mexico)
- Santiago de Chile Air Show (Chile)
- World Football Cup (Latin America)

MIDDLE EAST, NORTHERN AFRICA, AND INDONESIA
- Muslim holidays such as
  Dhul
  Dhul oa'da
  Jumada-ul awwal I and II
  Ramadan
  Safar
  Shaaban
  Shawwal
  Rabi-ul awwa I and II

JEWISH HOLIDAYS
- Chanukkah
- Passover
- Rosh Hashanah
- Yom Kippur

CHRISTIAN HOLIDAYS
- Christmas
- Easter
- All Saints Day

Figure 13-3 Major Holidays and Events in Various Regions, Religions, and Cultures

- Prepare accurate lists, by container, of contents, with particular attention to correct serial numbers, where applicable.
- Number and label all cases and include case numbers on the manifest.
- Enter the weight; some countries calculate duty by weight.
- Prepare invoices listing the value of all items. Separate materials that will be sent back from those to be consumed on site, such as product literature, giveaways, prizes, and supplies.
- Containers should be readily (but not too easily) opened and resealed.
- Avoid having shipments arrive on holidays, weekends, or the preceding days (see Figure 13-3 for a list of holidays).
- Use a freight forwarder whose corresponding customs broker is local, is familiar with regulations, and knows local customs officials.

PREDEPARTURE INFORMATION

Educating participants, particularly those who are traveling abroad for the first time, on how to prepare for the trip and what they are likely to experience when they arrive is one of the primary responsibilities of a global meeting professional. Even sophisticated, experienced travelers can overlook some details that can be embarrassing or cause inconvenience on arrival at a foreign destination. The quality of your attendees' on-site experience will be related directly to the quality of the information you provide before their departure. Carefully managing the expectations of your participants and preparing them to accept things that may be different or unfamiliar will provide the foundation for a successful meeting abroad.

Include with your advance registration or confirmation materials information on the host country and the specific city or region. A detailed destination brochure, which is available from the convention bureau or national tourist office, should contain a good map and complete information on the country and city hosting the event. This usually includes history, culture, political structure, climate, sightseeing, shopping, facts about the currency, cultural customs, and electric current as well as specifics that apply to individual travelers' comfort and safety.

Although each destination has unique attributes and laws, certain characteristics pertain to any overseas journey. Following are some guidelines to assist your group in deriving the greatest benefit from the trip abroad:

- *Passport and visa requirements* (as noted in the section above). Explain visa policies, the address of the consulate, embassy or visa services, fees, and processing time. Recommend that attendees check the expiration date of their passports and remind them to bring photocopies and passport pictures.
- *Hotel information.* Enclose a hotel brochure with the full address, telephone number, fax number, e-mail address, Web site, and location map.

Provide the direct dialing country code and city code for relatives and business associates and telephone rates and surcharges for calls from the hotel.

- *Cultural information.* Describe useful details about cultural differences, local customs, taboos, dress codes, dining and social etiquette, festivals and holidays, and ethnic foods. Enclose a phrase book or a list of commonly used greetings and phrases.

- *Currency.* Suggest that travelers buy small-denomination packets for countries visited or transited. Traveler's checks in foreign currency often have a more favorable exchange rate. Provide the name, address, hours of operation, and location of bank or exchange office closest to the hotel as well as the location of the nearest ATM machines that will provide cash in the local currency.

- *Insurance.* Suggest special coverage or a floater for personal property and a casualty floater for rental cars (if the traveler's policy has exclusions). Provide sources for traveler's medical insurance.

- *Medical.* Clarify required and optional inoculations, if any. Suggest taking prescriptions for refills of medications and eyeglasses. Request a medical profile on elderly attendees, attendees with physical challenges or special needs, and anyone with dietary allergies or restrictions or who requires special attention.

- *Ground arrangements.* Supply information on transfers, vouchers (if used), courtesy transportation, taxi fares, and mass transit systems. Include baggage-handling arrangements, weight limitations, special tags if used, customs clearance points, and group expediting procedures.

- *Clothing.* Offer clothing and dress suggestions for men and women for social, business, and recreational activities according to the climate and customs of the location. Be particularly clear about what should and should not be worn by women visiting Islamic countries, where strict social codes for female attire are observed. On general principles, no matter what the dominant religion of a country is, it is considered disrespectful for women to enter houses of worship with arms, legs, and heads uncovered. The same applies to men in spite of the spate of shorts, tank tops, and sandals one now sees during the summer tourist season. It is possible to be comfortable and appropriately dressed for the locale, and it is your responsibility to guide your staff and attendees accordingly.

- *Government policies.* Detail restrictions on local travel, the amount of currency a person is permitted to bring into the country, alcoholic beverages, pets, drugs, firearms, and controlled substances. Cover tax information, especially if attendees will be able to reclaim VAT for their personal purchases upon departure.

- *Automobiles.* If your attendees will be renting cars, explain driving and highway laws and enclose car rental information and negotiated rates as well as insurance regulations.

Some meeting planners anticipate the needs of inexperienced travelers and enclose in their predeparture packets basic suggestions such as the following:

- Airport diagrams and transit procedures for individual travelers.
- Packing list: flashlight, umbrella, power adapter, travel alarm.
- Steps to take before leaving home: hold mail, stop newspapers, and so on.
- Customs regulations for returning residents.

By preparing your attendees with such commonsense and country-specific information, you will ease the stress of travel to unfamiliar destinations and help them avoid potential inconvenience, embarrassment, and other potential risks as well as ensuring the benefits of attending an international event.

GETTING THROUGH CUSTOMS

All countries tend to guard their frontiers against goods and materials imported without some form of tariff. Within the meetings industry, there are frequent exceptions to the rule involving importation of materials, equipment, and supplies that may be consumed or transported to another country or point of origin. Yet another set of rules applies to individual passenger baggage, gifts, and goods for personal consumption. The way these items are treated varies with category, use, and country, but the following guidelines apply to most destinations.

If your attendees are traveling together as a group, arrange for their luggage to be unloaded and cleared through customs together. The use of distinctive luggage tags and an arrangement with the airline can ensure the former; a DMC with special clearance to meet passengers inside the restricted arrivals area can arrange the latter and prevent language difficulties. Be sure everyone understands the limitations on currency and controlled substances such as liquor and cigarettes. Narcotics, of course, are anathema in almost all countries, and in some countries possession of drugs carries the death penalty.

Such exceptions aside, personal baggage tends to receive favorable, even casual treatment. A reasonable quantity of gifts can be included with personal baggage.

The other side of the coin is clearing customs upon the return home. Get the latest information and disseminate it to participants on regulations governing the following:

- The amount of gifts and purchases that may be brought home duty-free.
- What items should be declared and listed individually.
- What items carry a quantity limit and what is prohibited altogether.
- The amount of duty payable on goods that exceed the exemption.
- Currency or form of payment acceptable to the customs bureau.

TRAVEL SECURITY

Not all travelers have the same risk profile, and there are threats other than terrorism, such as theft and mugging, to guard against. High-risk participants should be given special training. Low-risk travelers need only take certain commonsense precautions. Here are a few that should be passed on to your attendees:

- Go through your wallet or purse and weed out items not needed abroad, such as extra credit cards, voter registration, military ID, and/or business cards, especially if the bearer is a highly placed executive.
- Avoid the use of expensive luggage or distinctive luggage tags that pinpoint you as an executive or a wealthy traveler.
- Dress to project a low profile and to blend in at your destination. Leave business suits in your luggage and wear comfortable casual clothing while traveling. Avoid designer fashions and clothing with cartoon characters, printed messages, or slogans.
- Never wear expensive jewelry. If you need it abroad, conceal it on your person and keep it in the hotel safe with your important documents.
- Remember that travelers who fly first class are presumed to be wealthy and are therefore targets for hostage taking.
- Try to avoid peak travel times. If possible, stay away from crowded areas at the airport. Get boarding passes in advance and check luggage at the curb, if permitted.
- Take a minimum of carry-on luggage. It can restrict your movement in case of trouble.
- Stay out of cocktail lounges and avoid excessive alcohol. You need to remain alert while traveling.

ON-SITE BRIEFING

Depending on the group, a briefing session on the day of arrival often is organized to orient the attendees to their new environment, or a welcome packet with the same information is given out at the time of registration or hotel check-in. Topics include the following:

- *General orientation.* Using an area map, show the hotel location in relationship to local attractions, the city center, shopping, banks, and so on. Cover rapid transit, taxis and fares, and tipping for various services.
- *Cultural.* Explain protocol and etiquette for business and social activities, proper formal and familiar forms of address, and, when appropriate, protocol for dignitaries and guests.
- *Attire.* Review correct dress for sessions, functions, and recreational activities. Specify attire that may be in poor taste by local standards.

- *Services.* Provide the location of international business centers and services, banks, currency exchanges, and an American Express office near the hotel.
- *Shopping.* Cover local bargains, negotiating practices, caveats, and recommended shops. Explain VAT refund procedures and credit card purchases.
- *Security.* In a potential risk area, advise on precautions, conduct, keeping a low profile, and emergency information. Designate a staff person to be notified in case of trouble.
- *Other emergencies.* Provide the address of the local consulate, phone number, and contact information as well as law enforcement policies and procedures if detained or arrested. If possible, provide the name of a host government official with knowledge of the event.
- *Phrase book.* Provide a pocket-size card or booklet of phrases in the host language and helpful expressions and social niceties.

By preparing your attendees with such commonsense and country-specific information, you will ease the stress of travel to unfamiliar destinations; help them avoid potential inconvenience, embarrassment, and other potential risks; and ensure the benefits of attending an international event.

▌KEY POINTS

In choosing a carrier for your event, consider reputation, security, cost, and scheduling, as well as services such as assistance with group reservations and customs clearance.

Consult the destination's National Tourist Organization (NTO) for up-to-date information about passports and visa requirements. Inform attendees of the importance of getting all requisite documents in advance and keeping them safeguarded at all times.

When shipping goods overseas, it is advisable to work with a freight forwarder and customs broker whose expertise in completing required documentation can prevent costly delivery and clearance delays.

Inform attendees before departure about passport and visa requirements, currency, medical and insurance information, appropriate clothing and transportation needs. Include information on how to safeguard their personal belongings and be less conspicuous as tourists in a foreign destination.

▌PASSPORT

Books

Axtell, Roger E., *Do's and Taboos of Hosting International Visitors,* John Wiley & Sons, New York, 1990.

Internet

Centers for Disease Control: www.cdc.gov/travel.
Global passport and visa services: www.global-passport.com.

U.S. customs: www.ustreas.gov.
US passport information: www.travel.state.gov/passport_services.
U.S. State Department Travel Warnings: www.travel.state.gov.

Chapter 14

SAFETY AND SECURITY

Murphy's Law of Meetings and Events
When nothing can go wrong, it will.
If you try to please everybody, somebody is not going to like it.
If you explain something so clearly that no one can misunderstand it,
someone will.

—Richard P. Werth, CPP

IN THIS CHAPTER

We will explore:

- How to know what you are protecting when planning a meeting, convention, or exhibition.
- How to conduct a risk assessment and analysis for an international event.
- How to manage the risk for an international event.
- How to purchase international health insurance and why it is important.
- How to plan for and handle medical emergencies.
- How to develop basic safety procedures.
- Why it is important to maintain copies of critical documents such as passports.
- How to plan for and handle weather contingencies.
- How to anticipate and manage strikes and work stoppages.
- How to purchase appropriate insurance for an event.

Few would argue that among an event planner's responsibilities, ensuring the safety and security of the participants is paramount. Unfortunately, it is human nature to avoid thinking about unpleasant occurrences, and event planners often are unaware of or unprepared to handle emergencies until it is too late. Needless to say, the time to figure out what to do in a crisis situation is before it occurs, not while it is occurring. Comprehensive risk assessment and contingency planning, as well as preparation of clear emergency response and crisis management plans, *must* be standard operating procedure for every planner.

The cataclysmic events of September 11, 2001, brought safety, crisis management, and contingency planning to the forefront of professional concerns among event industry professionals everywhere. Many of us were affected directly by the events of that day. Although one would not consider event planning a particularly hazardous activity, members of our profession, like many others just doing their jobs that day, were among those lost when the World Trade Center towers collapsed. Planners of and attendees at a corporate meeting and the food and beverage staff of Windows on the World perished. At the World Trade Center Marriott, a courageous planner and the hotel staff safely evacuated 330 members of the National Association of Business Economists before the hotel was obliterated by the falling towers. Thousands of people participating in meetings and events all around the world were stranded for days when all air travel into and out of the United States came to a halt. Planners who had never noticed or paid much attention to the phrase *force majeure* learned overnight how important it is to read and understand the contracts we sign.

There is no question that 9/11 and its aftermath had a profound effect on the level of awareness of planners and suppliers of how sensitive and vulnerable our industry was, and still is, to events that are both unforeseen and out of anyone's control. Unfortunately, our collective wake-up call did not end on that dreadful day. Since 9/11 the global events industry has been rocked by a terrorist bombing of a crowded tourist discotheque in Bali in 2002, the devastating effects of the SARS epidemic in 2003, and a series of events in 2004, including another devastating bombing in a busy central railway station in Madrid, four destructive hurricanes barreling through the state of Florida in six weeks, and the tsunami that killed hundreds of thousands of people, many of them tourists, throughout the Indian Ocean area. In 2005, the entire mass transit system in London was shut down by terrorist bombings and the city of New Orleans was completely devastated by the floods that followed Hurricane Katrina. It is the authors' fervent hope that nothing else will merit inclusion in this list of catastrophic events by the time this book is published.

Needless to say, it does not take a major disaster to shut down an event. A wide variety of more common threats and hazards can affect an event negatively at any time. Medical emergencies, weather-related crises, street crime, strikes, protests, and a variety of other incidents can threaten the well-being of attendees and must be anticipated. Remember that anticipating a threat or hazard is the first step toward preventing it from occurring or at least minimizing its negative effect. For example, although it is impossible to prevent a hurricane, avoiding hurricane-prone locations during hurricane season will remove the threat. If there is no choice of location and the risk is acknowledged, an adequate contingency plan and insurance will help minimize the potential losses associated with cancellation of the event. In the worst-case scenario, an emergency response plan will help safeguard the lives of attendees.

WHAT ARE YOU PROTECTING?

The safety and security of attendees and staff should always be the top priority. After people, safeguarding property, proprietary information, and the financial investment in the event is important. The success of the event, your professional reputation, and even the reputation of your company or organization may be at stake, and so adequate measures should be taken to protect all these tangible and intangible assets.

The value of the planner's responsibility cannot be underestimated. Richard P. ("Rick") Werth, CPP, former president of Event & Meeting Security Systems, uses the worksheet shown in Figure 14-1 to demonstrate the importance of providing adequate insurance and security from the outset. All too often, these basic risk management components are overlooked, added as an afterthought, or deemed too expensive to include in the event budget. Showing the "bottom line" total of what is at risk helps put the situation in perspective for senior managers who base decisions on quantifiable input. In addition to the actual cost of an event's logistic components, the value of all the "human capital" must be considered. What would it cost the company or organization to locate, recruit, and train employees to replace those lost in a disaster? How much business might be lost if the skill and experience of upper management attendees had to be replaced suddenly? When presented in this quantitative framework, the costs and benefits of adding the necessary funds to provide adequate risk management are obvious. Whether special insurance, security, or both, the incremental cost usually comes out to no more than 1 or 2 percent of the overall budget—well worth the proactive investment.

What Is the Value of Your Responsibilities?

Complete the following questions for your next event:

1. The dollar value of each executive/VIP attendee? $_____

2. The dollar value of each employee/attendee? $_____

3. The dollar value of each customer/guest attendee? $_____

4. The dollar value of any proprietary information/property? $_____

5. The total event financial investment? $_____
   (i.e., hotel(s), air/ground transportation, activities, meals, gifts, services, production equipment/systems, etc.)

6. The overall value of a successful event for the planner? $_____

                                               Total $_____

Now compare the per attendee costs:
Total event value/costs $_____ divided by # of attendees = $_____ per attendee
Total event security costs $_____ divided by # of attendees = $_____ per attendee

Are you effectively protecting that responsibility?

© www.eventsecurity.com

Figure 14-1 Calculating the Dollar Value of an Event Planner's Responsibility

▌RISK ASSESSMENT AND ANALYSIS

Global event planners recognize that just being overseas constitutes a risk. When you and your attendees are in another country where the culture, language, and customs may be very different, many things you may take for granted are not at all the same. This can be disconcerting under normal circumstances, but imagine being in an emergency situation and not having any of your familiar support systems available. Do you know how to dial 911 in Rome? Is it 911 or some other number? Is there even a number to call? Do you know how to call your hotel in Rio de Janeiro from a public telephone booth on the street? Do you know what is required to get an attendee admitted to a hospital emergency room in Singapore?

In his textbook *Event Risk Management and Safety,* Dr. Peter Tarlow notes, "Risk management is as much about asking the right questions as it is about getting the right answers." In the case of an event overseas, where so much may be unfamiliar, putting together a list of the right questions is essential. How do we know what questions to ask, especially when we will be working in a totally unfamiliar situation?

We suggest beginning with a "what if?" list of everything you can think of that could disrupt or shut down your event: all those awful things you never want to occur and never want to have to deal with. What if someone dies? What if there is an accident or someone gets seriously ill? What if the entire group gets seriously ill? What if there is a fire? What if all the power goes out? What if none of the meeting materials arrive? What if the keynote speaker doesn't arrive? What if none of the attendees arrive because there is an air traffic controllers' strike? What if one of the attendees is assaulted? What if one of the attendees is arrested for assaulting someone?

Once you make this list, you may feel overwhelmed because there are so many potential disasters. How could anyone prepare for all these eventualities? The answer is that no one can, and you certainly will not be able to predict or plan for every possible hazard. However, you can use your what if? list to focus on the occurrences that pose the greatest danger to the event and its participants. Take into account the profile of your event and the attendees, its location, the time of year, the local conditions, the program components, and any conditions that may be likely to occur.

Tyra Hilliard, JD, CMP, associate professor in the Department of Tourism and Convention Administration at the University of Nevada Las Vegas, suggests asking the following questions to assess the specific risk potential of a particular event:

- Is there anything of concern with regard to the timing of the event? The date? The season?
- Is there anything of concern with regard to the location: the specific destination or venue?
- Is there anything of concern with regard to attendees, for example, age, physical limitations, and political views?

- Is there anything of concern with regard to the program components, such as controversial content and potentially dangerous activities?
- What is exposed to loss?
- What specifically could cause a loss?
- Who would suffer a loss?
- What are the consequences?

Figure 14-2 summarizes some of the major security and risk concerns of experienced planners and security professionals. Does it resemble your list? Some concerns apply to every event, whether domestic or international. Death, illness, accident, and fire can occur anywhere at any time and must be at the top of every planner's list. Other concerns, such as weather, labor unrest, and political instability, may be specific to a location or current situation.

Now that you know what questions to ask, where can you get answers? There are a variety of resources, some of which you already may be working with, such as local representatives from the hotel or meeting facility, a DMC, or a tourist authority. The U.S. State Department and the embassy or consulate of the country in which you will be working, as well as the local, national, and international news services, can keep you abreast of political developments in the destination. The Centers for Disease Control (CDC), travel medicine Internet sites, and insurance companies provide up-to-date health information and immunization recommendations.

Last but certainly not least, do not underestimate the value of your professional network. There are highly experienced colleagues who have been planning meetings and events like yours all over the world for many years. Perhaps you know some. Many are members of Meeting Professionals International or the PCMA, and they participate in professional educational conferences and networking events organized at the local national and international levels by those associations. If you are not a member of one of

---

- Street crime
- Health/medical
- Facility security & safety
- Proprietary assets
- Weather
- Executive protection
- Terrorism
- Language
- Cultures & religion
- Customs & laws
- Strikes
- Politics
- Historical dates
- Driving standards

Figure 14-2 Event Security Risks and Concerns

these associations, you should consider joining, if only to expand your global resource network. Both MPI and PCMA have membership categories for students and practicing professionals.

RISK MANAGEMENT

A good risk manager looks at two variables: the probability of a disruptive event occurring and the severity of its consequences. If an event has a high probability of occurring and serious consequences, its relative risk is greater than that of one with a lower probability of occurrence and/or less serious consequences.

For example, if you are asked to organize a meeting in the Caribbean in August, the probability of a hurricane disrupting this event is considerably higher than it would be if you were holding the meeting in February or organizing it in a different geographic region. In light of the high probability of its occurrence and the potentially serious consequences, this is one risk you might want to avoid altogether. If this is not possible and you must hold the meeting in the Caribbean in August, you must manage the risk to the greatest extent possible.

One cornerstone of risk management is insurance; the other is contingency planning. You should purchase the appropriate cancellation/interruption insurance to protect the financial investment in the meeting and prepare a contingency plan to ensure continuity of the meeting if the venue has to be changed at the last moment. Last but not least, you should work with the local contacts to prepare an emergency response plan that includes evacuation of attendees and staff if you are already on-site when the hurricane threat becomes severe.

It is beyond the scope of this chapter to provide detailed instructions for the preparation of contingency and emergency response plans for all the potential risks involved in overseas events. However, there are a few major categories of concern that require mention, such as medical emergencies, safety and security, weather events, natural disasters and labor unrest.

MEDICAL EMERGENCIES

Health-related issues are the most common situations that require special attention overseas. Whether a trip is for business or pleasure, many people tend to be less aware of their environment when they travel and even less observant and cautious when they are members of an organized group. They also have a tendency to indulge in unusually careless or irresponsible behavior once they are removed from their familiar surroundings and daily responsibilities. As a result, accidents, sports injuries, increased food and alcohol consumption, food allergies, fatigue, and illness attributed to change in diet, behavior, and locale are more likely to arise.

Fortunately, many of these health risks can be prevented or minimized by predeparture information and education as well as on-site monitoring and supervision of activities and social events. As part of the routine risk assessment, an experienced planner will determine whether there are any special health issues related to the destination or facility and whether there are any special health requirements or recommendations in effect.

Life-threatening medical emergencies such as heart attack, stroke, and anaphylactic shock also can occur, as can serious injuries as a result of accidents or violent crime. At larger events, where several hundred people are in attendance, the chance of something happening increases proportionately. Paramedical technicians at the event site or on call for rapid response should be hired for large events, and on-site medical teams are recommended if the event is in a remote location.

However, the size of the event is not the determining factor in planning for health-related contingencies overseas. Even a small group requires special attention to detail, since obtaining medical care and navigating unfamiliar health care delivery systems can be daunting, especially if one is not fluent in the local language. This is where your local resources, such as the convention bureau, destination management company, and/or facility representatives, can be particularly useful. These colleagues will provide not only the information necessary to assess specific health risks associated with their particular locale but also information about emergency medical and dental facilities, personnel, and protocols.

In addition to providing attendees with health-related information before departure, it is important for a planner to obtain information in advance about each attendee's personal health concerns or medical needs. Privacy laws in the United States state that no one can be required to divulge his or her personal medical history to a third party; however, there is nothing wrong with asking for information that may be useful in a medical emergency if it is made clear that responding is optional and that any response will be kept strictly confidential. Knowledge of a particular condition or medication is extremely useful to emergency medical personnel, so by all means ask for this information. At the very least, you should know whether someone is allergic to any food, substance, animal, plant, or insect sting so that adequate preventive measures can be taken.

Participants also should be asked to bring a list of all prescription and nonprescription medications they are taking, preferably by generic names, since trade names may be different overseas. Most pharmacies can provide a computer printout of this information. Again, this information may be potentially life-saving in an emergency and at the very least will be useful if medication is lost or stolen and needs to be replaced.

Equally important, the name of a person not traveling with the attendee, his or her relationship to the traveler, and his or her day and evening telephone numbers and e-mail address should be obtained from everyone involved in the event, including the staff, before departure. Being able to contact someone who can provide critical medical information or access to that information if an attendee is unconscious may make the difference between life and death in some cases. In the worst-case scenario, if someone is seriously ill, is injured, or has died, being able to notify this designated contact is especially important.

BASIC SAFETY PRECAUTIONS

Fire, theft, criminal assault, and natural disasters are common threats to travelers everywhere and should be taken seriously. Planners who have never worked overseas should know that many of the safety precautions and building codes that are mandated by law in the United States do not exist in other countries. Alarm and sprinkler systems, multiple exits and escape routes that are clearly marked and lighted, dead-bolt locks, flame-resistant materials, wind- or earthquake-resistant construction, and strict building codes in hazard-prone areas are neither standard nor required in many areas of the world.

Accordingly, a comprehensive site inspection is not just advisable but mandatory from a risk management perspective. In addition to all the reasons noted in previous chapters for the importance of a preevent site visit, ensuring the safety and security of attendees is paramount. It is a planner's professional responsibility to be aware of any and all on-site hazards to prevent or mitigate their effects and protect attendees from potential harm of any kind. This proactive, preventive approach also helps protect both the planner and the sponsoring organization from legal action if there is an accident or untoward event. Liability is reduced if it can be shown that due diligence was taken to discover foreseeable hazards and remove them or warn attendees to be aware of them.

A safety and security site visit should include a tour of every facility in which the group will gather or stay, with specific attention to fire exits, escape routes, fire prevention equipment, alarm systems, placement of security personnel, and lighting in public areas. A briefing from the head of security should review the existing emergency response procedures and address every one of the planner's concerns. "If someone has a heart attack, whom do we call? What do you do? What should we do?" "If there is a fire while the meeting is in session, what happens? If there is a fire in the middle of the night, what happens? Is there an alarm? What does the alarm sound like? Will people hear the alarm in their rooms? Where can we instruct our people to gather outside in the event of an evacuation so that we can be sure that everyone is accounted for?" "What happens if all the power goes out? Is there a backup generator? How long until the emergency power comes on? How long does the emergency power last?" "Who will provide assistance, and will they speak English?"

As outlined in Chapter 12, basic safety precautions begin before departure with instructions sent to attendees. On-site, with the exception of providing protection for meeting rooms and exhibit areas, there is not much you can do to protect meeting participants from criminal acts if they are out and about on their own. However, you can and should advise them to take certain commonsense precautions to protect themselves, such as the following:

- Keep hotel room numbers confidential.
- Verify deliveries before opening the door. If in doubt, call the front desk.
- Make use of the hotel's safe deposit boxes for valuables and your passport. Carry only a photocopy of your passport when you leave the hotel and keep a second copy locked in your luggage.
- Dress and act inconspicuously. Avoid attracting attention to yourself.
- Leave expensive jewelry at home and carry a minimal amount of cash and only one or two credit cards.
- Keep a photocopy of your credit cards stored in your locked luggage along with a copy of your passport.
- In developing areas of the world, avoid public transportation and consider using hotel cars or private car services. Use these car services instead of taxis, especially if you do not speak the local language.

SPECIAL SECURITY ISSUES

In the wake of terrorist attacks and other forms of violence and disruption, hotels and other event facilities have increased the number of trained professional security personnel, many of them former law enforcement or security service officers. You should be as familiar with the hotel security director as you are with the sales manager and convention services manager, as this is the person with whom you will want to review contingency provisions for your staff, VIPs, attendees, and facilities.

When you are dealing with security-sensitive participants—key executives, heads of state, high-ranking government officials, or controversial speakers—or if either the venue or the sponsoring organization has a history of problems, a security assessment is advisable.

You may wish to retain a security consultant or private security company to conduct an assessment of the city and facility and to check the employment records of the staff who will be in contact with the attendees and coordinate with both the regional security officer (RSO) of the local consulate and the local law enforcement agencies.

Security professionals also form a threat assessment team that includes the meeting planner or the designated member of the event planning group, along with local support personnel. They will contract for guards, designate "frozen" or restricted areas, enforce badge access, and, if warranted, sweep the premises for surveillance devices and explosives. Other precautions in security-sensitive meetings include prescreening of registrants and staff; the use of photo ID badges; uniformed and plainclothes guards; visual or electronic inspection of parcels, purses, and briefcases; and press blackouts.

As with any other specialized service, ask for references, especially from colleagues with groups similar to yours who have used their services in the same destination. What you want and need is someone who has experience, cultural savvy, professional connections, and personal relationships with security personnel in the country where you will be holding the event. This is particularly important in Latin America, Asia, the Middle East, and Africa, where cultural sensitivity and long-standing relationships are key. In many countries it is against the law for a foreign national to carry a loaded firearm, and so if this kind of protection is deemed necessary, your U.S. security personnel will have to obtain special permission from the local authorities or rely on trusted local contacts to provide this additional protection.

WEATHER CONTINGENCIES AND NATURAL DISASTERS

As was discussed in the risk assessment section above, although it is impossible to control the weather, certain weather events, such as hurricanes, can be anticipated and avoided altogether by choosing a different venue. Others, such as tornadoes, flash floods, and blizzards, are unpredictable and therefore require careful contingency planning.

Natural disasters such as harsh weather, hurricanes, tornadoes, and tsunamis can be disruptive even when they occur in other parts of the world. A hurricane in Miami or a blizzard in London can delay delegates to a conference in Manila. Meeting professionals need to keep abreast of weather conditions in places where substantial numbers of delegates originate as well as at the meeting site and plan accordingly.

STRIKES AND PROTESTS

Labor disputes that occur during an event can be extremely disruptive and demand flexibility and some ingenuity. In highly unionized countries such as France, Italy, and Germany, strikes, slowdowns, and periodic curtailment of critical services have become almost routine. Everything from public transportation to air traffic control to garbage collection can shut down on a few days' notice, wreaking havoc with the meeting schedule and off-site events. For these kinds of disruptions, contingency planning requires the knowledge and cooperation of the local support personnel, especially the DMC and hotel and/or convention facility management. Engage them in an honest dialogue about the current political and economic situation, labor issues, potential disturbances, and how any disruptions can be minimized. Understand that events may have to be altered, activities canceled, exhibits pared down, and banquet arrangements revised, if necessary. It is in these situations especially that patience and the ability to improvise will be required of you and your team. As difficult as it will be to accept that some things are out of your control, you will have to resign yourself to doing the best you can in the circumstances.

Contingency planning is an inherent responsibility of a meeting planner. It is intended to ensure that unanticipated emergencies do not become disruptive crises. Some element of the meeting that may be considered routine or benign at home may be controversial in your chosen location overseas. If some element of the meeting is controversial, you can anticipate demonstrations and make provisions to ensure that they do not disrupt the event.

Generally, demonstrators voice opposition to the sponsoring organization, a particular speaker or dignitary, or the program participants as a group. They cannot be ignored lest a peaceful protest turn into an angry confrontation. Passive measures call for the cooperation of security and law enforcement officials and publicity blackouts. Active measures may require giving protesters a forum for their grievance at a controlled meeting with organization leaders or perhaps an area where they can display literature on their cause. If you know that you may be faced with this kind of situation, be sure to enlist the assistance of not only special security personnel but also experienced public relations professionals to manage the external communications with both the demonstrators and the local authorities while you concentrate on the well-being of the attendees.

INSURANCE

There is insurance available to reduce the liability and financial loss associated with every one of the possible disruptions or crises mentioned in this chapter, including natural disasters and terrorist attacks. Cancellation and interruption insurance generally costs 1 to 2 percent of the overall event budget and is available for events overseas as well as in the United States. For large meetings with large budgets especially, the cost-benefit ratio of cancellation and interruption insurance is positive.

In addition to each attendee's individual health insurance, it is worthwhile to explore travel group insurance that can be purchased for a specific trip during a specified period. This additional insurance covers medical emergency evacuation that standard policies do not and is worth the minimal premium.

Regardless of the source, weather, other forces of nature, or an attack by human malefactors, if a disaster occurs, remember that you and your group will be competing with everyone else affected by the event for available resources and assistance. This is difficult even in your own neighborhood; for this reason, advance preparation is especially important overseas. If the proper contingency planning has been done and the appropriate backup personnel and procedures are in place, you will be in a better position to assist your attendees in the midst of chaos around you.

KEY POINTS

Anticipating a potential threat or hazard is the first step toward preventing its occurrence or minimizing its negative effect.

The safety and security of attendees and staff should always be the first priority.

Failure to include appropriate risk management as a planning component can have major financial effects as well as serious safety and security consequences.

Risk management includes a listing of all possible events that might disrupt the a meeting, a prioritizing of the probability of each event occurring and an analysis of the severity of each disruptive event's consequences.

Health related issues are the most common situations that require special attention overseas.

A comprehensive site inspection is mandatory from a risk management perspective. It not only safeguards attendees from potential hazards but also protects the planner and his or her sponsoring organization for legal action in the event of an accident or untoward event.

Contingency plans should be created for possible weather related disruptions, natural disasters, strikes, demonstrations that have a high probability of occurring.

When dealing with high profile, security-sensitive participants, it is advisable to retain the services of professional security consultant or company.

Insurance is available to reduce the liability and financial of most potential disruptions.

PASSPORT

Books

Berlonghi, Alexander, *The Special Event Risk Management Manual,* Berlonghi, Dana Point, CA, 1990.

Tarlow, Peter, *Event Risk Management and Safety,* John Wiley & Sons, New York, 2002.

Internet

American Society for Industrial Security: www.asisonline.org.

American Society of Safety Engineers: www.asse.org.

National Fire Protection Association (NFPA): www.nfpa.org.

MEDEX (international medical insurance): www.medexassist.com.

Insurex Expo-Sure (U.K.-based company that ensures events outside the United States): www.expo-sure.com.

Chapter 15

EVENT TECHNOLOGY

Computers will never replace humans entirely. Someone has to complain about the errors.

Prosper Eckert, Univac First Computer Architect

IN THIS CHAPTER

We will explore:

- The need for meeting professionals to communicate on a global scale.
- Telephone and related communication options available in other countries.
- Computer software and Web sites and their use in event management.
- New developments in meeting technology at home and abroad.
- The role of audiovisual technology in meetings and events.
- How video standards vary worldwide and their impact on audiovisuals in program support.
- Understanding the impact of culture on the production of audiovisual media for events.

What does technology mean to the meetings industry? It enables and strengthens the meeting as a medium for disseminating information, often in competition with other media. What does technology mean to the meeting professional? In today's complex world, it means more efficient planning, more dependable implementation, greater mobility, the ability to disseminate information efficiently, and the benefits of reliable global communication. To meeting participants, technology offers the opportunity to conduct business affairs while attending an event and, conversely, subject to some caveats, to participate in the meeting without leaving their homes or places of employment.

▌COMMUNICATING ON A GLOBAL SCALE

Meeting professionals and participants alike have a profound need to communicate, often across great distances. Technology has made it possible to send messages and data from place to place with relative ease, even in remote parts of the world. Text messaging, satellite relay, instant messages, cellular phones, e-mail, and data transmission are as much a part of business communications today as the telephone, telex, and typewriter were in the twentieth century.

In a typical two-month period, a meeting professional may spend a week in Kyoto setting up a world congress, stop off in Manila for a site inspection, attend an industry tradeshow in Las Vegas, manage a sales meeting in Toronto, and speak at a symposium on meetings in Puerto Vallarta. Similarly, delegates attending international events find it essential to maintain contact with clients, family, friends, and associates. For them and for those who provide the facilities, transportation, and services they require, recent developments in telecommunication are more than milestones in technological advances; they are essential tools that enable them to perform efficiently.

Kurt, the manager of conferences for a multinational corporation, finds many ways to keep in touch. He can place phone calls from a plane, review messages "pushed" to his Blackberry personal data assistant, and obtain approval proofs of a promotional piece in three languages via fax or e-mail.

A professional congress organizer, Luciana, uses a laptop computer to develop elements of the Meeting Prospectus and confirmation letters while on a premeeting coordination trip in Monaco. Her satellite phone enables her to transmit the material to her staff in Milan and receive additional input from her client.

CALLING HOME

In most developed countries, people who travel are able to stay in constant communication thanks to the cellular telephone networks that dominate the globe. Specialized equipment allows cellular systems to offer data access and fax transmission in addition to voice communication. Britain's PCN (Personal Communication Network), which went online in the 1990s, provides users of lightweight pocket-size telephones with a number assigned to the user rather than the instrument.

Most hotels today offer business travelers guest-room telephones equipped with the RJ-11 port, which permits the user to hook up a modem or a portable fax. Some have high-speed connections in guest and meeting rooms via a CAT-5 networking cable. Thomas Cook Express enables clients to make airline reservations by using ordinary touch-tone telephones.

Keeping pace with the need for mobile communications, the sky phone, which has long been standard on most transcontinental flights in North America, can be found on international airlines in Europe and Asia. Several carriers have added seat phones, and SkyTel has expanded its services to include pagers and voice messaging.

British Airways offers rental pagers and cell phones to international passengers. SAS has gone it one better and makes word-processing equipment available to its business-class passengers at no cost. A number of airlines have added the convenience of in-flight data ports and improvements in air-to-ground communications.

The convenience of all this electronic wizardry has not come without cost. Even before all the new toys began appearing, travelers were becoming alarmed at the excessive surcharges added by hotels for local and long-distance telephone calls. In the United States, the emergence of the Alternative Operator System (AOS) in the early 1990s offered hotels and restaurants a handsome revenue source, with the unwary traveler footing the inflated bill. In other countries, government-owned telephone systems, usually under the postal authorities, impose high taxes on telecommunications.

Faced with customer resentment, several international hotel chains have taken steps to ameliorate the situation. Stouffer Hotels and Resorts took the lead by eliminating surcharges on credit card 800 calls and faxes and limiting the charges on all other calls. Other hotels that tried AOS have gone back to traditional telephone providers.

An innovative solution to the perceived telephone rate abuses was organized by AT&T under the name Teleplan Plus, which enabled hotels in Europe to offer their guests AT&T service for calls to the United States and Canada. Member hotels agree to limit surcharges in exchange for promotional assistance from AT&T. They also agree to provide a choice of calling methods and inform guests of the availability of that service.

Another feature popular with callers worldwide who place frequent calls to North America is USADirect Service. Linked with AT&T's calling card, USADirect puts travelers in direct contact with an AT&T international operator. Callers to the United States also can take advantage of discount rate periods and avoid surcharges. Access numbers change, and new access numbers are added as the number of telephone providers increases worldwide. Check ww.usa.att.cpm/traveler/index.jsp for current listings.

In a similar vein, hotel chains such as Ciga, Hilton International, Inter-Continental, and Steigenberger are showing increased sensitivity to the needs of delegates and business travelers from other countries. In addition to surcharge-free calls, many offer their growing international clientele fax and data transmission as well as voice mail in their own language.

More and more hotels, airlines, and car rental companies are recognizing the needs of the business travel market for fast, mobile, and cost-effective communications on a global scale and are making a commitment to provide those services.

COMPUTER SOFTWARE

Technology is not a static commodity. It is fluctuating, and the meetings industry's need to manipulate data to fit different needs is dynamic and subject to change.

That is a caveat that should precede any discussion of or articles on computer software. As the dynamics of event management continuously evolve and mutate, the tools we utilize must keep pace. Nowhere is this more evident than in the management of global events. Even as data on available software changed while this book was being researched, it is very likely that some of the information given here will be obsolete a year from the book's publication. Presumably, the various software programs described here will be modified to keep pace. Dynamics notwithstanding, the function of data management is relatively constant. A full-featured meeting management software product ideally automates many of the administrative and logistic functions associated with managing events of all kinds. To appreciate how event management software can best serve those who are responsible for managing international events, let us trace the various meeting functions chronologically.

The use of computer software starts with laying out a timetable for the meeting. Ideally, the program should have the ability to generate a diagram that traces the key planning phases on a time line, identifies the tasks and deadlines associated with each phase, and tracks progress, alerting the user to daily tasks in order of priority.

Once the meeting parameters have been set and a timetable has been established, the next task for the computer is site selection. Web sites for destinations throughout the world are all computer-accessible, as are venue listings now appearing on CDs and DVDs. Most enable users to take virtual tours that allow them to view guest rooms and recreational amenities and evaluate meeting rooms and exhibit halls. Some of the more advanced allow the viewer to diagram ideal seating arrangements, staging, projection, and exhibit floor plans.

A TYPICAL APPLICATION

A substantial percentage of a meeting professional's function relates to registration procedures and financial management. As a minimum, PC-based and Web-based registration programs should offer the following elements:

- Flexible event and session registration
- Accommodations and itinerary tracking
- Speaker and exhibitor assignment
- Confirmation letters and mailing labels
- Typeset high-quality name badges and signs
- Delegate lists, session and event counts, and other reports
- Budget and financial summaries

At this point a document, variously called the meeting plan or the staging guide, begins to take shape. Although many planners prefer the familiar printed text, generating the various elements of the plan—checklists, function forms, budget reports, rosters, correspondence, contracts, and so on—is a task for the computer. Today's electronic palmtop organizers and laptops are equal to the task and offer voice, fax, and e-mail communication as well.

Also around this time business, educational, and social agendas must be generated. The software must be up to the task, scheduling a variety of program elements—particularly concurrent sessions—and the physical and logistic elements that pertain to each, such as room assignments, speaker designations, and audiovisual support.

As delegate responses begin to arrive, the data are entered into a registration data bank. Information from the conference registration form will enable organizers to create reports summarizing, among other things, attendance analyses, alphabetical rosters by category (delegate, spouse, speaker, exhibitor, etc.), and nationality. These menus also generate confirmation letters, payment receipts, selected seminar schedules, name badges, and seminar rosters. The program should enable users to assess the effectiveness of their mailing list.

The same software allows users to track and confirm accommodations, function space, and travel arrangements, where applicable. Unless hotel reservations are made directly with the hotel or via a housing bureau, the database should be capable of generating rooming lists and confirmations. If travel arrangements are made through an official airline, the data can be exported to provide arrival and departure times and flights. These things are especially helpful as a confirmation of hotel reservation dates and meal guarantees and for organizing airport reception.

A flexible event management program takes much of the effort out of function controls. All meeting elements, from conference headquarters and registration area, through educational sessions and social events, to the final banquet and departure, are assigned a function number. Conference programs, event orders, and instructions for support requirements are generated from this master résumé.

Automated tasks are assigned to on-site operations, beginning with an agenda for the preconference meeting with the facility staff and ending with postconference evaluations and the settlement of accounts. In between, the system enables the meeting executive and staff to anticipate and manage the myriad details involved in even a small conference. Serving as a master checklist, it schedules tasks related to all staff functions and events, highlights uncompleted tasks, and checks for conflicting activities.

Industry Web sites and some of the globally oriented software currently available for the foregoing tasks are listed in Appendix 2.

TECHNOLOGY TOOLS

Beyond automating the various elements of planning and managing events, computer technology is having a great impact on the industry. It is influencing not only the mechanics of the meeting but the dynamics as well. Today one finds computer-generated graphics, multimedia presentations, and interactive response systems as an intrinsic part of many conference programs, especially plenary sessions. Even in smaller breakout sessions held at technologically advanced venues, one expects to find a laptop computer combined with a projection system replacing the ubiquitous slide projector and giving the presenter far greater flexibility than ever before. We are finding purpose-built conference rooms in which each participant has access to a computer, an exponential leap forward pioneered by the Heathrow Conference Center 25 years ago.

Hotels in Asia and Europe that cater to business travelers as well as exhibit halls in key destinations are going beyond high-speed Internet access and offering wireless access. There are some caveats with wi-fi, however. The first is limited capacity; it may use the same bandwidths as cell phones and pagers. That factor also influences security, which is limited. Some of the more progressive hotels that cater to meetings are offering meeting executives and attendees in-room state-of-the-art desktop computer systems.

The ubiquitous name badge has undergone a metamorphosis thanks to the microchip. Radio frequency identification (RFID) enables the system to identify and track the wearer. What may seem invasive at first glance can be a benefit to the wearer, enabling instant location in case of an emergency and immediate notification of messages. For the event sponsor, it serves to document attendance at each event and verify visitor count and booth traffic at exhibitions. Developers are working on the privacy issue with an implanted chip that enables the wearer to turn off the tracking function.

WEB CONFERENCING

Webcasts can serve as a safe alternative for sensitive, high-profile events such as global business meetings that are subject to protest and political intimidation. When unruly mobs threatened to disrupt the World Bank's Conference on Development Economics, the Washington-based organization opted for a webcast. Registrants were encouraged to e-mail their questions before and during the webcast, and presenters were videotaped at a studio whose location was kept secret. An added benefit of this Web-based conference was that instead of the 300 participants who normally attended, the conference drew an audience of 1,800 viewers from more than 100 countries.

WIRELESS CONNECTIVITY

After beginning as a convenience in North America, wi-fi has been gaining worldwide acceptance. The need to communicate effectively without telephone terminals or wall sockets has generated a broad range of wireless options.

Driven by radio-wave technology, miniaturization, and wireless networks, manufacturers worldwide are providing a steady stream of new equipment for personal and business use. For meeting or exhibit applications, wireless systems simplify setup and allow better performance at lower cost. In fact, facilities often waive fees for wi-fi usage as an incentive.

▌AUDIOVISUALS AT MEETINGS ABROAD

You wouldn't think that meeting veterans who have faced virtually every AV problem at their domestic meetings, from blown projector lamps to scratches on their DVDs, would face taking their programs abroad with trepidation. However, some are reluctant to venture into what they consider uncharted waters simply because they don't understand the differences and don't know where to find out. The following pointers should clear up some of the perceived mystique.

Meeting professionals who organize events that utilize extensive audiovisuals often are faced with the dilemma of shipping equipment or renting it on-site. The decision may be complicated by variations in standards and electric current. On-site rental of audiovisual equipment may need to be outsourced, depending on the hotel's audiovisual inventory, to a local AV supplier. However, conference centers and the newer conference hotels in most meeting venues tend to have extensive audiovisual apparatus that often rivals that found in North American cities.

Professional standards and levels of expertise vary widely from one country to another, just as they do from site to site in domestic venues. The in-house AV contractor you have come to expect in the United States and Canada is relatively rare in some parts of the world. Except for conference centers, in most overseas venues you will be dealing with an audiovisual rental (hire) firm, though there may be a house engineer or other staff members who are AV-literate. The supervisory staff will be multilingual, but don't expect bilingual stagehands, camera operators, and projectionists.

Meeting rooms vary widely in other parts of the world. Older hotels with their grand ballrooms boast elaborate chandeliers that interfere with projection and unusual shapes and pillars that make seating arrangements a problem. Meeting professionals look for a meeting environment free of those obstructions. As in domestic venues, the ideal configuration is a room that has a length at least twice its width and that permits adequate seating with side aisles. Allowance needs to be made for staging, screen placement, and sight lines if projected visuals are used (see Figure 15-1).

PRODUCTION MEDIA

Comparable in sophistication and quality, AV media are different around the globe; 16-mm film is a universal standard, and overhead and slide projectors are still in limited use in some venues. Sound equipment—microphones, speakers, mixers, and the like—is pretty much the same the world over.

Presenters who use slides—a few still do—should be cautioned that although 35-mm double-frame slides are universal, the projection trays in which they are housed are different. The standard carousel tray will not fit on a European Kodak SAV projector.

Multi-imaging is used widely throughout the world, employing state-of-the-art video media such as DVDs and streaming video. However, you will

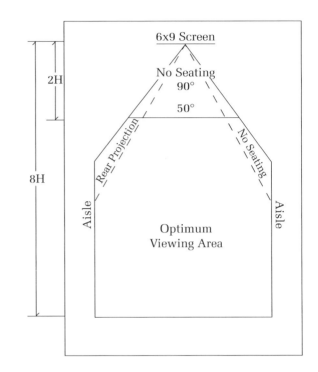

Figure 15-1 Seating for AV
Projection

face some disparities in video standards. Television monitors, cameras, and tape and DVD players are manufactured to different video specifications that may not be compatible with your software. There is more on this later in this chapter.

NTSC, the Japanese and North American standard for video, is not compatible with the PAL formats found in most of Europe, Australia, parts of Africa, and Southeast Asia nor with the SECAM system used in France, Germany, Russia, and much of the Middle East.

To show a video program in a country with a different standard, the video must be converted to the appropriate format. If video is to be used, determine the standard in the host country and then locate a production company that can make the conversion. Since DVDs and some variations of a digital medium seem destined to be the primary technology for the near future, it may be informative to expand on this topic.

Andrew Wright of Premier Images, a prominent business video producer based in Oakland, California, explains: "When authoring a DVD, producers are able to allow or lock playback of the disk in certain regions of the world. Players and computers are sold with region numbers, so they can only play a DVD with a matching region code. A DVD purchased in the United States may not play anywhere else. The rationale for these restrictions is that motion picture studios want to control the home release of movies in different countries. Theatrical releases aren't simultaneous (a movie may come out on video in the United States when it's just hitting screens in Europe)."

Wright points out that studios sell distribution rights to different foreign distributors and need to guarantee an exclusive market. Therefore, they require that the DVD standard include codes that can be used to prevent playback of certain discs in specific geographic regions. Each player is given a code for the region in which it is sold, and discs that are not coded for a region cannot be played. The bottom line is that a disc bought in one country may not play on a player in another country.

VIDEO STANDARDS

There are eight regions ("locales"), each of which is assigned a number. Players and discs often are identified by the region number superimposed on a world globe. If a disc plays in more than one region, it will have more than one number on the globe:

1. United States, Canada, U.S. territories
2. Japan, Europe, South Africa, and Middle East (including Egypt)
3. Southeast Asia and East Asia (including Hong Kong)
4. Australia, New Zealand, Pacific islands, Central America, Mexico, South America, and the Caribbean
5. Eastern Europe, Russia, Indian subcontinent, Africa, North Korea, and Mongolia
6. China
7. Reserved
8. Special international venues (airplanes, cruise ships, etc.)

"The good news," says Wright, "is that North American nontheatrical production firms authoring a DVD for a client can encode it for all regions so that it will play anywhere—but it still needs to be in the correct format."

(*Background note:* It's relatively easy to shoot NTSC and convert it to PAL during the editing process.)

MEDIA PRODUCTION FOR MULTICULTURAL AUDIENCES

In some cases, program sound elements recorded in English may cause problems in comprehension by foreign attendees even when simultaneous interpretation is provided. Translation of the narrative track and playback in multiple languages is the best solution. Discriminate sound tracks on film, audio/videotape, and DVD (you can rent a movie and listen in English, Spanish or French) make this option feasible at the presentation phase. However, before you reach that stage, the following principles should be part of your planning during production:

- Have the English script translated by professionals who are native to each country.
- Verify the translation with people familiar with the vernacular.
- Avoid abstract concepts in the script unless they can be conveyed symbolically. Keep in mind that other cultures interpret symbols and even colors differently.
- Keep words to a minimum on text and title visuals.
- Use generic visuals that focus on pictures, numbers, and universal symbols.
- If English is the conference language, be sure the narrator avoids slang and idiomatic language. (This is also true of narration to be translated.)

These technical considerations should not deter you from incorporating recorded visual imagery and sound in an international meeting. On the contrary, music and visuals can be powerful aids in establishing effective communications and ensuring comprehension.

What tomorrow will bring is only conjecture. Computer teleconferences? Certainly. Holographic three-dimensional image projection in which conferees are projected around a table at a distant location? Possibly; the technology already exists, as seen in the final *Star Wars* episode *Revenge of the Sith*. However, there is some reassurance for technophobes. Technology may have a major impact on meetings, but high tech will not replace what the futurist John Naisbit calls "high touch": the need for people to interact on a personal level. It is in automating the labor of planning and managing events that technology holds the greatest promise.

Your future, whether it is high tech, high touch or both, will most certainly be expanded and enriched as you plan your meetings, conventions and exhibitions around the world. The authors hope that you will continue to use this book as a reference and best practices guide along the exciting career path you have chosen. It is a rewarding and worthwhile journey and we wish you *bon voyage, au revoir* and good luck!

KEY POINTS

Communicating between Borders

Staying connected internationally may be accomplished by using cell phones, high-speed lines, air phones during flight, calling cards, and business rooms at hotels.

Meeting Software

Meeting planning computer software allows a planner to make itineraries, make reservations, register people, and make financials and budgets.

Global Connectivity

Wireless connectivity, Web conferencing, and radio frequency identification are keeping business travelers connected. It is essential to have these services available to professionals during an international meeting.

AV Support

When you are planning audiovisual, ensure equipment and media compatibility and be certain that DVDs and the software are formatted correctly.

Multicultural Media

Be sure to consider cultural differences in translating English-language videos and DVDs into the represented tongues. Avoid slang and jargon.

PASSPORT

Books

Ball, Corbin, *Ultimate Technology Guide for Meeting Professionals* (e-book), www.mpifoundation.org.

Wright, Rudy R., and E.J. Siwek, *The Meeting Spectrum,* HRD Press, Amherst, MA, 2005.

Appendix 1

MAJOR MEETING INDUSTRY ASSOCIATIONS AND ORGANIZATIONS

- **American Society of Association Executives (ASAE)** has an international department to support association executives and their suppliers who are operating globally; maintains relations with 13 other societies of association executives worldwide. In Washington, DC, (202) 371-0940, www.asaenet.org.
- **Asian Association of Convention and Visitor Bureaus (AACVB)** provides information and contacts in Asia. Contact the association c/o Macau Government Tourist Office, Gomes, Macau, (853) 798-4156/57, www.aacvb.org.
- **British Association of Conference Destinations** represents eighty conference destinations and more than 3,000 venues throughout the British Isles. Provides venue location service, news, conference support, and education and training. In Birmingham, UK, (44) 0 121 212 1400, www.bacd.org.uk.
- **Convention Industry Council (CIC)** represents more than thirty national and international organizations in the meetings, conventions, exhibitions, and travel and tourism industries. Certified Meeting Professional program offered in Europe and Asia. McLean, VA, (703) 610-9030, www.conventionindustry.org.
- **Destination Marketing Association International (DMAI),** formerly International Association of Convention and Visitors Bureaus, publishes a directory listing 1,000 cities and member bureaus around the world, (202) 296-7888; www.iacvb.org; CVB Directory www.officialtravelguide.com.
- **European Federation of Conference Towns (EFCT)** provides many services to U.S. meeting planners. Has a directory of more than 100 European convention destinations in thirty-four countries that can handle 300 or more delegates. Based in Brussels, Belgium. (32) 2 732 69 54; www.efct.com.
- **International Congress & Convention Association (ICCA)** about 600 members in 80 countries representing specialists in handling, transporting, and accommodating international events; extensive database on more than 7,300 international meetings; in Amsterdam, Netherlands, (31) 20 398 1919, www.iccaworld.com.
- **International Association of Congress Centres (AIPC)** publishes AIPC and ICCA "General Conditions for Contracts with Congress Centres," which have been adopted by nearly 200 congress centers worldwide; defines keywords and offers

quality standards for congress, conference, and convention centers worldwide; Brussels, Belgium, (32) 2 534 59 53, www.aipc.org.

- **The International Association of Professional Congress Organizers (IAPCO)** can put you in touch with member PCOs in specific countries; IAPCO Secretariat, in London, (44) 20 87496171, www.iapco.org.
- **The International Special Event Society (ISES)** can put you in touch with event planners and a wide variety of event suppliers (caterers, decorators, entertainers, etc.) in many countries throughout the world. (800) 688-ISES (4737) or www.ises.com
- **Meeting Professionals International (MPI)** offers a global network of colleagues, continuing education, and a resource center that sells literature; maintains a European and a Canadian office; in Dallas, (972) 702-3000, www.mpiweb.org.
- **Meetings & Events Australia** 1,600 members in Australia and the Asia/Pacific region; P.O. Box 1477, Neutral Bay NSW 2089, Australia, (61) 2 9904 9922, www.miaanet.com.au.
- **The Professional Convention Management Association (PCMA)** continuing education on international meeting planning; in Chicago, (877) 827-7262, (312) 423-7262, www.pcma.org.
- **The Society of Incentive & Travel Executives (SITE)** educational conferences and workshops on international business challenges; constituents in key international destinations can be consulted or linked into a developing incentive program; in Chicago, (312) 321-5148, www.site-intl.org.

Resources above excerpted from the 2005 Beyond Borders Resource Guide and reprinted with permission from **Beyond Borders 2005,** *an Annual Guide to Taking Your Meeting Outside the USA, June 2005. A supplement to Corporate Meetings & Incentives, Association Meetings, Medical Meetings, Insurance Conference Planner, and Religious Conference Manager, published by The Meetings Group, www.meetingsnet.com.*

- **Confederación de Entidades Organizadores de Congresos y Afines de America Latina (COCAL)** Ibero-American regional professional association of PCOs from Argentina, Brazil, Colombia, Costa Rica, Cuba, Guatemala, Mexico, Paraguay, Peru, Uruguay, Venezuela and Spain, www.cocalonline.com

▌TRADE SHOWS

AIME (Asia/Pacific Incentives & Meeting Expo) – www.aime.com.au
EIBTM (European Incentive Business Travel and Meetings Exposition) – www.eibtm.com
IMEX – www.imex-frankfurt.com
THE MOTIVATION SHOW – www.themotivationshow.com

Appendix 2

MEETING SOFTWARE AND SERVICES

Product Category	Company	Web Site	Product Name or Description
Association Management	1st Priority Software, Inc.	www.1stprioritysoftware.com	Membrosia
Association Management	Amlink Technologies USA	www.amlinkevents.com	EventsPro
Association Management	AVECTRA	www.avectra.com	TASS—The Association Software System
Association Management	EKEBA International	www.ekeba.com	Complete Event Manager
Association Management	Peopleware, Inc.	www.peopleware.com	PeoplewarePro
Audio Conferencing	Conference Archives Inc.	www.conferencearchives.com	ConferenceOnDemand
Audio Conferencing	Connex International	www.connexintl.com	Connex International
Badge Making	Avery Dennison	www.avery.com	LabelPro
Badge Making	PhotoBadge.com	www.photobadge.com	Asure ID Enterprise Edition
Badge Making	The Laser's Edge	www.badgepro.com	BadgePRO Plus
Communications	Association Network	www.theassociationnetwork.com	Event Express
Communications	Digitell Inc.	www.digitellinc.com	iPlan2Go
Communications	ExpoSoft Solutions Inc.	www.exposoft.net	Product/Exhibitor Locator
Communications	FLASHpoint Technologies LLC	www.flashpointtech.com	FLASHfire Chats
Communications	Rockpointe Broadcasting Corp.	www.rockpointe.com	Video Conferencing
Communications	Tradeshow Multimedia (TMI)	www.tmiexpos.com	ShowMail—The Internet Message Center
Communications	WebEx Communications	www.webex.com	iPresentation Suite 4.0
Consultants/Speakers	Meeting U.	www.meeting-u.com	Speaker/Trainer
Consultants/Speakers	Meetingworks	www.meetingworks.com	Services
Convention and Visitors Bureau Management	Newmarket International	www.newmarketinc.com	NetMetro Bureaus
Data Management	EventMaker Online	www.eventmakeronline.com	EventMaker
Data Management	Laser Registration	www.laser-registration.com	RegBrowser
Data Management	The Conference Exchange	www.confex.com	Online Abstract System
E-Learning	E-Conference, Inc.	www.e-conference.com	E-Conference, Inc.
E-Learning	PlaceWare, Inc.	main.placeware.com	PlaceWare Meeting Center 2000
E-Marketing	Cvent	www.cvent.com	Cvent
E-Marketing	ShowSite	www.showsitesolution.com	Interactive Event and ShowXpress
E-Marketing	thesmartpicture.com	www.thesmartpicture.com	Smart Picture for Events
Facility Management	CEO Software, Inc.	www.ceosoft.com	Scheduler Plus 2001
Facility Management	EventBooking.com	www.eventbooking.com	EventBooking
Facility Management	Network Simplicity	www.netsimplicity.com	Meeting Room Manager 2002
Facility Management	Resource Information & Control	www.riccorp.com	ConCentRIC'S

Category	Company	Website	Product/Service
Global Web Portal	Comworld	www.comworld.net	Global events/sevices website
Groupware	Group Systems.com	www.groupsystems.com	Meeting Room, GSOnline
Housing	PASSKEY.COM, Inc.	www.passkey.com	Passkey.com ResDesk
Housing	ConventionNet	www.conventionnet.com	Visitor Housing
Housing	Pegasus Solutions Companies	www.pegs.com	Wyndtrac, LLC
Housing	Software Management, Inc.	www.softwaremgt.com	Housing 3000
Incentive Management	TimeSaver Software	www.timesaversoftware.com	Golf Trend Analyzer
Marketing	Data Tech SmartSoft Inc.	www.smartsoftusa.com	Veri-A-Code
Meeting Management	123signup.com	www.123signup.com	123Signup Event Manager
Meeting Management	Dean Evans & Associates	www.dea.com	EMS Professional, Virtual EM
Meeting Management	Ambassadors International	www.ambassadors.com	Enterprise Event Solution 3.0
Meeting Management	gomembers inc.	www.gomembers.com	MeetingTrak
Meeting Management	Impact Solutions, Inc.	www.impactsolutions.com	MaxEvent
Meeting Management	ISIS Corp.	www.isisgold.com	ISIS Gold
Meeting Management	Meeting Expectations	www.meetingexpectations.com	Site Selection Services
Meeting Management	PC/NAMETAG	www.pcnametag.com	PC/Nametag Pro
Meeting Management	RegOnline	www.regonline.com	RegOnline Online Event Registration
Meeting Management	EventPro Software	www.eventpro-planner.com	EventPro Planner1D17
Program Content	Conf. Reports & Internet Services	www.conferencereports.com	Conference Reports and Internet Services
Registration	seeUthere Technologies	www.seeuthere.com	seeUthere Enterprise
Registration	b-there, a unit of Starcite, Inc	www.b-there.com	b-there.com ERS (Event Registration System)
Registration	EventRegistration.com	www.eventregistration.com	The Event Assistant
Registration	International Conference Mgmt.	www.conference.com	Credit Card Manager
Registration	MeetingWare International, Inc	www.meetingware.com	MeetingWare Registration
Registration	Worldwide Registration Systems	www.wwrs.net	Online Web-based registration
Resource Guide	Incentives & Meetings Intl.	www.i-mi.com	International venues
Resource Guide	Expoworld.net Ltd	www.expoworld.net	ExpoWorld.net
Resource Guide	Official Meeting Facilities Guide	www.omfg.com	OMFG.COM
Resource Guide	Bedouk International	www.bedouk.com	International venues
Room Diagramming	Event Software Corp.	www.eventsoft.com	3D Event Designer

Product Category	Company	Web Site	Product Name or Description
Room Diagramming	Applied Computer Technology	www.expocad.com	Expocad VR2
Scheduling	Atlantic Decisions	www.ad-usa.com	Conference Room Manager
Scheduling	Meeting Maker, Inc.	meetingmaker6.com	MeetingMaker 6
Site Selection	BusinessMeetings.com Ltd.	www.businessmeetings.com	BusinessMeetings.com
Site Selection	MADSearch International, Inc.	www.madsearch.com	MADSearch.com
Site Selection	MeetingLocations.com	www.meetinglocations.com	Online Facility Search Database
Site Selection	HotelsOnline Directory	www.hotelsonline.com	HotelsOnline
Site Selection	Industry Meetings Network	www.industrymeetings.com	ProposalExpress
Site Selection	Market Stream, LLC	www.marketstream.com	STARdates
Site Selection	MeetingMakers	www.meetingmakers.com	MeetingMakers
Site Selection	MPBID.COM	www.mpbid.com	The Hotel Rooms Exchange
Site Selection	Starcite	www.starcite.com	Global Site Selection & Resources
Site Selection	Unique Venues	www.uniquevenues.com	Meeting Services Website
Speaker Management	Walters Speaker Services	www.walters-intl.com	Speakers
Speaker Management	World Class Speakers/Entertainers	www.speak.com	Speakers
Surveys	Scantron Service Group	www.scantronservicegroup.com	Scanning
Surveys	Principia Products, Inc.	www.principiaproducts.com	Remark Office OMR, version 5.0
Surveys	SurveyConnect	www.surveyconnect.com	Survey Select Expert
Surveys	TRAQ-IT	www.traqit.com	TRAQ-IT
Surveys	Autodata Systems	www.autodata.com	Survey Plus 2000
Surveys	Creative Research Systems	www.surveysystem.com	The Survey System
Surveys	MarketTools, Inc.	www.markettools.com	Zoomerang
Surveys	Research Systems	www.surveyview.com	Surveyview
Trade Show Management	Acteva, Inc.	www.acteva.com	ExpoManager
Trade Show Management	HEMKO Systems Corp.	www.hemkosys.com	EMS—Exhibition Management System
Trade Show Management	iTradeFair	www.itradefair.com	Interactive Online Venues (IOV) software
Trade Show Management	Netronix Corporation	www.eshow2000.com	eshow2000
Travel Management	Double Eagle Services	www.doubleeagleservicesinc.com	TourTrak
Travel Management	GetThere.com	www.getthere.com	DirectMobile
Travel Management	Tr-IPS Services	www.Tr-IPS.com	Tr-IPS
Video Production	Premier Images	www.video11.com	Meeting/Exhibition Continuity

Category	Company	Website	Product
Virtual Trade Shows	Unisfair	www.unisfair.com	GMEP—Global Mass Event Platform
Web Conferencing	1st Virtual Communications	www.fvc.com	CUseeMe
Web Conferencing	Avistar	www.avistar.com	Avistar
Web Conferencing	Communicast.com	www.communicast.com	Communicast
Web Conferencing	ConferZone	www.conferzone.com	E-conferencing
Web Conferencing	EventCom by Marriott	www.marriott.com/eventcom	Global conferencing
Web Conferencing	HealthAnswers, Inc.	www.healthanswersinc.com	Conference.CAST
Web Conferencing	iShow.com	www.ishow.com	iShow.com
Web Conferencing	Latitude Communications	www.latitude.com	Meeting Place
Web Conferencing	MindBlazer	www.mindblazer.com	MindBlazer
Web Conferencing	Netspoke	www.netspoke.com	iMeet, Inc.
Web Conferencing	Premiere Conferencing	www.premconf.com	Premiere Conferencing
Web Conferencing	WebEx Communications	www.webex.com	Multimedia communications
Web Conferencing	Winnov	www.winnov.com	Winnov
Web Conferencing	Wire One Technologies, Inc.	www.wireone.com	Wire One Technologies, Inc.
Web-Based Tools	ConventionPlanit	www.conventionplanit.com	Meetings Industry Link
Web-Based Tools	iNetEvents, Inc.	www.iNetEvents.com	iNetEvents Hosted Event
Web-Based Tools	Meetings on the Net	www.meetingsonthenet.com	Meetings on the Net
Web-Based Tools	Plansoft Corporation	www.plansoft.com	Internet Sales Support Solutions (SSS)

Appendix 3

CHECKLISTS

A3.1 GLOBAL MEETING PLANNING CHECKLIST FROM A TO Z

Use this checklist as a guide when you are planning and organizing a meeting outside your home country. Its purpose is to highlight aspects of the planning process that you may take for granted when planning a meeting at home or not be aware of. Some items on this list relate to specific meeting planning activities, and others refer to cross-cultural issues that can have a major impact on the implementation of your program.

This is also a useful checklist for risk management, which is based on an orderly approach to each component of the planning process. Potential difficulties can be identified, anticipated, and addressed. When the meeting will be taking place in an unfamiliar environment where the language, culture, and business practices are not familiar to you or your attendees, the potential "risks" are increased. This exercise is one way to organize your "what if?" scenarios. Add your insights as you discover them.

A
Accessibility
Affordability
Airline service
Appeal to attendees
Allocation of staff resources
Availability of required resources
Audiovisual requirements

B
Backup systems
Broadband availability
Budget caps
Budget cuts

C
Climate
Climate control (heating and
    air-conditioning)
Communications
Concurrent local events
Contingency funds
Contracts
Credit
Credit cards
Crime
Crisis management
Cultural attractions
Culture shock

Currencies
Customs (materials entry)
Customs (social)
Customs brokers

D
"Developing" countries
Destination management companies
Dress
Drugs
Duty-free regulations

E
Economic stability
Electricity
Electronic funds transfer (EFT)
Emergency services
Embassies and consulates
Energy and environmental regulations
Entertainment
Ethnocentrism
Etiquette
Expectations of attendees
Exchange rates
Excursions

F
Facilities for disabled attendees
Food and beverage quality and service
Forward contracts
Freight forwarders

G
Gifts
Gratuities
Ground operations

H
Health care services and facilities
Holidays
Hotel accommodations
Hygiene

I
Immunizations
Insurance
Internet

J
Jingoism
Jokes

K
Kissing

L
Language
Laws
Liability

M
Management and staff time
Marketing
Medical assistance and facilities
Meeting space
Metric system
Money

N
Negotiations
Networking

O
Off-site activities
On-site resources
Options contracts

P
Passports
Political stability
Professional Congress Organizers
Pre- and postevent programs
Promotion
Protocol

Q
Quality assurance
Quality control

R
Recreation
Religion
Rooms (meeting, sleeping)

S
Safety and security
Scheduling
Sex
Shipping
Shopping
Signage
Simultaneous interpretation

Site selection
Site visit(s)
Special events
Sports
Staffing issues
State Department advisories

T
Taxes (VAT, IVA, GST, etc.)
Telephones
Temporary staff
Temptations
Terrorists
Time, concepts of
Time zones
Tipping
Translation
Transportation
Travel costs

U
Unexpected, unforeseen, unheard of

V
Vendors
Venue
Video standards
Visas

W
Welcome materials
Wireless networks

X
Xenophobia
X-ray machines (airports)

▮ A3.2   SITE VISIT CHECKLIST

When	Department	What to Check/Ask/Notice	Information Noted
Before setting off Airport		■ Check what currency is used. ■ Check to see if any countries will will require a visa. ■ Check how many terminals. ■ Is there one terminal for domestic flights and one for international? ■ Check customs; what is the procedure? ■ Check luggage procedure. Do you have to pay to get a luggage cart? ■ Check suitable area for welcome desk, if required.	
Hotel	Accommodation	■ Check standard of rooms (and facilities). ■ Check high-speed Internet availability in sleeping rooms. ■ Check breakdown of room type allocated within reserved block. ■ Check potential added value (e.g., comp rooms and upgrades possible, VIP welcome gifts). ■ Check-in and check-out times and flexibility (occupancy night before group's arrival?).	

When	Department	What to Check/Ask/Notice	Information Noted
		▪ Check specific location of rooms. ▪ Satellite check-in available? Required? ▪ Confirm procedure for room payments (are credit card details required?). ▪ Passport details required? ▪ Storage for luggage, bellmen gratuities. ▪ Room delivery charges if applicable. ▪ Car parking; check if this is required. ▪ Where is breakfast served? Will it be private? ▪ What type of breakfast is served? ▪ Hours of breakfast service? ▪ Can an earlier breakfast be served?	
	Meeting space and breakout rooms	**Check main meeting room:** ▪ Size appropriate to the meeting requirements. ▪ Ceiling height, any obstructions. ▪ Natural daylight, blackout facilities. ▪ Check in-house PA system facilities/microphone provision. ▪ Check staging and lectern provision (microphone? light?). ▪ Check availability of floral decorations for stage area. ▪ Electrical outlets and location of lighting controls. ▪ High-speed Internet connection if required. ▪ Check air-conditioning: controlled in room or elsewhere? ▪ Check location of fire exits. ▪ Check to see what type of lighting is in the room and where the controls are. ▪ Check sight lines. ▪ Check blackout facilities. ▪ Confirm provision of meeting materials/water, etc. ▪ Check access for unloading. ▪ Is any lift equipment available? ▪ Check any potential noise problems.	

When	Department	What to Check/Ask/Notice	Information Noted
		▪ Location of rooms in relation to each other (breakouts/meals).	
		▪ Location in relation to restrooms.	
		▪ Location in relation to public elevators.	
		▪ General standard of décor and cleanliness.	
		▪ Is there three-phase power?	
		▪ Check what linen is used to cover tables.	
		▪ Charges for setup and access.	
		▪ What time do we have to vacate the main meeting room at the end of the conference?	
		▪ Is there an in-house technician on site 24/7?	
		▪ Check the size of the tables to be used.	
		▪ Does a fire marshal have to check and agree about stage and screen placement?	
	Food and beverage	▪ Where are refreshments to be served?	
		▪ What is served in each of the breaks?	
		▪ How many stations will there be?	
		▪ What kind of lunch is served if lunch is included in a delegate rate?	
		▪ Is lunch private?	
		▪ What is the location of lunch with regard to the meeting room?	
		▪ Where will cocktail reception be held, and is this area private?	
		▪ Where are the restrooms?	
		▪ Where is the nearest bar, or is it a portable one?	
		▪ Until what time does the bar stay open in the evening?	
		▪ What time do the public eating outlets close?	
	Audiovisual (AV)	▪ In-house audiovisual company? Is it required?	
		▪ Get a prospectus for the AV company; arrange a suitable time to meet and discuss equipment and setup.	

When	Department	What to Check/Ask/Notice	Information Noted
		▪ Get a breakdown of all the types and makes of equipment to be used.	
		▪ Check that all technicians understand and can speak English, if required.	
		▪ Ask for references from previous clients.	
		▪ Check technician dress code during meeting hours when on the job.	
		▪ Check deposit, payment and cancellation terms.	
	Signage	▪ Does facility have signposts, tripods? Specify what type.	
		▪ Measure lectern for logo if required.	
		▪ What materials do we need to put up the signs?	
		▪ Check that it is acceptable to put signs up around the hotel.	
		▪ Walk from each meeting room to check how much signage is required.	
	General	▪ Check other meetings taking place in the hotel at the same time, especially in the same industry.	
		▪ Check business center facilities and hours of operation.	
		▪ Identify staff operations working office/area as required (location, power points, telephone, etc.).	
		▪ Get the telephone number of a local office supplier.	
		▪ Check equipment: what should be hired, cost, reliability.	
		▪ Deliveries to the venue; confirm procedure.	
		▪ Does the hotel have leisure facilities, and what are hours of operation?	
		▪ Check the operating staffing structure in the hotel: duty manager, night porter, operations manager.	
		▪ Check the usual conditions around the time of the conference.	

When	Department	What to Check/Ask/Notice	Information Noted
		▪ Check if the hotel exchanges currency. If not, where is the nearest ATM?	
		▪ Check power voltage with concierge. Does the hotel have a supply of adapters?	
		▪ Does the hotel have a courtesy bus into town or to the airport?	
Destination management company		▪ Check transfer time from the hotel to airport.	
		▪ Check timings of rush hour traffic.	
		▪ Check transit time from the airport to the hotel.	
		▪ Check whether off site venues have their own caterers or use outside caterers.	
		▪ Check off site venue restroom facilities; how many?	
		▪ Check off site venue access: walking distance, footwear, etc.	
		▪ Does the support staff wear uniforms?	
		▪ Check English proficiency of support staff if required.	
		▪ Get information on other general tours.	
		▪ Check response time for cars not prebooked.	
		▪ Check types of cars used. How many are available?	
		▪ Check that all drivers speak English if required.	
		▪ Check deposit, payment and cancellation terms.	
		▪ Get ideas for room gifts.	
		▪ Obtain sample menus and brochures for all dinner venues.	
Items to collect or bring back		▪ Hotel brochures.	
		▪ Hotel conference pack: relevant details for site visit report.	
		▪ Gift items.	
		▪ Maps of the local area.	
		▪ General information for the local area, leaflets.	
		▪ Postcards (site visit report).	
		▪ Photographs.	
		▪ List of local suppliers and emergency members.	

A3.3 CONFERENCE, MEETING, EVENT SAFETY, AND SECURITY CHECKLIST

Name of Event: _____ Date: _____

Location: _____

Name of Facility: _____

Purpose of Facility: Meeting _____ Conference _____ Party _____ Hotel _____

Trade Show _____ Dinner _____ Convention _____ Special Event _____

Other _____

Address: _____

City: _____ State/Province: _____

Country: _____ Zip/Postal Code: _____

Telephone #: _____ Fax #: _____

Contact Name: _____ Phone #: _____

Security/Safety Contact Name: _____

Security Phone #: _____

Other Information: _____

_____

Date of Site Inspection: _____

_____

Note: Obtain copies of facility floor plan, facility diagrams, room dimensions, local maps, security and safety information, and other venue-related information.

PART I: SAFETY

Some questions require only a yes, no, or not applicable (NA) answer. Longer lines are provided for information that may help you later in the planning stages for that site.

Who from the event staff will be responsible for safety during the event? _____

_____

Emergency Action Plans   **Indicate Yes/No/NA**

1. Does the facility have an emergency action plan?   _____

   What is the date of the plan?   _____

2. Did you review the plan?   _____

Emergency Action Plans   **Indicate Yes/No/NA**

3. Does the plan include current information for:

   Fire _____ Medical _____ Security _____ Evacuation _____

   Contingencies _____ Weather/Acts of God _____ Communication _____

   Emergency contact information _____

4. Are employees trained in the plan response?   _____

   Date the facility last tested the plan _____

Life Safety and Fire

5. Date of the last fire/safety inspection _____

   What agency conducted the inspection? _____

   Did the facility pass the inspection?   _____

6. Are there current and adequate life safety systems?

   and programs throughout the facility(s)?   _____

   Fire sprinkler systems   _____

   Smoke/heat detectors   _____

   Manual fire alarm pull stations   _____

   Emergency exits   _____

   Emergency lighting   _____

   Portable fire extinguishers   _____

7. Date the life safety systems were last tested _____

8. Date the employees were last trained in system response _____

9. Does the system sound a public alarm automatically when
   activated?   _____

10. What actions does the staff take when a fire is reported? _____

11. How is the fire department notified of the alarm?

    Automatically _____ Telephone Call _____ Other _____

12. How is the evacuation of guests with physical impairments managed in emer-

    gencies? _____

13. Are emergency/fire exits properly marked, easily accessible, and in proper work-

    ing order? _____

14. Does the facility have emergency electrical power?   _____

    What does it operate? _____

    How long can it operate? _____

15. Do the elevators have automatic recall to the ground floor in a fire
emergency? _____

16. Do the elevators have emergency instructions and telephones? _____

    Where are the phones answered? _____

17. Is each floor in the stairwells marked with the floor numbers? _____

    Can you access the floor from the stairwell? _____

18. Are stairwells pressurized or ventilated for smoke? _____

Medical

1. What medical services are available at the facility during the event? _____

   _____

2. How are attendees charged for medical services? _____

   _____

3. Is there an in-house doctor for the hotel? _____

4. What is the distance to the closest walk-in medical clinic for nonemergencies?

   _____ miles

   Name: _____

   Address: _____

   Phone #: _____ Hours of operation: _____

5. What is the distance to the closest quality emergency care hospital? _____ miles

   Name: _____

   Address: _____

   Phone # _____

6. Do the demographics of the attendees and the nature of activities
   dictate additional on-site medical personnel/services? _____
   Who is recommended? _____

   Phone #: _____ Cost ($): _____

7. What employees at the facility are trained in CPR and first aid?

   All security personnel? _____

   Wait staff? _____

   Housekeeping? _____

   Maintenance personnel? _____

   Management? _____

8. Are any employees certified as Medical First Responders? _____

Identify departments and shift(s): _____

9. What is the response time for the following emergency services:

	Response Time and Distance		Telephone #
Ambulance	_____	_____	_____
Fire Department	_____	_____	_____
Police	_____	_____	_____
Hospital	NA	_____	_____

Other Safety Issues

1. How will the attendees be informed (welcome/registration packets, opening day briefing, etc.) about basic facility, event, and travel safety tips? _____

2. Are the following appropriately **licensed, insured,** and **experienced** to provide the services requested?

    All modes of transportation? _____

    Special activity vendors (boat, bike, helicopter and jeep tours, snorkeling/scuba diving trips, etc.)? _____

    Facility/special venue? _____

3. Do these vendors have the appropriate type and amount of safety equipment for the activity? _____

4. Does the equipment meet recognized and acceptable safety standards? _____

5. Will the pretrip registration material ascertain any special requirements (medical, disabled assistance, special meals, etc.), and how can you contact a designated person in case of an emergency both at the event and at home? _____

6. Will the program and/or facility be in compliance with the requirements of the Americans with Disabilities Act (ADA)? _____

7. Is the number of attendees being placed on airline flights or ground transportation distributed to avoid too many senior executives, top sales personnel, special guests, and so on, in case of a crisis? _____

8. Will the facility monitor local and international weather during transportation periods during the event? _____

9. Will the staff know what actions should be taken in a storm watch and a storm warning? _____

10. Will the facility provide useful emergency equipment such as a good first-aid kit (aspirin, sinus, stomach, and cold medications, etc.), flashlights, and a cellular phone in the event control room? _____

11. Has the facility determined the history of any acts of nature (earthquakes, hurricanes, floods, tornadoes, severe storms, etc.), fires, safety or environmental incidents, etc., that have affected and/or could affect the venue or program? _____

12. Is the facility prepared to manage the situations listed above? _____

13. Are there any known construction projects before or during the event that would affect transportation, accommodations, or special activities? _____

14. Who on your staff can brief the event staff on how to manage safety and emergency issues? _____

15. Do any event activities (fireworks, overload, etc.) require the local fire department's approval or attendance? _____

16. Are hallways, steps, stairwells, walkways, sidewalks, paths, pool areas, etc., properly maintained and lighted? _____

17. Do swimming pools, beaches, etc., have full-time certified lifeguards and safety equipment rules? Are they well maintained? _____

     What hours are the lifeguards on duty? _____

18. For an international trip, have you identified competent medical facilities and doctors? _____

     Name:_____

     Phone #: _____

19. For an international trip, does it require any special vaccinations, health guidelines, medical supplies, or travel precautions for the attendees? _____

20. For an international trip, are there any unique safety issues or considerations (language, safety standards, medical standards or concerns, evacuations, etc.) for this event, and how will you manage them? _____

     Describe: _____

     _____

     _____

Safety/Health Elements

Number of **NO** answers: _____   Number of **YES** answers: _____

Does the Facility Appear/Feel **SAFE** to you? Yes _____ No _____

Why: _____

On a scale of 1 (low) to 5 (high), how would you rate the overall safety of the facility?

                              1 2 3 4 5

Comments: _____

_____

_____

SECURITY

1. Who from the event staff will be responsible for security during the event? _____

   _____

2. Did you assess the level of security risk at the facility, transportation routes, activity venues, and the surrounding environment you are considering? _____

3. Did you speak with the senior person responsible for security and safety at the hotel/facility to determine the types of problems (crime, demonstrations, fires or related false alarms, labor problems, negative publicity, terrorism, etc.) they have had, are experiencing, or are anticipating? (Don't hesitate to press for specific answers.) _____

   Describe: _____

   _____

   _____

4. Did you contact the local law enforcement agency or other resources to obtain current crime concerns and recommendations for the venue(s) being considered? _____

   Describe: _____

   _____

   _____

5. Does any of this information indicate crime-related problems or concerns that are not acceptable to the programs? _____

6. What action will be taken to eliminate the concerns? _____

   _____

7. Does the nature of the event require special access control procedures such as name badges, company identification, tickets, and unique invitations? _____

8. How will access be managed? _____

9. Will there be different types of identification for staff, vendors, guests, special access authorization, etc.? _____

   Staff: _____ *Special Guest:* _____ *Vendors:* _____

10. Will there be any celebrity or other VIP guest who will require special security arrangements? _____

11. Will the access management process and identification procedure be communicated before the event to all attendees, event staff, security, etc.? _____

12. Will there be cash or high-value gifts for the event? _____

    How will it be protected? _____

13. Have you identified special-use rooms (event control room, gift/ equipment storage, presentation rooms, entertainers/green rooms, etc.) that need limited (rekeyed) access? _____

14. Will any competitor companies, associations, high-profile domestic or foreign government dignitaries, VIPs, or activities disrupt, interrupt, or delay your activities by using this facility before, during, or immediately after your event? _____

Identify: _____

_____

_____

_____

15. How will the facility reduce disruptions to your program? _____

_____

_____

16. Are there any known or possible threats against the company, associations, senior management, guests, or attendees? _____

   Describe: _____

   Who will manage? _____

17. Will proprietary and confidential information or property be on-site? If so, will it require additional security and/or electronic inspections [Technical Surveillance Counter Measures (TSCM sweeps)] and monitoring services? _____

18. If proprietary information is on-site, will a paper shredder that cross-cuts the material into unreadable sizes be available? _____

19. Will a locking container be needed for storing documents and other valuables that cannot or should not be secured in another location? _____

20. Based on the nature of event, the location, or the event program, will attendees be provided with customized written safety, health, and security tips? _____

21. Does the hotel/facility display the event/activities and their rooms on public announcement boards or televisions? _____

22. Are the exteriors of the facility and the parking areas well lighted? _____

   Exterior: _____   *Parking Areas:* _____

23. What hours is the hotel/facility secured during nonbusiness hours or hours of darkness? _____

24. Does security patrol the interior and exterior of the facility? _____

   How often?

   Interior: _____   *Exterior:* _____

HOTEL SECURITY

1. Do the hotel's sleeping rooms provide:

   Deadbolt door locks? _____

   Door viewing device/"peepholes"? _____

   Additional locking devices? _____

   Do all doors (including patio and

   connecting doors) and windows lock and

   work properly? _____

   Is there a posted emergency action plan? _____

   Centrally monitored smoke/fire detectors? _____

   Fire sprinkler system? _____

2. What type of guest-room door key and door lock system is in use?

   Standard Key: ____ Card Access: ____ Other: ____

   Are room numbers marked on the key/card? ____

3. How often are the keys or access card combinations to the room changed? _____

   Date of last change: _____

4. How is guest-room key security maintained at the front desk? _____

   _____

5. How often are guest-room keys inventoried at the front desk? _____

   _____

6. If a hotel guest does not respond to a requested wake-up call, what actions are

   taken? _____

   _____

7. Does the hotel have safe deposit boxes or room safes? _____

   If not, what are your options? _____

Security Personnel

1. Does the facility have security personnel? _____

   Proprietary:_____ Contract:_____ Other:_____

2. How many security officers and supervisors per shift?

   First shift _____ Second shift _____ Third shift _____

3. Are all security personnel certified in CPR/first aid? _____

   What is the date of the last training? _____

4. What other types of security and safety training are conducted? _____

   _____

5. How are fire, medical, weather, and other emergencies handled? _____

_____

6. If extra security personnel are required for the event, who provides them and at what cost?

    Hotel/facility: _____ Contracted company: _____

    Off-duty police: _____ Other: _____

7. Based on the nature of the event, the location, the client, and the attendees, where will security services need to be?

    Totally transparent: _____ Semivisible at specific spots: _____

    Highly visible: _____

8. What performance criteria will you use for good security personnel (*effectively supervised, well trained, competent, mature, helpful, diligent,* etc.), and how will you obtain that performance level?

_____

_____

9. Will you use a special event security contract agreement for contract security personnel? _____

10. Will clearly written security duties and responsibilities be provided to security personnel? _____

    Who will brief them on their duties? _____

11. Will security (or off-duty police) personnel be in uniform? _____

    What type of uniform?

    Blazer and slacks uniform? _____

    Plain clothes? _____

    Official uniform? _____

12. Did you contact your government's international affairs office (U.S. Department of State) and/or in-country/city resources for current security and safety information? _____

    Describe: _____

13. Are there any unique security issues (language, crime, customs, laws, medical emergencies, evacuations, etc.) for this event, and how will you manage them? _____

    Describe: _____

_____

Security Elements

Number of **NO** answers: _____   Number of **YES** answers: _____

Does the Facility Appear/Feel **SECURE** to you? Yes _____ No _____

Why: _____

On a scale of 1 (low) to 5 (high), how would you rate the overall safety of the facility?

1   2   3   4   5

Comments: _____

_____

_____

_____

_____

_____

Communication Systems

1. Who on the event staff will be responsible for communication systems during the event? _____

2. Will the event require rental communications equipment? _____

   Portable radio: _____   How many: _____

   Pagers: _____   How many: _____

   Cellular phones: _____   How many: _____

   Spare equipment: _____   How many: _____

3. Will the equipment clearly work (consider any human-made or natural barriers that may disrupt the signal) in, around, and between the facility and venues (airport, hotel, special activity locations, etc.)?   _____

4. Will each piece of communication equipment be numbered and an inventory maintained of who is assigned the equipment?   _____

5. Will the staff be trained in the effective use of the equipment, and an event staff contact list distributed?   _____

6. Will the attendees be provided (in advance) an event contact card to be given to their offices, family members, trusted neighbors, baby-sitters, etc., in case of an emergency at home?   _____

7. Will the attendees be provided with information on-site that indicates the name of their accommodations, telephone number, address, and how to contact the event staff in an emergency?   _____

8. Will there be an event staff member accessible to the attendees and facility staff at all times?   _____

9. Will you provide the hotel/facility with an event staff on-call list for the front desk, telephone operators, and security? _____

Contingency Planning

1. Who on the event staff will be responsible for contingency planning? _____

_____

2. How would the facility or venue manage problems such as tornadoes, hurricanes, floods, large snow storms, ice storms, severe heat or significant human-made problems (fire, environmental, etc.), and terrorist acts?

   Describe: _____

_____

_____

3. Are you prepared to manage your program in a natural and/or human-made emergency or disaster? _____

4. Will the event staff know the appropriate emergency action procedures and contact numbers and be briefed on how to manage an emergency? _____

5. Will you have accurate and current information for:

   Guest/staff travel arrangements?   _____

   Transportation schedules?   _____

   Guest/staff sleeping room assignments?   _____

   Meeting room assignments?   _____

   Special activities participation?   _____

6. Will you have a method to account for/locate attendees en route, during, and after the event in case of an emergency? _____

7. In an emergency, what will you do if you require an alternative:

   Accommodations?   _____

   Meeting space?   _____

   Transportation?   _____

   Communications?   _____

   Food and beverage?   _____

   Special activities?   _____

8. Do you have an emergency air evacuation plan (medical and nonmedical evacuations)? _____

9. If you have to evacuate the facility, how will you account for each attendee? ____

_____

10. Have you selected one or two specific areas where attendees will gather in an evacuation? _____

_____

11. Do the attendees know which area(s) they are to go to in an evacuation? _____

_____

12. Do you have a system or plan to communicate with or notify the attendees in an emergency?   _____

13. Are you prepared to communicate and work with government emergency service agencies?   _____

14. What emergency communication equipment is available to you? _____

_____

15. Who is the senior event decision maker? _____

16. Who are the senior attendee/public relations representatives? _____

_____

17. Do you have the names and emergency contact numbers for the following:

Doctor(s) _____   Dentist(s) _____

Hospital(s) _____   Accommodation(s) _____

Police _____   Weather _____

Fire _____   Communications _____

Extra security _____   Meeting space _____

Transportation _____   Security consultant _____

Evacuation service(s) _____   Charter jet service(s) _____

Emergency preparedness office (local) _____

State Department/external affairs office(s) _____

Embassy/consulate(s) _____

Other _____

Miscellaneous

1. Does the nature of the event, location, attendees, or value of the property on-site require special or additional insurance for the following:

Medical/health _____ Luggage _____ Liability _____

Transportation _____ Theft _____ Event cancellation _____

2. If corporate, charter, or private aircraft are used, will they require special security arrangements?   _____

3. Do you have the corporate, charter, or private aircraft tail numbers, flight schedule, type of aircraft, and manifest? _____

4. Do you know how to reach the flight crew and private hanger (fixed base operations) 24 hours a day? _____

5. On international trips, do you have immigration and customs requirements for entering and departing the country as well as the requirements when returning home? _____

Total Number of NO/YES Answers

Number of **NO** answers: _____ Number of **YES** answers: _____

Does this facility meet your safety and security needs for this event? _____

Courtesy of Richard P. Werth, CPP

Appendix 4

CRITERIA FOR VENUE SELECTION

DESTINATION CRITERIA

1. Does the city or region have a good range of conference hotels and facilities?
2. Are there adequate direct flights from major gateways and a choice of airlines?
3. Is the area politically stable and compatible?
4. Are climatic and seasonal factors favorable?
5. Are there adequate ground transportation and support services?
6. Does the destination enhance the objectives of the conference?
7. Will attendees be attracted by the destination's assets?
8. Is there a compatible host organization in a related field?
9. Do customs and immigration accommodate foreign travelers?
10. Are overseas liaison offices established in major cities?
11. Does the destination offer a variety of cultural and recreational attractions?
12. Are there restrictions imposed by attendees' governments because of the destination?

FACILITY CRITERIA (HOTEL SITES)

1. Does the hotel have adequate room capacity on the dates required?
2. Are there enough meeting rooms for programs on the dates scheduled? Are they adequate in size, number, and appointments?
3. Is the hotel of a quality consistent with the attendees' expectations?
4. Are room rates within the organization's budget range?
5. Are management and staff trained to handle international conference? (e.g., key staff members multilingual and trained for convention service)?
6. Is the hotel readily accessible from the airport?
7. Can the hotel meet technical requirements in terms of computers, simultaneous interpretation, audiovisual equipment, tables, platforms, and related meeting room needs?
8. Are food and beverage policies and facilities suited to meeting groups?
9. Will there be other meetings that may conflict?
10. Does the hotel have a suitable emergency plan and qualified security staff?

FACILITY CRITERIA (HALLS AND AUDITORIUMS)

1. Is the facility convenient to headquarters hotel(s)?
2. Is key staff well trained and permanent? Multilingual?
3. Are facilities adequate in capacity, size, number, and appointments?
4. Are there adequate provisions for lighting, sound, and technical support?
5. Will outside contractors be required for specialized services?
6. Does the secretariat office have suitable communications, computers, and office equipment?
7. Are simultaneous interpretation booths and systems provided?
8. Does the staging fit needs of the program? Is the stage fully lighted and draped?
9. Are catering facilities available on-site?
10. Are medical, security, and other emergency facilities and trained staff available?

Appendix 5

SAMPLE QUIZ

TEST YOUR GLOBAL MEETING PLANNING IQ

Choose the best answer:

1. Preliminary site information can be obtained from all the following except:
   A. National tourist office (NTO) or convention and visitors bureau (CVB)
   B. Internet
   C. Centers for Disease Control (CDC)
   D. Industry colleagues or coworkers
   E. U.S. Department of State

2. Outside the United States, the equivalent of a destination management company (DMC) is a:
   A. TGV
   B. PCO
   C. VAT
   D. DMC
   E. B and D

3. Hotel contracts in Europe are:
   A. Rarely in English
   B. Nonnegotiable
   C. All the same, according to European Union standards
   D. Identical in format to those found in the United States
   E. None of the above

4. Meeting room charges overseas are:
   A. Usually waived if the room block and food and beverage (F&B) expenses are large enough
   B. Never allowed on the master account
   C. Rarely waived even when room and F&B charges are significant
   D. Discounted only if a twenty-four-hour hold is not required
   E. A and D

5. In Scotland, when you are invited to see the "syndicate rooms," you have been asked to:
   A. Visit the local union hangout
   B. Tour the suites used by visiting labor leaders at their last conclave
   C. Look at breakout meeting space
   D. Check out the action in the casino
   E. Visit the local newspaper offices

6. A 10 percent devaluation of the dollar will:
   A. Add 10 percent profits to your budget
   B. Decrease the amount you owe vendors by 10 percent
   C. Infuriate customs officials
   D. Increase your meeting costs by 10 percent
   E. Provide extra money on site for unexpected emergencies

7. To provide simultaneous interpretation into three languages you must hire:
   A. Three interpreters
   B. Three translators
   C. Six interpreters
   D. Three interpreters and three translators
   E. Six translators

8. SECAM, PAL, and NTSC are:
   A. South American economic treaties
   B. European meeting industry associations
   C. Taxes similar to the VAT and IVA
   D. Herbal stimulants sold over the counter in most Asian countries
   E. Video standards

9. The midday meal in most of Europe and Latin America is:
   A. Not necessarily at midday
   B. The main meal of the day
   C. A light meal easily consumed during a 60-minute lunch hour
   D. A and B
   E. A and C

10. Outside of North America, a "stand" often refers to:
    A. A podium
    B. A position paper
    C. An exhibit booth
    D. A confrontation
    E. A night table

Appendix 6

PROGRAM GUIDELINES FOR GLOBAL MEETINGS

SCHEDULING FLEXIBILITY
    Avoid overprogramming
    Consider time-zone factors
    Offer pre- and postconference options
PROGRAM MATERIALS
LANGUAGE CONSIDERATIONS
    Translation
    Working with interpreters
SESSION FORMATS
    Emphasis on plenary sessions
    Avoid working lunches
    Allow for cultural differences in learning styles
PROVIDE FOR INTERACTION
    Social events
    Informal discussion groups
PREPARE PRESENTERS
    Visual aids
    Distinct, idiom-free language
    Outline or abstract
    Global perspective
    Repeated questions and summarizes
CONFORM TO PROTOCOL
AUDIOVISUAL SUPPORT

Appendix 7

GUIDELINES FOR HOSTING INTERNATIONAL VISITORS

1. Be aware of cultural differences in business etiquette, forms of address, relationships, learning styles, values, eating habits, and protocol.
2. Address visitors by title and family name until invited to use a less formal form. Learn or ask the proper pronunciation and avoid abbreviating given names or the use of nicknames.
3. Avoid slang and colloquial terms and expressions. Shun sports references such as "can't get to first base" and "you play ball with me." Don't use acronyms that may not be understood.
4. Certain English words may mean something else in another culture. Stick to basics.
5. Cultivate a basic understanding of metrics. Most of the world uses metric measurements and Celsius temperature references.
6. Be cautious in using gestures. Some that are prevalent in our culture may be offensive in others. For instance, joining the thumb and forefinger in the "okay" sign means money to the Japanese, zero to the French, and an obscenity to Brazilians and Greeks.
7. Avoid national stereotypes. Just as U.S. regional characteristics and values differ greatly, other countries have widely divergent cultures and subcultures.
8. If you know some social phrases in the visitors' language ("hello," "please," "thank you," etc.), by all means use them. It will make them feel welcome and gratified that you are making the effort. But first be sure to ascertain nationality, especially among Asians.
9. Seek out visitors who speak a language in which you have a degree of fluency and make use of your language skills. The visitors will be appreciative and tolerant of occasional mistakes.
10. If drawn into conversations, avoid political topics and professional sports. Discuss business matters only after you have established a relationship. Family, individual sports, hobbies, and travel are good conversational openers.
11. Personal space varies with cultures. Latin Americans and Middle-Eastern visitors like close proximity during conversation. Most Asians and northern Europeans prefer some distance.

12. Time sensitivity fluctuates with culture. As a rule, people in the northern countries value punctuality and are time-conscious. Those in the southern regions are more casual about time and view a lack of promptness with greater latitude.

13. If you anticipate spending time with a particular visitor, brush up on his or her country's history, geography, culture, and current events. The Web is a great resource for that kind of information.

14. Humor is universal but understanding is not. Funny anecdotes and jokes that are readily understood can be great conversational gambits and enhance relationships.

—Extracted from *Developing Multicultural Competence* by Rudy R. Wright

Appendix 8

GLOSSARY OF INTERNATIONAL FINANCIAL TERMS

Arbitration
Taking advantage of price differences prevailing in different markets for a currency. Works against buy-sell differentials of currencies sold or bought.

Bank draft
A check drawn on a domestic financial institution with a face value expressed in a foreign currency. Is generally subject to the spot price at the time the draft is bought.

Carnet
A "visa" for goods and equipment to enter and exit a country with a bond posted to guarantee that the goods and the equipment will be reexported to avoid duty-free charges at both ends.

Chart points
High or lows established by a currency after each trading day. Used in predicting short-term trends when analyzed over extended period. Also called "trading ranges."

Convertibility
A currency, whether in foreign exchange or bank notes, usually is called convertible if the holder can change it freely to another currency.

Cross-rates
Price levels established between two other world currencies expressed in the domestic currency (e.g., euro versus Swiss francs in pounds sterling). Applies when a trip entails several countries and you wish to convert foreign currency to another currency rather than exchanging it for your own.

Currency options
Options or calls to purchase a foreign currency at a predetermined price during a set period as a "hedge" against currency fluctuations; sold at varying prices.

Dealer position
A risk position that reflects net exposure to a given currency.

Forward rates and transactions
Future purchase of a currency based on its current rate. Useful to lock in a rate for future expense to permit a planner to act upon rates. Can be locked in for two years with a nominal deposit. Not available for all currencies.

Fundamental analysis
Predicting currency trends on the basis of world influences and events.

Future transactions
Similar to forward transactions but more complex. Available on limited currencies through commodity brokers.

Letter of credit (L/C)
A monetary instrument issued by a bank that allows the holder to draw funds against the letter at correspondent banks abroad. Funds are available generally in U.S. dollars or a foreign currency at the spot price at the time the letter is issued.

Long position
A working credit balance in a foreign currency (i.e., your own).

Opening rates
Rates quoted when trading begins for the day. Generally measured in U.S. dollars.

Resistance position
The price level beyond which there is no or limited demand by buyers.

Short position
A working debit balance (i.e., your own).

Spot price
The rate for immediate purchase of currencies in dollars or euros daily or even from minute to minute in a competitive market.

Support point
The price level below which a currency is not readily available to buy.

Swap transactions
Combination of a spot purchase of currency with a simultaneous forward sale or vice versa. Generally uses the forward price.

Technical analysis
The use of chart points, trading volume, and other money market influences to predict currency price movements.

Trading range
The price range in which a currency trades expressed in domestic funds or U.S. dollars. Usually somewhere between resistance and support points.

Value date
The date on which monies must be paid to the parties for spot or current exchange operations. It is the second working day after the date on which the transaction is concluded.

—Courtesy of Jonathan T. Howe, Esq.

Appendix 9

SAMPLE SCHEDULES

A9.1   OVERVIEW OF MEETING SCHEDULE

MARKETING MEETING
Hotel Arts, Barcelona
Overview for Staff

	Thursday 04 October	Friday 05 October	Saturday 06 October	Sunday 07 October
Operations Room	09.00–18.00	07.00–18.00	07.00–18.00	07.00–15.00
Hospitality Desk (Gaudi foyer)		07.45–17.00	07.45–17.30	07.45–13.00
Breakfast	Breakfast 07.00–10.30 Café Veranda	Breakfast 07.00–10.30 Café Veranda	Private Breakfast 07.00–08.30 Pao Casals	Private Breakfast 07.00–08.30 Granados
Morning	Arrivals	Speaker Training I Meeting 08.30–12.30 Gaudi 1	Directors Meeting 08.30–12.15 Gaudi 1 and 2	Speaker Training II Meeting 08.30–13.00 Gaudi 1
Luncheon	Arrivals	Private Buffet Luncheon: 12.15–13.15 Granados	Private Buffet Luncheon: 12.30–13.30 Pao Casals	Private Buffet Luncheon: 12.45–14.00 Granados

Afternoon	Arrivals	Speaker Training I Meeting 13.15–17.00 Gaudi 1	Breakout Groups A/B/C/D 13.30–14.45: Gaudi 1 and 2 E 13.30–14.45: Gaudi 3 *Directors Meeting* Closing Session 15.15–17.30:	Departures
Evening	Group Dinner: La Bona Cuina Restaurant Bus departs at 20.00 *Dress: business casual, no jeans. Please wear comfortable footwear.*	Directors Welcome Reception & Dinner Café Veranda Restaurant Hotel Arts Reception 19.45–20.30 Dinner 20.00 onward *Dress business casual, no jeans*	Speaker Training II Reception & Dinner La Fitora Restaurant 19.45 meet in the hotel lobby *Dress: business casual, no jeans. Please wear comfortable footwear.*	Departures

A9.2 DAY-BY-DAY MEETING SCHEDULE: FERTILITY CONGRESS (SALVADOR DE BAHIA)

DATE/TIME	EVENT	LOCATION	STAFF	COMMENTS
MON 03 MAY				
08:30	Leave for Secretariat	Lobby	Staff	
09:00	Meeting with organizing committee	Secretariat	Staff	Confirms sign-ups on Tues 04
	Registration status for speakers + guests			Letter to PCO authorizing badges/passes
	Parking			for faculty and client personnel access to
	Signs			VIP room for material storage; parking pass.
	Materials storage on Fri 07 May			
10:30–11:00	To airport		JM/PP	
	To hotel		CK/VJ	CK front desk/suite throughout day for check-in; get dinner count
11:30	Smith arrival	Airport	DMC	
12:00	Jones/Black arrival	Airport	DMC/JM/PP	
14:45	White/Brown arrival	Airport	DMC	
19:00	Advance Rincon Gaucho		VJ	Two vegetarian meals, special order
19:30	Leave hotel for Rincon Gaucho	Lobby	CK/JM/PP	
20:00–22:30	Dinner	Rincon Gaucho	CK/JM/PP	
TUE 04 MAY				
09:00	Leave for Congress Center to pick up registration materials	Lobby	CK/VJ	Lists for badges/congress bags/spot for posters Get VIP room key Contact: Teresa/PCO
09:00	Leave for city tour with Jones and Black (others TBD up to 6)	Lobby	JM	Back by 14:00 Other tours TBD
PM TBD	Johnson/Alba return from Itaparica			
12:50	James arrival	Airport	DMC	
14:45 PM	Simon arrival	Airport	DMC	

Time	Activity	Location	Person(s)	Notes
6:00–18:00	Slide review Place posters in Congress Center	Hotel—Rm 648	JM/PP	CK on call for slide review
18:45	Advance Yemenja restaurant		VJ	
19:15	Leave for Yemenja	Lobby	JM/PP	
19:45–22:30	Dinner	Yemenja	JM/PP	Two vegetarian special orders
WED 05 MAY				
06:00 AM	To Congress Center	Lobby	CK/VJ/PP DMC	Transport symposium materials (hand trucks) Store in VIP room 4th floor Send vans back to hotel
07:00	Orientation/placement of hostesses (10) Begin handing out reminders	Convention Center	CK/VJ	Exact location TBD CK/VJ/PP remain in Congress Center
08:00	JM to Congress Center	Lobby		Van remains to bring her back
10:00	JM returns to hotel			
10:30	Set up barrier/tables Box lunches arrive—transport to 3rd flr	Yemenja I Foyer	CK VJ	PP floater
11:00	Faculty transfer to Congress Center	Hotel Lobby	JM	2 vans—remain at CC Bring speakers to 3rd floor
12:30–14:30 PM	Androgen symposium	Yemenja I	All staff	Return transfer to hotel for those who want it
14:45 PM	Ames arrival	Airport	DMC	CK at check-in
16:15	Smith departure	Hotel lobby	DMC/CK	
17:00–18:30	Progesterone symposium slide review	Hotel—Rm 648	CK/JM/PP	
TBD	Congress transfer to Pelourinho		JM/PP	Speakers to have dinner with Congress group—special invitation. JM/PP with clients
THU 06 May				
09:00	Advance boat	Pier	VJ	
09:45–17:00	Boat excursion to Itaparica		VJ/JM/PP/DMC	
14:45	Lewis arrival	Airport	DMC	CK at hotel check-in

DATE/TIME	EVENT	LOCATION	STAFF	COMMENTS
16:00–18:00	Slide review Place posters in Congress Center	Hotel—Rm 648	JM/PP VJ	CK on call for slide review
18:45	Advance Yemenja restaurant		VJ	
19:15	Leave for Yemenja	Lobby	JM/PP	
19:45–22:30	Dinner	Yemenja	JM/PP	Two vegetarian special orders
WED 05 MAY 06:00 AM	To Congress Center	Lobby	CK/VJ/PP DMC	Transport symposium materials (hand trucks) Store in VIP room 4th floor Send vans back to hotel
07:00	Orientation/placement of hostesses (10) Begin handing out reminders	Convention Center	CK/VJ	Exact location TBD CK/VJ/PP remain in Congress Center
08:00	JM to Congress Center	Lobby		Van remains to bring her back
10:00	JM returns to hotel			
10:30	Set up barrier/tables Box lunches arrive—transport to 3rd flr	Yemenja I Foyer	CK VJ	PP floater
11:00	Faculty transfer to Congress Center	Hotel Lobby	JM	2 vans—remain at CC Bring speakers to 3rd floor
12:30–14:30 PM	Androgen symposium	Yemenja I	All staff	Return transfer to hotel for those who want it
14:45 PM	Ames arrival	Airport	DMC	CK at check-in
16:15	Smith departure	Hotel lobby	DMC/CK	
17:00–18:30	Progesterone symposium slide review	Hotel—Rm 648	CK/JM/PP	
TBD	Congress transfer to Pelourinho		JM/PP	Speakers to have dinner with Congress group—special invitation. JM/PP with clients
THU 06 May 09:00	Advance boat	Pier	VJ	
09:45 –17:00	Boat excursion to Itaparica		VJ/JM/PP/DMC	
14:45	Lewis arrival	Airport	DMC	CK at hotel check-in

Time	Activity	Location	Staff	Notes
Evening	TBD—Congress closing banquet			
FRI 07 MAY 06:00	To Congress Center	Lobby	CK/VJ/PP	Transport symposium reminders (hand trucks) Send vans back to hotel
07:00	Placement of hostesses (6) Begin handing out reminders	Convention Center	CK/VJ	
12:30	Set up tables	Yemenja 2 foyer	CK	PP floater
	Transfer meeting guides		VJ	
	Faculty transfer to Congress Center	Hotel lobby	JM	Two vans—remain at CC Bring speakers to 4th floor
14:00 –16:00	Progesterone symposium	Yemenja 2	All staff	Return transfer to hotel for those who want it
16:15 PM	James departure	Lobby	CK	
19:30 PM	Transfer to dinner # TBD	Lobby	JM/PP	Jones/Black Birthday cake for Jones
SAT 08 MAY 12:30	Jones/Black departure	Lobby	Staff/DMC	
14:00	White/Brown departure	Lobby	Staff/DMC	
15:00	Simon departure	Lobby	Staff/DMC	
16:15 PM	Ames departure	Lobby	Staff/DMC	
SUN 09 MAY 06:00	CK/VJ departure	Lobby	DMC	
12:30	JM/PP departure	Lobby	DMC	
13:00	Lewis departure	Lobby	DMC	

Appendix 10

BUDGET WORKSHEET

EVENT:
PARTICIPANTS: **GUESTS:**   **COST PER PERSON:**

▌FIXED EXPENSES

MEETING ROOM RENTALS
STAFF EXPENSES
Transportation (including site visits)
Lodging
PCO/DMC fees
PROGRAM
Speaker fees
Speaker expenses
Program elements
Translation/interpretation
Leisure activities
Entertainment
PRODUCTION AND STAGING
Audiovisual production
AV rental, staff, staging
MARKETING
Production and printing
Web site development
Mailing
SHIPPING
Freight and customs fees
Broker fees
MISCELLANEOUS
CONTINGENCY

Appendix 11

FORMS

A11.1 FORM FOR DEPARTURE RECONFIRMATION

We will reconfirm your return as follows:

Name _____

**Departing
to** _____

Date _____

Airline/Flight# _____

**Time of
Departure** _____

PLEASE CHECK ONE:

_____ The information above is correct

_____ I have changed my departure reservations to:

    Date_____

    Airline/Flight# _____

    Time of Departure _____

_____ Please change my departure reservations, if possible

If you would like to change your return flight, please fill in the information below and bring it with your ticket to the operations room no less than 72 hours before the day of your departure. It may not be possible to make the change you request; however, we will do our best to accommodate your request.

CHANGE RETURN FLIGHT RESERVATIONS TO:

Date _____

Airline/Flight# _____

**Time of
Departure** _____

_____

Signature   **Date**

A11.2   AIRPORT TRANSFER DEPARTURE CONFIRMATION

Name _____

**Room
Number** _____   _____

Name of accompanying traveler (if applicable) _____

**Date of
Departure** _____

Flight _____   **Time** _____

Departure time to airport _____

If your return flight information above is not correct or has changed, please bring this form to the operations room as soon as possible.

Please review your charges and check out of the hotel before meeting the transportation staff in the lobby at your designated departure time.

A11.3   SCHEDULE LOG FOR EVENT ATTENDEES

FAMILY	FIRST NAME	DAY 1 Bfast	LUNCH	BREAK	DINNER	DAY 2 Bfast	BREAK	LUNCH	BREAK	DAY 3 Bfast	BREAK	LUNCH	Special Needs
TOTAL FOR GUARANTEE		0	0	0	0	0	0	0	0	0	0	0	

Appendix 12

CASE STUDIES

A12.1 CASE STUDY: INTERNATIONAL CONGRESS

The recognition by industrial nations of the vulnerability of institutions and industrial facilities to acts of terrorism and violence has led to the convening of a world congress to explore ways to prevent and combat the problem. An ad hoc steering committee consisting of corporate security executives, government agency and military leaders, and manufacturers of security systems and devices has underwritten the development cost and funded a secretariat to plan and implement the congress.

Participants from sixteen countries are to be invited to attend, and a total of 250 delegates and 130 exhibitors are anticipated. Delegates are corporate directors of security, members of private and government law-enforcement agencies, and high-ranking military officers. Seven hold deputy ministerial rank, and the honorary chairperson is a full minister. Housing requirements for staff and speakers call for 270 single or double rooms and 18 suites. Exhibitors may be housed at a separate hotel if the secretariat determines that the headquarters hotel lacks the capacity. No spouses are invited, though 10 percent of the delegates are expected to have accompanying guests sharing rooms.

The steering committee has designated Geneva, Switzerland, as the focal point for venue selection. Plans call for a four-day conference in September of next year. The business agenda will cover four days of plenary sessions, forums, workshops, and exhibitions. Adequate space for forty exhibit stands will be required and preference is for the exhibit area to be in the same facility as the meeting rooms.

As many as six small-group sessions (forty to sixty attendees) and hands-on workshops may run concurrently. Food and beverage requirements include an opening gala reception, breakfast and lunch each day (with probable luncheon speakers), two onsite dinners, and two free evenings, with one possibly organized as a dine-around.

As conference executive for one of the participating organizations, you have been seconded to the secretariat to help assess and select a destination and meeting venues.

DISCUSSION POINTS

1. Refer to Chapter 3 for guidance on destination assessment.
2. Conduct Web-based site research in order to recommend which venue(s) in Geneva can accommodate the meeting. The hotels should have adequate space for the exhibits or be in close proximity to an exhibition facility that does.
3. Prepare a table of the first two choices showing facility name, number of guest rooms, committed capacity, group rate, number of meeting rooms, and their capacities by seating configuration.

A12.2 CASE STUDY: CORPORATE CONFERENCE

Safecor International, a multinational manufacturer of lighting systems that is head-quartered in Vancouver, markets its products through licensees in Europe, Latin America, and the Pacific Rim. Plans have been announced to hold a new product launch in fourteen months. Principal executives of licensee companies and regional offices, North American distributors, and corporate executives and staff will attend. Additional invitees—potential buyers and users—include corporate security executives, workers in law enforcement and government agencies, and military personnel.

Participants from 23 countries are expected to attend for a total of 235 invitees, 3 speakers, 34 exhibitors, and 20 corporate staff. The geographical distribution is as follows:

Asia-Pacific	28%
South and Central America	12%
Other regions	6%
Europe	20%
Canada and United States	32%

Principal gateways for participants are Asia-Pacific: Hong Kong, Manila, Sydney, Taipei, Tokyo; Europe: Amsterdam, Frankfurt, London, Milan, Paris and Vienna; South and Central America: Buenos Aires, Bogota, Mexico, Sao Paulo; and Canada and United States: Atlanta, Chicago, Dallas, Los Angeles, Montreal, New York, Toronto, and Vancouver. Housing requirements, including staff and speakers, call for 275 single or double rooms and 12 suites. No guests or spouses are invited, though 10 percent of the delegates are expected to have accompanying persons sharing rooms. Special amenities for all attendees are appropriate.

The conference committee has designated Singapore as the venue. Safecor has a regional office and licensees at that site. Plans call for a four-day conference after the arrival day and departure on day 6. The business agenda will cover three and a half days of general sessions, forums, workshops, and exhibitions. Adequate space for sixteen two- by four-meter perimeter exhibit stands and two four-by-eight meter island stands will be required. As many as six small-group sessions (forty to sixty attendees) and hands-on workshops may run concurrently on the second through fourth days. A conference office, an information center, a speakers lounge, and a press room are to be staffed during conference hours.

Food and beverage requirements include an opening gala reception, breakfast and lunch each day, two on-site dinners, and two free evenings, with one possibly organized as a dine-around. The afternoon of the third day is open time. Two hospitality suites capable of accommodating 40 and 100, respectively, are to be stocked and staffed between the hours of 5 P.M. and midnight.

As conference executive for one of the participating subsidiaries, you have been assigned to the conference committee to help research and recommend a destination; assess and arrange transportation and destination services; and negotiate and contract for hotel rooms, function space, and support services. You will work closely with the program committee to ensure that its requirements are met.

You will work with other meeting professionals from the home office, professionals from other subsidiaries, and licensees. Your first meeting as a conference committee is this week. All meeting operations will be managed by the senior meeting executive, supported by a local Professional Congress Organizer (PCO) (to be retained), and select corporate staff augmented by licensee or branch office staff employed at the destination city.

DISCUSSION POINTS

1. Determine what airlines have the best routing from each origination point.
2. Conduct a destination assessment, using the appropriate Web sites, to select a hotel or hotels capable of housing delegates and supporting the meeting requirements.
3. Would you recommend contacting a PCO and/or a destination management company for local support? If so, conduct an online search for qualified candidates.
4. Be prepared to recommend a tentative program schedule to include social activities and meals.

A12.3   CASE STUDY: CORPORATE INCENTIVE TRIP

It is April 30, a Sunday and the last day of an incentive trip you have been implementing in Madrid, Spain, this week. On this final day, the schedule calls for an optional final tour for those who would like to see the countryside or a day at leisure in the city.

At 09:00, 120 of the 300 participants and their spouses and guests leave the downtown hotel in three buses for their tour outside the city. The itinerary includes lunch at a country restaurant and a visit to a crafts museum and shopping outlet on the way back to town. It is raining heavily, but all the activities are indoors, and so the group takes off cheerfully. The buses are scheduled to be back at the hotel by 16:00 to leave time for everyone to relax and dress for the gala awards dinner to be held at a hacienda ten kilometers outside of town. Departure for dinner is scheduled for 20:30.

At 16:00 the buses have not returned. At 16:30 you ask your destination management company (DMC) to find out what might be causing the delay. He returns with unexpected and disturbing news: None of the three buses are responding to either the dispatcher's radio calls or calls to the drivers' personal cellular telephones. The DMC also has tried to reach the guides on the buses, and all their cellular phones are busy as well.

At 17:00 you still have received no information as to the location, condition, and estimated time of arrival of the three buses. Both the DMC and the bus company are at a loss to explain the situation but are trying to find out where and when the buses were last seen. The senior company representative on site, who sent his wife and daughter on the tour while he spent the day at the local subsidiary office, has just come down to the staff operations room to find out what is going on.

By 17:30 your operations contact from the DMC is visibly perplexed and assuring you that this has never happened before and that both he and the bus company are at a loss to explain the mysterious loss of the three buses. A telephone call to the first stop, the restaurant, established that the group arrived at 12:30, ate lunch, and departed at 14:00. No one was ill, everything was fine, and all three buses left together in the direction of Madrid. However, a call to the next scheduled stop, the crafts museum, was most disturbing. The group, which was scheduled to arrive at 14:30, never showed up and never called to cancel the arrangements. Nothing has been heard from any of the guides assigned to each bus, and you have not heard from your staff accompanying the tour. All attempts to make contact via cellular phone have been in vain.

At 18:00 you hear from the DMC that there is still no response to the dispatcher's continuous efforts to contact the buses by both radio and cellular phone. The silence is as ominous as it is inexplicable. The police and the equivalent of the highway patrol have been contacted, but there has been no information from them either.

Some of the senior managers who sent their spouses on the tour are waiting in the lobby of the hotel, and the anxiety and tension are mounting. You have a basic emergency response plan that covers a variety of scenarios: fire, serious illness or injury, violent crime, bomb threats, terrorist activity, labor unrest, and so on. Unfortunately, you did not anticipate the wholesale disappearance of three buses with 120 guests on them. Have they been beamed up to a UFO? Just what would be an effective emergency response to an alien abduction of your guests, anyway?

At 19:00, three hours after the buses were due to return to the hotel, you finally receive word from the DMC that the drivers have made radio contact. The good news is that all the passengers are safe and sound. The bad news is that they are still an hour and a half outside the city, stuck in what will be described in the next morning's newspaper as the worst traffic jam in the history of Madrid. Apparently, the rain and the continuing dismal forecast prompted a million or more *Madrileños,* who had left town on Friday for the long May Day weekend, to return home a day earlier. This early and unexpected surge of traffic on what was supposed to be a quiet holiday Sunday caught everyone by surprise and, beginning around midday, paralyzed every major highway within a 100-kilometer radius of Madrid. Cellular telephone lines jammed as thousands of people attempted to call each other either from the highway or from home to find out what was going on. The three buses, which had been inching their way back to Madrid since leaving the restaurant at 14:00, were out of radio range until they were close enough to the city five hours later.

You are relieved that the dreadful accident you had been envisaging has not occurred; however, you and your team now have an additional logistical challenge. Transportation to the gala dinner, the final social highlight of the meeting, is scheduled to begin at 20:30, which is about the time the tour participants are due to return from their highway ordeal. After six and a half hours returning to the city on a bus, they may not even want to go to dinner, especially when getting there will entail getting onto another bus to leave the city again. You reconfirmed all arrangements for the dinner at 10:00 this morning, guaranteeing 250 meals, the flamenco troupe, lavish decorations, and everything down to a rose for each female guest upon arrival. Now you are looking at the prospect of having only half your guests attend and the entire program ending on a disastrous rather than celebratory note.

Half of your group will be arriving in an hour, tired, angry, and not in the mood to celebrate anything other than getting off the bus they have been trapped in for the last six hours. At the same time, the rest of the participants will be expecting to board a bus to go to a fabulous farewell evening of gourmet food, world-class entertainment, and cheerful camaraderie.

The success of the entire program, the thousands of dollars spent on the final evening, and the image and credibility of your senior managers and your department are in jeopardy. Your senior management wants to meet with you in twenty minutes to find out how you plan to salvage the evening, the program, and, quite possibly, your job.

DISCUSSION QUESTIONS

1. What are the key elements of this situation that require attention?
2. Is there anything about the situation that you could have anticipated either from your experience in your home country or from a site visit to Madrid before the program?
3. At what point during the day do you think senior management should have been advised that there was a concern about the location and possible safety of the tour group? Why?
4. Describe your plan of action and for the final evening, addressing the needs and concerns of the following:
   - The participants who spent all day on the bus and may not want to attend the dinner
   - The participants who did not go on the tour and are looking forward to the dinner
   - Your senior managers, who are angry and concerned

A12.4   CASE STUDY: HOW TO AVOID FALLING INTO THE VAT TRAP

The National Association of Widget Builders decided after extensive deliberation to hold its first international meeting in Stockholm, Sweden. Stockholm was selected because of the enormous potential for international networking with the Swedish widget-manufacturing industry. Furthermore, the association wants to expand its international (non-U.S.) membership through this new initiative.

During the planning for the meeting, the budget was analyzed thoroughly by the U.S. accounting firm. The meeting planner and budget committee for the association concurred that the accounting firm had scrutinized the budget carefully. However, at the conclusion of the meeting the association fell into what is often called the VAT trap.

At the conclusion of the meeting, when all invoices were received, the total cost of the event was not the previously budgeted $200,000 but, rather, $250,000. When the meeting planner and her accountants reviewed the invoices, they noted that the term *VAT* appeared at the bottom of each invoice and resulted in an increase in the cost of goods and services of 25 percent. In addition, the 500 persons from North America who attended the meeting were unpleasantly surprised by the VAT charges, and their comments resulted in negative evaluations of the meeting.

When the executive director of the association asked the meeting planner to explain these charges, she answered, "I did not know about VAT." The executive director explained that ignorance was no excuse for this omission in the budget and that it therefore would affect her annual review negatively. Furthermore, the association decided to seek a new accounting firm. Finally, and perhaps most important, the annual budget was reduced for the following year by $50,000 to make up the previous year's loss.

How does a meeting planner avoid the VAT trap?

The VAT trap often occurs when a meeting organizer does not realize that in many European and other countries the government may attach a value-added tax (referred to in some countries as a goods and services tax, GST or IVA which is the equivalent in Spanish-, Portuguese-, and Italian-speaking countries). This tax can range from 5 percent to 25 percent on top of the amount charged by the vendor.

In addition, attendees at your meeting may be charged VAT or its equivalent. You must inform them in advance about the VAT policies in the country where the meeting is being held and provide instructions for reclaiming these taxes if possible.

Although it is possible to apply for a VAT refund, there are no uniform procedures for doing this. Therefore, if the event organizer does not plan for this additional cost, it may affect the budget negatively. To avoid the VAT trap, the meeting planner should ask all vendors to include the following information on their quotes and bids:

- The amount of VAT should be factored into the quoted or bid amount.
- The procedures for receiving a VAT refund should be delineated carefully.
- The proper certifications or documents to collect the VAT refund should be provided by the vendor at the time of purchase.

DISCUSSION QUESTIONS

1. How do you determine if VAT is charged in the country where a meeting is being held?
2. How do you determine which goods and services are taxed and which are not?
3. How do you budget carefully to include all VAT charges?
4. How do you reclaim VAT?
5. How do you inform your meeting attendees about VAT policies and reclaim?

▍A12.5   CASE STUDY: RISK MANAGEMENT

Today is Thursday, three days before your meeting begins. You are on-site in Rio de Janeiro, and all is going well so far. Your destination management company (DMC) has been keeping track of the inevitable arrival changes. Your team is getting welcome packets together, incorporating last-minute changes into the day-by-day schedule, checking VIP amenities, and preparing for the next morning's arrival of your boss and several other senior managers.

Good news! Your project coordinator has just verified that all the printed material shipped from the United States has cleared customs and will be delivered to the hotel tomorrow. You were concerned about this shipment, since it was sent directly from the printer and not through your office. Fortunately, the shipping department did everything right and the local company you have hired to receive, store, and transport the materials has come through.

You congratulate yourself on choosing a company whose affiliated customs broker once worked as a customs inspector. This person is more connected than a chain-link fence and clearly knows the ins and outs of the system. As it turns out, the customs agents and federal police are threatening to go on strike, and things are even slower than usual. You are particularly grateful that all your materials are safely in your possession.

Your major challenge at the moment is to get the learning center constructed on time. This combination exhibit and training area has been specially designed and will be constructed by a local company in one of the hotel's two ballrooms. The only components being shipped from your home country are the computers that will be the core of this high-tech learning center. Your information technology (IT) manager, Tony, is in charge of this equipment and has made all the shipping arrangements directly with a freight forwarder in your home city that has been recommended highly by several colleagues.

Your company has invested over half a million dollars in the development of the new computers that will be introduced in the learning center. The CEO, who will be in attendance, considers both the learning center and the new state-of-the-art hardware to be the cornerstone of a new corporate image campaign. Both local and international media have been invited for a special preview demonstration of the company's new training resources. Because your company will be manufacturing the machines in Brazil for distribution throughout South America, your country's ambassador and the Brazilian minister of commerce will be in attendance. There will be significant local press coverage of the event and a global press videoconference to announce the new product to the North American, European, and Asian markets.

When you go over to the exhibit site, you note with satisfaction that the construction of the learning center is proceeding on schedule. Tony is scheduled to test each unit in situ this afternoon, but you know the machinery is delicate, Murphy's law knows no boundaries, and the stakes are too high to leave anything to the last minute. Everyone is nervous about the computers because they are the CEO's pet project, and expectations are very high for their debut.

By the way, where *are* the computers? You realize that with all your running around the past few days, you haven't actually seen them. They should have arrived and been cleared through customs by now. You assume that this is the case and make a mental note to check with Tony.

You ask the construction supervisor when he thinks the computers can be installed for testing. He gives you a blank look and says, "Whenever Tony tracks them down. Didn't he tell you they got lost somewhere en route to Rio de Janeiro? He's been going crazy for the past two days trying to find out what got screwed up."

At 10:00 that same Thursday, you locate Tony and he tells you the following:

- The six cartons of computer equipment were shipped from your home base three weeks ago.
- The cartons were shipped to Rio de Janeiro via common carrier and should have arrived within a week, plenty of time to clear customs even with the work slowdown.

- He has been in constant contact with the shipping company, and his contact there has traced the container with the cartons to Santiago, Chile.
- He's really sorry he hasn't said anything up to now, but the guy at the shipping company promised him that everything would work out, and so he decided not bother you about it.
- He just spoke to the guy at the shipping company, who is *really* sorry about the screw-up, swears this has *never* happened before, and says don't worry, the cartons should be leaving on a plane to Brazil tomorrow morning, once the other contents of the container finally have been released.

You make a valiant attempt to neither shriek at Tony nor physically injure him. You consider first homicide, then suicide, then both for a moment. None of these are viable alternatives at this juncture, and so you take a deep breath and start mobilizing your resources.

After a sleepless night worrying about the wayward computers, you receive a fax at 10:00 on Friday morning, informing you that they are on a plane bound for Brazil and are due to arrive at 13:30 that afternoon. That's the good news. The bad news is that they will arrive in São Paulo and you are in Rio de Janeiro. The even worse news is that the equipment must clear customs in São Paulo because it is the initial port of entry into the country. After being trucked to Rio (approximately four hours' transit time if road conditions are favorable), the shipment will then have to clear customs again, since Rio is the original port of entry noted on the official paperwork.

You will have to pay significant customs duty on the equipment in both São Paulo and Rio, but this is the least of your problems at the moment. Customs offices shut down for the weekend at 18:00 everywhere in the country and do not open again until Monday morning, the day the meeting begins with a media breakfast to show off the new hardware.

You are now racing against the clock and about to blow the meeting budget into the stratosphere. Your boss is in a panic and is suggesting that you "call out the big guns." The senior VP of administration has contacts at your country's embassy, and the CEO has played golf with the Brazilian secretary of commerce. One call from him to the appropriate official and the equipment surely will be released immediately. Your boss is adamant. The company's reputation and your jobs are on the line. It's time to throw some weight around and use your company's influence as a global, multimillion-dollar firm to salvage the situation.

At the same time, your local support team is advising *against* the "big guns" option. They ask you to trust their experience and judgment and give them some more time to do what they do best. They have mobilized all their contacts within the system in both São Paulo and Rio and are hopeful that they will be able to work something out, even though customs will technically shut down for the weekend at 18:00. Your local colleagues cannot guarantee that they will be successful, but they *can* guarantee that if the big guns are called in, the computers will be held in customs indefinitely or be released at an exorbitant "duty" many times greater than what is currently being negotiated.

As project team leader, you have to make a decision now. Your very nervous boss respects your experience and judgment enough to follow whatever course of action you recommend, but you had better be right. If you are not, you will be looking for a place to make copies of your résumé within a matter of days.

DISCUSSION POINTS

1. Read over the first six paragraphs of this case study carefully. Highlight or underline everything that you think may be a potential risk factor and note down why. How many did you identify?
2. As the project team leader, you have several critical issues to resolve once you learn about the missing hardware. What are they, and which should you address first?
3. After Tony informs you that the computers have not arrived, you mobilize your resources. Just who are your key resources at this point, and how will you use them most effectively to resolve the situation?
4. Your boss is urging you to call in the big guns, but your local support network is advising just the opposite. You have been given the responsibility and authority to decide the course of action, and your job is on the line. What do you decide to do and why?

▌A12.5 VIDEO PRESENTATION CHALLENGE

Global Merchandising, Inc., of San Francisco, a distributor of office equipment, is planning a new market introduction of its product line in Hong Kong, Copenhagen, and Rio de Janeiro. A key feature of the program is a multi-image video presentation of Global's products.

As the staff member person responsible for managing the company's meetings and events, you have been given the task of finding, in addition to the usual facilities and support services, a competent audiovisual (AV) rental firm in each city. It is also your responsibility to advise the marketing staff on the video standards employed in each destination.

DISCUSSION POINTS

1. Contact by Web site each city's convention bureau for a list of AV support firms.
2. Ascertain the video standards pertaining to each of the proposed sites (Chapter 15).
3. Using the Internet, locate a Bay Area video production company capable of converting the videos to the appropriate standards.
4. Prepare a brief memorandum explaining to management why the conversion is necessary.

INDEX

Printed in the USA/Agawam, MA
June 17, 2014

591284.002